Determining
U.S. Foreign Policy
Toward Russia:

An Overview of the Issues
Related to U.S. and Russian
Foreign Policy

Determining U.S. Foreign Policy Toward Russia:

An Overview of the Issues Related to U.S. and Russian Foreign Policy

Robert C. Rowland
Communication Studies
The University of Kansas

National Textbook Company
a division of NTC/CONTEMPORARY PUBLISHING GROUP
Lincolnwood, Illinois USA

ISBN: 0-8442-0432-3

Published by National Textbook Company,
a division of NTC/Contemporary Publishing Group, Inc.,
4255 West Touhy Avenue,
Lincolnwood (Chicago), Illinois 60646-1975 U.S.A.

890 VP 0987654321

Contents

Chapter Three: Economic, Political, and Social Issues in U.S. Foreign Policy Toward Russia   59

Chapter Four: Defense Issues in U.S.-Russian Relations   91

Chapter Five: Strategic Dimensions in Debating About U.S. Foreign Policy Toward Russia   129

Outline of Selected Affirmative and Negative Arguments   138

Bibliography   145

Introduction

There is no question about the timeliness and importance of a close consideration of United States foreign policy toward Russia. For 45 years, from the end of the Second World War to the end of the Cold War, United States foreign and defense policy was dominated by issues relating to the Soviet Union. From the Marshall plan to the Strategic Defense Initiative, the United States aimed at deterring the Soviets from aggression and maintaining the Western alliance.

In that context, most foreign policy debates were reduced to questions of means, as opposed to a consideration of ends. Liberals and conservatives, Republicans and Democrats were united in opposition to the Soviets. The point of debate on foreign relations was over the best means of opposing the Soviets. With the death of the Soviet Union on Christmas day 1991, the universe of U.S. foreign policy radically was altered.

Of course, even more fundamentally, the situation facing Russia is dramatically different than the situation that faced the Soviet Union. Almost no one saw the death of Soviet communism coming. The collapse of the Warsaw Pact, the end of the Cold War, the dismemberment of the Soviet Union, and the movement of a new Russian state from communism and totalitarianism toward a market economy and democracy all came with dizzying speed. And there also has been a move from "empire" back to the nation state. As Henry Kissinger has observed, "Russia is living within borders it has not known since Peter the Great" (D *U.S. National Goals* 5). Put simply, the people of Russia have lived through an economic, political, and social revolution in the last seven years. That revolution is not yet over.

In the political situation I have described there is no question of the importance of U.S. policy toward Russia. Deputy Secretary of State Strobe Talbott spoke about that subject in an address at Stanford University in September 1997. He said that

> Russia in 1997 is still in the throes of a titanic struggle. We Americans have a huge stake in how that struggle turns out. Our goal, like that of many Russians, is to see Russia become a normal, modern state—democratic in its governance, abiding by its own constitution and by its own laws, market-oriented and prosperous in its economic development, at peace with itself and with the rest of the world. (P "The End" 22)

Talbott sees two possible futures for Russia:

> A Russia that reflects their aspirations is likely to be part of the solution to the world's many problems. Conversely, a Russia that erects barriers against what it sees as a hostile world and that believes the best defense is a good offense—such a Russia could be, in the 21st century just as it was in much of the 20th, one of the biggest of the problems we and our children face. (P "The End" 23)

As Talbott makes clear, the stakes involved in U.S. foreign policy toward Russia are very high. This point was emphasized by one of the foremost experts on the Soviet Union, Harvard's Richard Pipes. Pipes, while noting that Russia is not now an enemy, concludes that "it might become one" (P 78). It is the risk that Russia once again could be our enemy, above all else, that makes the topic of U.S. foreign policy toward Russia so important.

Some might disagree and say that with the end of the Soviet Union, Russia simply isn't that important to the United States. In one sense, that is correct. On a day to day basis, the situation in Russia has relatively little impact on the United States. Russia does not have much effect on our economy, and the United States, as the only remaining superpower, has vastly more influence in the world than any other nation. On the other hand, there are any number of things that could happen in Russia that would have a vast impact on the United States. David Remnick emphasizes the importance of U.S. foreign policy toward Russia, when he labels the country as a "giant developing nation with nuclear weapons" (P "How Russia" 14). How Russia "develops" could shape world history in the 21st century, just as it did the 20th. The issue is particularly important since in the words of Richard Pipes, "The situation in today's Russia is highly volatile" (P 68).

Nor is the problem posed by Russia for the United States likely to go away soon. Strobe Talbott argues that the process of the "continuing transformation of Russia into a democratic, stable, secure, prosperous state, at peace with its neighbors" "will take a generation or more, and it will require steady support from the international community, led by the U.S." (P "Managing" 59).

Therefore, a consideration of the topic—Resolved: That the United States should substantially change its foreign policy toward Russia—is quite important. At this point in history, the United States is preeminent, perhaps even more so than after the end of the Second World War. There is, however, a grave danger that goes with such preeminence, complacency. If the United States is going to successfully deal with problems involving Russia, then careful analysis and action is needed now. There already are signs of the danger of complacency, including cuts in U.S. assistance programs to help Russia protect and dismantle its nuclear arsenal. Given the more than forty years in which Americans lived under the threat of Soviet nuclear attack, the fact that a program to dismantle Russian nuclear weapons faces funding shortfalls is astounding.

In sum, a consideration of U.S. foreign policy toward Russia is quite important. Russian-U.S. relations remain one of the crucial factors in the world. And, despite the importance of the issue, there has not been nearly as much close policy analysis as one might expect. For example, there are far fewer Congressional Hearings directly on U.S.-Russian relations than I expected to find. These two factors indicate the importance of a close analysis of the status of U.S.-Russian foreign relations.

A Note on Sources

The topic of U.S. foreign policy toward Russia is either a relatively narrow one, or an enormously broad one, depending upon how you define the subject area. If the topic is defined to focus on foreign relations issues between Russia and the United States, then it is easily defined and can be researched by utilizing obvious key words like U.S. foreign policy and Russia. On the other hand, if the topic is defined in such a way that any action of the United States government that tangentially impacts Russia is included, then it becomes nearly limitless. Under the second approach, for example, campaign finance reform limiting foreign donations would be defined as an aspect of U.S. foreign policy toward Russia. For reasons that I will explain in the first chapter, I think the narrower approach to U.S.-Russian relations is more appropriate.

In researching that narrowly defined subject area, two issues are of crucial importance: timeliness and expertise. The political situation changes so rapidly in Russia that it is essential that information be as up to date as possible. It also is important to make certain that any given source actually has adequate experience and expertise in the area.

One implication is that unlike other recent topics, I did not find books to be as useful as other sources. As noted, the situation in Russia is evolving so rapidly that by the time a book is written and published, it may no longer be up to date. In addition, many books on the topic have a broadly historical focus on the end of the Soviet Union and the beginning of reform. That historical focus is useful for providing background information but is not usually directly relevant for a consideration of what future U.S. policy toward Russia should be. For example, Anders Aslund, a Swedish economist who has advised the Russian government, has written an excellent book, *How Russia Became a Market Economy*. Although the copyright date is 1995, so much has happened since then that the book is primarily useful for its description of past economic reform efforts.

If books are a less important resource than is often the case, periodicals and the *Congressional Record* are proportionately more important sources of information. Periodicals, including scholarly journals, are especially useful for providing information that is up to date and also backed up with academic expertise. There are four journals that often print especially useful essays about U.S.-Russian relations. In the March/April 1997 issue of *Current*, Anatol Lieven wrote about "The Future of Russia: Will It Be Freedom or Anarchy?" and Adam Garfinkle focused on "Expanding NATO: Implications for America." Both essays provide useful summaries of positions relating to U.S. foreign policy toward Russia. Similarly, there are several useful essays in the October 1997 *Current History*. Marshall Goldman's discussion of "Russia's Reform Effort: Is There Growth at the End of the Tunnel?" and Michael McFaul's consideration of "Democracy Unfolds in Russia" were particularly helpful. *Foreign Affairs* also often publishes insightful analyses of U.S.-Russian relations. Finally, the most important source for explaining and justifying current policy is the *U.S.*

Department of State Dispatch, a publication of the State Department, which often includes speeches or position papers relating to U.S. foreign policy toward Russia.

One other point concerning periodicals is important. As on almost any topic, there is no source as good as the *New York Times* for staying up to date on what is happening on Russia.

Because many of the issues at the core the resolution, especially NATO expansion and nuclear weapons concerns, are often debated in Congress, the *Congressional Record* provides an invaluable discussion of current U.S. policy and prospects for the future. One other comment about the *Congressional Record* is important. The titles of sections in the Record often tell you very little about what is in fact being discussed. For example, the bibliography includes a title "The Trip to South Africa," which actually includes a substantial focus on Russia.

While the *Congressional Record* was a more important source than is often the case, as noted earlier, Congressional hearings were less important. Perhaps because the focus of Congress has been on NATO expansion, Russian arms and technology sales, and strategic defense issues relating to arms control, there hasn't been very much general scrutiny of U.S.-Russian relations.

Conclusion

In the following chapters, I will explore the major issues relating to U.S. foreign policy toward Russia. In the first chapter, I will discuss the meaning of the resolution, focusing on why a relatively narrow definition of "U.S. foreign policy toward Russia" is more sensible than a broad interpretation of the language. The second chapter will focus on three main issues: recent changes in the Russian political and economic systems, the scope of U.S. foreign policy toward Russia since the end of the Cold War, and three possible general mechanisms for altering U.S. policy: direct policy change, foreign assistance programs, and use of sanctions or threats as a means of changing Russian actions. The third chapter will focus on economic, political, and social aspects of U.S. policy toward Russia. In other words, I will discuss alternative policies that might be used to strengthen Russia's political system or economy or deal with social problems such as gaps in health care and various environmental crises. In the fourth chapter, I will focus on defense issues involved in U.S.-Russian relations and trade concerns that are directly related to defense. In the final chapter, I will describe the characteristics of an effective affirmative and negative strategy. It is followed by a number of outlines of potential affirmative and negative arguments.

Throughout the book I have used an internal citation scheme that references material in the bibliography. The bibliography is divided into the following sections: books and book chapters (B), Congressional Record (CR), documents (D), and periodicals (P). For every source that I cite, I include a reference indicating the type of source, the author's name (or title of the work if there is no listed author), enough of a citation to identify the work in the bibliography, and where relevant a page reference. So the source (P Cooper "Expanding" 435) is a reference to p. 435 of Mary H. Cooper's essay titled "Expanding NATO: Does adding new members pose serious risks?" which was published in the periodical *CQ Researcher*. I cited a portion of the title of the essay because several essays by Cooper are included in the periodical section of the bibliography. If there had been only one essay by Cooper in the bibliography then I would not have included the short title. The reader should find the bibliography to be useful in researching U.S. foreign policy toward Russia.

1 The Parameters of United States Foreign Policy Toward Russia

The primary purposes of a debate resolution are to focus the subject of debate on a limited policy area and divide ground between those who propose and oppose change. In relation to a discussion of U.S. policy toward Russia, both of those purposes will be important.

This year's resolution states:

"Resolved: That the United States should substantially change its foreign policy toward Russia. "

The crucial issue on this year's resolution concerns the definition of the word *toward* in relation to the terms *U.S. foreign policy* and of course *Russia*. If U.S. foreign policy toward Russia is defined in the same way that both foreign policy practitioners and experts would understand the phrase, then the meaning of the topic is relatively clear. The focus of the resolution is on three types of actions that the United States can take in its relations with Russia: foreign aid to Russia, sanctions or threats aimed at Russia, and direct policy changes in U.S. relations with Russia, such as changing the targeting of nuclear weapons that literally have been or could be aimed at Russia. Defined in this way, *U.S. foreign policy toward Russia* covers a wide variety of important issues, but the area is still limited and, therefore, quite debatable for both the proponent and opponent of change.

On the other hand, it could be argued that the words *U.S. foreign policy toward Russia* have a much more expansive meaning than the one I just described. In this view, any policy action that indirectly influences U.S. foreign policy toward Russia is included within the resolution. So, for instance, a proposal that the United States should spend more money on research and development would be included in the resolution because increased spending on R & D would make U.S. companies more competitive and therefore able to get more of the Russian market. A proposal to increase spending on education could be resolutional by the same logic. And in the area of foreign relations, any change that indirectly influenced Russia would be considered resolutional. Obviously, this second interpretation moves the focus of debate away from timely issues relating directly to Russia and also has the effect of making the resolution extremely broad. For both of these reasons (and others that I will discuss in a moment), the narrower interpretation is preferable.

Debating Topicality

Topicality in academic debate serves a similar purpose to discussion in the law about the proper scope of the meaning of terms in statutes, contracts, and so forth. Such argument is quite important in the real world to determine issues like the coverage available under health insurance policy or the specific actions mandated in legislation.

The first step in preparing a strong topicality position is research. The advocate should gather definitions from the major dictionaries (*Webster's* and so forth), specialized dictionaries, and legal dictionaries. Legal dictionaries, including *Black's Law Dictionary* and *Corpus Juris Secundum* (*CJS*), are quite useful because they provide definitions of terms as they were used in the context of a particular court case. By matching particular legal definitions to a specific context, it may be possible to build a strong argument for the superiority of a given interpretation of a term. The term "substantially," for instance, may have a very different meaning in relation to changing the foreign policy of the United States, as opposed to renewable energy policy.

Contextual research on the meaning of terms in a particular subject area is also important. A contextual definition is a definition of a term within a particular context area. Within the subject of foreign policy, for instance, defense issues are routinely considered. While an advocate could draw a distinction between foreign policy and defense policy, a consideration of contextual definitions would not support such an action. As this example indicates, the advocate should be alert for definitions found in policy analyses of U.S. foreign policy toward Russia. The way that the terms are used in journals on foreign relations, in statements by officials in the State Department published in the *U.S. Department of State Dispatch,* and also the way that they are used by those who create indexes of periodicals or other sources, provide particularly useful data for building a topicality position. For example, indexes *never* include a discussion of research and development in the subject area heading such as U.S. foreign policy, Russia. On the other hand, articles on NATO expansion often are included there. That difference in indexing provides strong evidence that NATO expansion falls directly into the resolution, while the research and development policy does not.

The second step in getting ready to debate topicality is to prepare the argument itself. Negative debaters often simply present definitions and then assert that the affirmative proposal does not meet them. A better approach is to *both* present the definition and explain why it makes the affirmative plan nontopical. The easiest way to do this is to include within the topicality argument a statement of why the definition means that the affirmative is illegitimate. There are three particular reasons that can be used to demonstrate that an interpretation is irrational. The negative might argue that the affirmative interpretation is not acceptable because it makes the topic overly broad, stretches the meaning of a term to such a degree that the topic no longer distinguishes between the affirmative and negative, or unfairly divides ground. In essence, the negative would be arguing that the affirmative interpretation is unsound because it makes the resolution undebatable or shifts the focus away from timely issues concerning U.S.-Russian foreign relations.

The process of developing arguments and responding to topicality for the affirmative is essentially similar to what I have described for the negative, with one exception. The affirmative demonstrates that the negative interpretation restricts the resolution to an excessive degree and therefore ignores issues that are at the core of U.S.-Russian relations. Contextual definitions are even more powerful aids for the affirmative than the negative because they can be cited to demonstrate that affirmative proposal would be considered by real policy makers to fall within the subject area of the resolution.

This brief discussion of the process of debating topicality serves as an introduction to a consideration of definitional issues involved in debating about U.S. foreign policy toward Russia.

United States Foreign Policy Toward Russia

The topic area for this year's resolution asks: "What is the best foreign policy for the United States to implement toward Russia?" And the particular resolution states

"Resolved: That the United States should substantially change its foreign policy toward Russia. "

United States

The first important term in the resolution is *United States*. In relation to U.S. foreign policy toward Russia, the term *United States* seems to mean the Federal Government, including the executive branch, Congress, and the Federal Courts. According to *Black's Law Dictionary,* United States:

> has several meanings. It may be merely the name of a sovereign occupying the position analogous to that of other sovereigns in the family of nations, it may designate territory over which sovereignty of United States extends, or it may be the collective name of the states which are united by and under the Constitution.

In this instance, the third meaning is obviously the correct one. While the term can refer to any group of "united states," the topic is certainly referring to the United States of America. The fact that the term *United States* is capitalized is one indication of that point. Nor does it make sense to consider the resolution as referring to the territory of the nation. Obviously, then the resolution is referring to the government of the union of the states, in other words the Federal Government.

It could be argued that *United States* literally includes within it the governments of the states and that, therefore, it would be permissible for individual states to take action. Of course, under our system, only the Federal Government may take actions in foreign policy. Moreover, the resolution calls for the United States to substantially change "its" foreign policy. The use of its as a possessive indicates that the resolution calls for action by the Federal Government alone.

One other issue relates to the meaning of United States. It could be argued that U.S. foundations play an important role in U.S. foreign policy toward Russia. The billionaire George Soros has given very large sums of money to Russia. Thus, someone might claim that the best means of substantially changing U.S. foreign policy would be for U.S. foundations to increase their giving to Russia.

An interpretation of the resolution allowing for a change in foundation policy or even the personal policy of George Soros would be illegitimate. First, as I noted earlier, the word *its* indicates that the foreign policy to be changed belongs to the United States. The assistance programs of the Ford Foundation or Mr. Soros, belong respectively to the organization and a particular billionaire. The United States does not control those programs.

The second reason that such an interpretation is unacceptable relates to the idea of fiat in academic debate. Fiat is the assumption for the purpose of debate that a given policy has been adopted. It is needed in order to overcome political objections to a policy action. The negative cannot legitimately argue that such and such a policy will not be implemented. It is only the burden of the affirmative to prove the desirability of policy action. But there has to be some reasonable limit to fiat or the affirmative could "fiat" the action of individuals, in this case Mr. Soros. The obvious place to define the boundary of acceptable fiat is with normal governmental action. If there is a governmental mechanism for policy change to occur, as there clearly is in the case of changing the foreign policy of the Federal Government, then the action meets a reasonable definition of fiat.

In sum, the term *United States* refers to the central government of the United States.

Should

The second important term in the resolution is *should,* which means "ought to, but not necessarily will." In other words, debate must focus not on what the United States will do but on what it ought to do. As explained earlier, the term *should* allows the affirmative to focus on the desirability of action, not its political likelihood.

It is important to recognize, however, that while political arguments cannot be made to deny the right of the affirmative to advocate a policy, there may be cases in which the popularity of a proposed policy is relevant for considering the effectiveness of the policy. An example may make this point clear. Recently, Bill Bradley, then a United States Senator from New Jersey, argued for targeted aid programs to help Russia deal with an environmental crisis in Russia. Given the magnitude of the various environmental problems facing Russia, such programs might be enormously expensive. Even so, it would not be legitimate for the opponent of change to argue that Congress would not pass such a program, even though it is clear that the present Congress would never take that action. It is important that debate include ideas that are not yet politically feasible. Remember that not that many years ago, calls for equal rights for all Americans were not politically acceptable in Congress. Obviously, it was important that we talk about the need for equality in order to create the preconditions for legislation to guarantee equal rights under law for all Americans.

While the political feasibility argument would be ruled out of order as a "should-would" argument, the negative might legitimately be able to argue that in the current political situation passing an immense aid program for Russia would be counterproductive. They would argue that establishing such a program would produce a massive backlash among Americans who would be angry that Congress was expending large resources on Russia, rather than doing so on programs for all Americans. Essentially that argument is made in the *Congressional Record,* "Providing Housing for Russian Soldiers While Americans are Uprooted by Military Base Closings." Some in Congress are extremely angry that the United States is providing a small amount of aid to help Russian soldiers find housing. Obviously, that program is based on the premise that instability in Russia is more likely if soldiers lack a place to live. My point is that if some protest obviously reasonable programs to decrease the chance of a military coup in Russia, there could be much greater protest against expanded environmental assistance that might look just like a handout to many Americans.

Therefore, the negative could argue based on the protest in the present system that the likely effect of the plan would be to cause Congress either to cut other crucial aid to Russia or even eliminate all foreign aid. That latter result seems quite realistic given how unpopular foreign aid is with Congress and the people. Against this position, it would not be legitimate for the affirmative to say that it is a "should-would" argument. The backlash disadvantage deals not with whether a plan is politically feasible but with the effects of passing the plan in the present system.

The important point to remember is that the word *should* gives the affirmative the right to assume that the plan is enacted through whatever normal means apply in the area, in this case action by the President and/or Congress. But the word *should* does not give the advocate of change the right to ignore the effects of the plan in producing some sort of public backlash.

Substantially

The next important term in the resolution is *substantially,* which designates the aim of policy action, a major alteration in U.S. foreign policy toward Russia. According to *Black's, substantially* means "essentially; without material qualification; in the main; in accordance; materially; in a substantial manner." Similarly, *Webster's New Twentieth Century Dictionary* states that *substantially* means "in a substantial manner; solidly; firmly; with strength" or "largely; essentially; in the main." *CJS* notes that the term means "in the main; essentially; solidly; actually; really; truly; competently" and cites a recent case in which the term was used to mean "Strongly; for the most part."

CJS cites a number of cases in which the meaning of the root term, *substantial,* must be understood in context. *CJS* also says that *substantial* means "of or pertaining to substance or main part of something."

Clearly, the primary function of *substantially* in the resolution is to indicate that the change in U.S. foreign policy toward Russia must be major. The change must be "of substance" or of the main part of our foreign policy. However, it is also important to note that *substantially* is a "a relative and elastic term which should be interpreted in accordance with the context in which it is used" (*CJS*).

Given the definitions of *substantial* and *substantially,* the negative should be prepared to argue that the affirmative can only fulfill the resolution if they make a major alteration in the substance of U.S. foreign policy toward Russia. In this view, a change in study-abroad programs or even in U.S. medical assistance would not be a substantial one. Rather, to be resolutional, the change in policy must be both major in magnitude and also in substance. This means that the affirmative must propose a considerable alteration in the direction of present policy.

There are, however, several problems with a topicality argument stating that the term *substantially* requires the affirmative to make a major and substantive alteration in U.S. policy. First, as noted earlier, the term does not have a single clear meaning and is used in a variety of ways in different contexts. Second, the advocate of change should argue that their proposed action meets the term *substantially* by producing major benefits. They also might argue that in the context of U.S. foreign policy toward Russia the change is truly substantial. Since the advocates for any policy action inevitably claim that their proposal is significant in some way, the affirmative should be able to find contextual evidence supporting their interpretation that the proposal meets the meaning of *substantially.*

Third, the affirmative should argue that a strict interpretation of *substantially* would arbitrarily restrict the proponent of change to an unreasonably narrow resolution. It could be argued that to require the affirmative to advocate both a major change and one that alters the substantive nature of U.S. foreign policy is unreasonably restrictive. In this view, many substantial changes have been only in the magnitude of support. Surely, it could be argued, an increase in aid to Russia by 10 or 20% would be a substantial change in the given policy environment.

Closely associated with this view, the affirmative should argue that since there is no clear definition of *substantially* in the context of foreign policy, it would be unreasonable to apply an extremely strict definition of the term. Again, the affirmative should rely on sources defending the importance of their policy proposal to indicate that it would represent a substantial change from current policy.

All of this means that the term *substantially* is unlikely to be of much use to the opponent of change in limiting the resolution, except in relation to proposals that call for very small alterations in U.S. foreign policy. If the affirmative can demonstrate the importance of their proposal, that will go a long way toward demonstrating the substantial nature of the change involved.

Change

The term *change* means to "make or become different" *(Oxford American Dictionary.)* According to *Black's Law Dictionary, change* means to "make different in some particular; put one thing in place of another."

Change is obviously a vague term. It's function in the resolution is to require the affirmative to alter current policy. Of course, that alteration also must be a substantial one.

Change has two important implications for understanding the resolution. First, the affirmative must be able to indicate that they are altering current policy. There are some instances where this requirement may be important. In relation to NATO expansion, for instance, there is a strong argument that the current policy of the United States is to move on a process of gradually expanding NATO to include all those nations of Central and Eastern Europe that meet appropriate criteria for NATO membership. Arguably, an affirmative calling for admission of a particular nation or set of nations, say the three Baltic republics of Latvia, Estonia, and Lithuania, would be embracing the present system, at least if the three states meet the standards for NATO admission. Of course, the affirmative could argue that the states don't meet those standards, but this would seem to set up major disadvantages.

On the other hand, almost any advocate of the resolution will be able to argue that their proposal in some way alters current policy. For example, in relation to NATO expansion, it could be argued that present policy is to move slowly and that a more rapid process is needed. Thus, *change* is unlikely to be of much use in limiting the resolution, and use of the term *change* makes the resolution nondirectional. One could change U.S. policy toward Russia either by speeding up NATO expansion or slowing it down. Both policies represent an alteration in current U.S. relations with Russia and, therefore, meet the definition of *change*. This nondirectionality dramatically reduces the counterplan options of the negative. Since any change in policy meets the resolution, it would be resolutional for the negative to defend a counterplan that substantially altered U.S. policy toward Russia.

It could be argued that it is permissible for the negative to advocate a policy position that falls within the resolution (a topical counterplan), as long as that counterplan is competitive with the affirmative proposal. The only justification for this position is on strategic, rather than principled theoretical grounds. First, if the negative advocates resolutional action, then they in no way are negating the resolution. Imagine that in Congressional debate on the topic "Resolved: That social security reform is needed," a Senator opposed a call for limiting benefits by saying that the real need was for a change in the age at which someone could collect benefits. The proponent of the limit on benefits might say, "OK that is true too, but your position in no way negates the general resolution calling for reform of Social Security." As long as debate focuses on resolutions, as opposed to particular public policies, it is not permissible for the negative to advocate resolutional action.

Second, if the negative is allowed to advocate topical counterplans, that will decrease the incentive for research on specific proposals for change. Obviously, it is harder to research the specifics of an affirmative proposal than to advocate the same topical alternative in debate after debate. The result would be reduced clash.

What about the requirement that a topical counterplan must be competitive. In most instances, this restriction will rule out resolutional counterplans on this topic. For example, it would be possible both to expand NATO and to expand health assistance programs to Russia. It should be noted, however, that allowing resolutional counterplans, if they are competitive, has the effect of encouraging specious competitiveness arguments. For example, a team defending expanded health assistance programs might argue that Congress is capable of considering only one policy at a given time and that, consequently, it would be impossible to implement both expanded health assistance and expansion of NATO. While I think that argument is obviously false, since Congress often acts in multiple ways on a given issue, the truly unfortunate aspect is that allowing topical counterplans encourages this kind of faulty analysis.

Thus, because of the nature of resolutional advocacy, the importance of clearly dividing ground between the affirmative and negative, and the need to encourage research and clash, topical counterplans should not be accepted.

Its

The next term in the resolution is *its*. *Its* is a possessive, which specifies the "foreign policy" to be altered. In this case, it refers to the United States. The affirmative must alter the foreign policy of the United States in order to fulfill the resolution.

The only way that *its* might play a role in a debate would be if the opponent of change argued that the United States currently lacked any policy on a given aspect of our relations to Russia. Therefore, it would be argued, the affirmative could not meet the resolution because the United State lacked a policy to be altered.

The obvious problem with this analysis is that no policy is a policy. If the United States has no set policy on species preservation in Russia, that is in fact a policy of doing nothing about the species destruction problem.

Foreign Policy

The next important term in the resolution is *foreign policy*. According to *Webster's New Twentieth Century Dictionary, foreign* means "of, from, characteristic of, or dealing with another country or countries." *Black's* defines *foreign* as "belonging to another nation or country." *The Oxford American Dictionary* defines the term as "dealing with or involving other countries."

A policy is "the course or general plan of action adopted by a government or party or person" *(The Oxford American Dictionary)*. A similar definition is cited by *Webster's New Twentieth Century Dictionary,* which says a policy is "any governing principle, plan, or course of action." *Black's* adds that a policy encompasses "The general principles by which a government is guided in its management of public affairs, the legislature in its measures."

Put together, *foreign policy* would seem to mean "the plan or program dealing with another nation." This interpretation is also contextually supported. The journal *Foreign Policy* focuses on the programs of the United States in relation to other nations. And articles on U.S. foreign policy routinely focus on aid, trade, defense issues and so forth as are relevant to the relations between the United States and one or more other nations. Moreover, a synonym for *foreign policy* is *foreign affairs,* which is defined by *Webster's New Twentieth Century Dictionary* as "matters concerning the policy of a country in its relations with other countries."

There are several sub-issues that relate to the meaning of *foreign policy.* The first concerns the contrast between foreign and domestic. According to *Webster's New Twentieth Century, domestic* means "pertaining to one's own country; not foreign." The importance of this definition is that it indicates that *foreign* and *domestic* are exclusive terms. A domestic policy is, in this view, not a foreign policy. The contrasting nature of foreign and domestic policy is important as one of several arguments for limiting the resolution to policies such as trade, foreign assistance, sanctions on trade, military policy, threats, negotiations, and agreements between the United States and other nations, that are commonly interpreted as part of our foreign policy. Note that issues like the minimum wage are generally considered to be domestic policies, although the minimum wage may have some effect on international relations. Clearly, a higher minimum wage decreases the competitiveness of the United States in world trade by increasing labor costs. But even though there is a relationship between raising the minimum wage and decreasing U.S. foreign trade, the minimum wage is always considered to be a domestic issue.

Thus, the contrast between the meaning of *domestic* and *foreign* suggests that the negative should argue that there is a clear distinction between the two terms. In addition, the standard for distinguishing between foreign and domestic policy is one of the directness of the relationship. If the policy directly alters a plan or program dealing with a foreign nation, it is a foreign policy. If it alters a plan or program dealing with the United States that indirectly influences our relations with other nations, the proposal is a domestic policy and, according to this logic, outside of the resolution.

There are additional reasons for preferring an interpretation of *foreign policy* restricting the term to actions that are tied to direct changes in U.S. actions in relation to another nation. One way to get at this point is to consider the subject areas that are discussed in a general analysis of United States-Russian relations. In a book edited by Sharyl Cross and Marina A. Oborotova, *The New Chapter in United States–Russian Relations,* there are chapters dealing directly with United States and Russian foreign policy toward the other nation. There are chapters dealing with arms control and other defense issues. There are chapters dealing with economic relations, human rights, the chance of U.S.-Russian cooperation in the Middle East, and even environmental relations. But all of these chapters focus on a direct relationship between the United States and Russia. There are no chapters that focus on U.S. policy toward France or Germany because those subjects would not be perceived as directly related to U.S. policy toward Russia.

This view is supported by the treatment of U.S. relations with China in any number of analyses. Commentators writing about U.S. foreign policy toward China never argue that a policy toward China is also toward Russia (see P Doherty "The Heat"). Nor do journals or indexes list articles in that manner. For example, an article in *Reader's Digest* which argues that China is a greater threat than Russia (P Zakaria) was indexed under topics relating to U.S. foreign policy toward Russia. But it was indexed under that topic because it dealt directly with the subject. On the other hand, articles that deal with U.S. foreign policy toward China are never indexed under the topic area relating to Russia.

Thus, it would seem that *foreign policy* is both an expansive and a limited term. It is expansive in the sense that it includes all aspects of United States relations with Russia. The expansive nature of the term is indicated by the subjects considered in Congressional hearings and the subjects included within the topic in various indexes. On the other hand, the term is limited in that it excludes domestic policies that indirectly influence our relations with Russia and policies that are primarily directed at other nations, but that arguably relate to Russia in some way.

An additional argument might be made distinguishing between foreign and defense policy. In this view, it could be argued that *foreign policy* and *defense policy* are terms of art that can be distinguished from each other. For example, a *Congressional Quarterly* article on the general topic of "Defense and Foreign Policy," dealt with foreign policy issues such as "NATO Enlargement" and "Bosnia Mission" first, before confronting issues such as "Missiles and Anti-Missiles," which fell under the defense policy label. This indicates that there is a distinction between foreign and defense policy (see P Towell "Senate Boosts" 1719–1722).

There is good reason, however, to believe that the two terms overlap substantially and that many defense policies also fall into the context of foreign policy. For example, in a recent essay on expanding NATO, Adam Garfinkle suggested that "The question of enlarging NATO has occasioned the most important foreign policy debate in the United States since the end of the Cold War, and rightly so" (P 23). Clearly, NATO expansion could be labelled a defense policy. At the same time, it also falls into the area of foreign policy. This suggests that defense policies that have implications relating to the conduct of United States foreign affairs or which directly relate to foreign nations, legitimately can be considered also to be part of the foreign policy of the United States. And the fact that some defense policies are not foreign policies, as in the *Congressional Quarterly* example cited above, does not mean that some defense policies are not also foreign policies.

Thus, the argument that policies like NATO enlargement or proposing trade sanctions on Russia because of arms sales to Iran fall into the area of defense policy, as opposed to foreign policy, is probably a weak one. It is worth adding that this argument has the unfortunate effect of excluding from the resolution issues directly related to the foreign relations of the United States and Russia.

The position that including a proposal within defense policy does not necessarily exclude it from foreign policy is also supported by contextual usage of the term *foreign policy*. Take the arms sales example mentioned above. It would not be uncommon to find that issue discussed in a Congressional hearing on either general defense policy or a hearing on the topic of U.S. foreign policy toward Russia. Thus, there are good reasons to reject as overly restrictive a distinction between foreign and defense (or military) policy.

In sum, the term *foreign policy* includes negotiations, trade concerns, defense issues, sanctions and other threats, foreign assistance, exchange programs, technology assistance or controls and other policies that directly relate to United States relations with Russia.

Toward

The next important term in the resolution is *toward,* which according to *CJS* "is said to be a word of somewhat indefinite meaning." On the other hand, *CJS* adds that the meaning is "controlled by the context" and cites a definition as "indicating, in one sense, direction in space and meaning in the direction of." *The Oxford American Dictionary* cites three useful definitions: "in the direction of," "in relation to," and "for the purpose of achieving or promoting" as in the government made moves "toward" strengthening Social Security.

These definitions suggest that the foreign policy to be changed must be in the direction of Russia or for the purpose of achieving some aim in relation to Russia. There is no question that all of the main subsets of foreign policy meet the definition of *toward*. For example, arms control negotiations are both "in the direction of Russia," in that they are conducted with Russian negotiators, and "for the purpose of" achieving reductions in missiles by both the United States and Russia. A similar point could be made about the other policies I listed.

The key question is whether polices that indirectly influence Russia are "toward" Russia. Of course, I already have argued that such indirect influence policies do not meet the definition of *foreign policy*. On the other hand, the affirmative could argue that the definition of *foreign policy* varies with the context. For example, regulation of technology is considered part of foreign policy today, while it would not have been considered to fall into that category in the 19th century.

It could be argued that any program that influences U.S.-Russian relations is in fact a policy *toward* Russia. As I explained earlier, that interpretation would open the resolution to a wealth of interpretations. It also would make topical any foreign policy concern with any nation, as long as that issue tangentially related to Russia.

Against this broad interpretation, the negative should argue that it is unacceptable because it produces an extremely expansive topic. The negative also should argue that the interpretation violates the purpose of the resolution that is to focus debate on the particular subject area of U.S. foreign policy in relation to Russia. If a host of domestic policies and foreign relations with a variety of nations are included within the resolution, then there is no longer a focus on U.S. foreign policy with Russia.

Second, the negative should argue that the expansive interpretation of *toward* is based on an unacceptable "effects" topicality. In this view, the proposed action is not directly topical; it does not alter a U.S. foreign policy in the direction of Russia. Rather, it alters a policy that has a secondary effect of influencing Russia. Effects topicality of this type is arguably illegitimate because it makes the judgment of topicality dependent on affirmative solvency. This is unacceptable because topicality is a jurisdictional issue that must be resolved prior to consideration of the substantive merit of the proposal. Of course, the advocate of change will argue that all proposals meet the standard of changing foreign policy based on their effects.

Third, the negative should argue that the broad interpretation does not meet the "for the purpose of achieving" definition. In this view, domestic policy changes or alterations of foreign policy toward other nations are not "for the purpose of achieving" some result with Russia. Rather, they are designed to achieve some alternative purpose and only indirectly influence U.S. policy toward Russia.

Fourth, the conclusion that to meet the resolution U.S. foreign policy must be changed in some way that is directly aimed at Russia is supported by a consideration of the context of U.S. foreign policy and Russia. A good illustration of this point is provided by a recent dispute over what has been called the "special relationship" of the United States with Armenia. Armenia, formerly part of the Soviet Union, is a small nation in the Caucasus that borders Georgia, Turkey, Iran, and Azerbaijan. A recent dispute over U.S. aid to Armenia focused on issues involved in the conflict between Armenia and Azerbaijan and also the amount of military aid received by Armenia from the Russians. In an article reporting on this dispute in the *Congressional Quarterly,* Carroll Doherty treats the foreign policy issue as one relating to, and therefore "toward," Armenia, except as it concerns the Russian arms sales, in which case it relates both to Russia and Armenia. It would seem, therefore, that foreign policy is toward a particular nation, such as Russia, when it directly impacts that nation and not toward that nation when it indirectly impacts the nation.

In the real world, policies that tangentially impact U.S.-Russian relations are not seen as part of the nation's foreign policy toward Russia. A recent dispute over Russian sales of high technology to Iran illustrates this point. The call for sanctions against Russia because of the technology transfers clearly falls within U.S. foreign policy toward Russia. Members of Congress talk about it in those terms, and articles related to the sanctions are indexed under topics relating to U.S. Russian relations. On the other hand, policies responding to the Iranian threat, but not directly aimed at Russia, are not considered part of our foreign policy toward Russia and are not indexed in that manner. A recent *Congressional Quarterly* article reported first on the call for sanctions and then discussed a proposal "to improve anti-missile systems protecting troops and allies in the Persian Gulf" (P Towell "House Poised" 2780). This latter action was discussed under a subheading "Anti-Missile Defense," and there was no mention of any linkage between the proposal and U.S. policy toward Russia. Similarly, an article on NATO expansion referred to related subjects such as a proposal to keep U.S. troops in Bosnia for a longer period as "collateral debates" (P Towell "NATO Expansion" 2416), indicating that they were not considered to fall in the category of U.S. foreign policy toward Russia. These examples indicate that policy makers draw a distinction between proposals that directly alter U.S. foreign policy toward Russia and policies that in some way respond to a situation involving Russia, but are not aimed at Russia specifically.

The same point can be made in relation to domestic policy concerns. Earlier, I mentioned the minimum wage as a policy that could indirectly influence U.S. relations with Russia. A higher minimum wage would make Russia more competitive in relation to the United States. But neither policy makers nor those who do indexes for periodicals, the *Congressional Record* and so forth would consider a minimum wage proposal as being toward Russia. Thus, there are strong reasons based on the context of the policy dispute to restrict the affirmative to changes in foreign policy that directly alter the United States relationship with Russia.

In sum, there are good reasons to prefer the restricted as opposed to the expansive definition of *toward*. The analysis of this term illustrates the important point that it is not enough to merely argue competing definitions. There are interpretations of the word *toward* that could be used to justify an extremely broad topic. Instead, the negative in this case (and the affirmative on other topicality positions) must provide reasons justifying their interpretation as superior. Those grounds will be tied to the purposes of debate resolutions, which are to define the scope of debate on a particular topic, to provide appropriate ground to both sides, and to define a topic area that is neither too narrow nor too broad to be debated.

Russia

The final term in the resolution is *Russia,* which obviously references the nation Russia. Russia is important in the resolution primarily to indicate the nation toward which the change in U.S. foreign policy must be taken.

It could be argued that the changed U.S. foreign policy must be relative to the nation and, therefore, to the government of Russia. I think this argument is clearly specious. First, the resolution could have specified the government of Russia, rather than simply Russia. Second, Russia as the name of the country includes more than merely the government. It encompasses the entire nation.

Third, a change in U.S. foreign policy in relation to the people of Russia is also a change toward the government of Russia. In the early days after the end of the Soviet Union, a great deal of U.S. aid was sent directly to the government of Russia. As I will indicate in the next chapter, that is no longer the case. Almost all U.S. foreign assistance is given directly to some nongovernmental group in Russia. The switch from aid to the government to aid to organizations in Russia clearly represented a substantial change in U.S. foreign policy toward Russia. As this example indicates, a policy that is aimed at the people of Russia is also aimed at the government of Russia.

Conclusion

The resolution calling for a change in U.S. foreign policy toward Russia is both timely and important. The scope of the resolution is large but not so large that it becomes undebatable. The danger is that the resolution will be stretched with a broad interpretation of *foreign policy* and *toward*.

Therefore, the most important topicality positions on the resolution for the negative are to develop strong defenses of the more restricted interpretations of *foreign policy* and *toward*. In developing those positions, both contextual material on U.S. foreign policy and Russia and principles tied to the purposes of debate resolutions can be utilized to support the argument. In addition, the negative should develop the argument that in order to meet the meaning of *substantially,* the affirmative must advocate a truly major change. As I noted earlier, this argument will be more difficult to maintain because of inherent ambiguities in the term *substantially.*

In developing these positions, both the proponent and opponent of change should approach topicality arguments in the same way that they do substantive claims. That is, they should research the positions and develop them in depth. In a sense a topicality argument is a lot like a disadvantage except that the impact relates not to the substantive effect of a plan but to the effect of a given interpretation on the universe of policies included within the resolution. In that way the "impact" of a topicality argument from the perspective of the negative generally will be that the affirmative position either shifts debate away from the appropriate context of the resolution or makes the resolution undebatable. The affirmative will make precisely the same kind of arguments but from their side of the resolution. So for example, the negative is likely to argue that a given interpretation is overly broad, while the affirmative would argue that the alternative interpretation is too narrow and denies appropriate ground to the advocate of change.

2 The Status of U.S. Foreign Policy and Russia

The purposes of this chapter are to provide an overview of the context of U.S. foreign policy toward Russia and a brief discussion of the major methods of implementing policy change toward Russia. In carrying out those purposes, I first will describe the present political and economic situation in Russia and then sketch the evolution of U.S. foreign policy toward Russia from the last years of the Soviet Union to the present. In the final section, I will discuss in general terms the pros and cons associated with the three primary methods of carrying out U.S. foreign policy toward Russia: direct policy action, foreign assistance, and sanctions or threats to change Russian policy.

Russia's Movement from a Totalitarian Communist System Toward the Free Market and Democracy

Unlike the nations of Western Europe and, for that matter, most of the nations of Central and Eastern Europe, Russia has almost no historical experience with liberal democracy. For over seventy years, Russia was a totalitarian society ruled by the Communist Party. In the Stalin era, millions (some experts say multiple tens of millions) of Russians were murdered in purges and famines caused by state policy. And even after Stalin, the Soviet Union remained a rigid totalitarian nation in which there was no freedom of expression, no democracy, and a large system of slave labor camps (the Gulag), in which political criminals were sent for long sentences.

And before the communists took power, Russia was an empire headed by the Czar. The point is that Russia had no significant experience with democracy before the end of the Soviet Union in 1991.

Only a decade ago, the idea that the Iron Curtain would be pulled down and that communist rule across the Soviet Union and Eastern Europe would end seemed like a pipe dream. Almost no one believed that it would happen in the foreseeable future and certainly not as rapidly as it did occur. The key point in the end of the Soviet Union was when Mikhail Gorbachev became the party chief.

Gorbachev and the End of the Soviet Union

Gorbachev became the leader of the Soviet Union in 1985 and introduced a program of "new thinking" (B Cross and Oborotova "The New Chapter" 2) that changed his nation and the world. He initiated reform efforts in both the domestic and the foreign policy arenas. In domestic policy, Gorbachev's two main initiatives were *glasnost* and *perestroika*.

Glasnost can be "translated as 'openness' but more literally as 'a public voice'" (B Linden and Prybyla 73). *Glasnost* was a reform designed to open up the Soviet system and make it more responsive. It led to "far reaching public debate," resulting in "searching criticism and exposure of the regime's despotic past" (B Linden and Prybyla 73). Civic organizations were founded and "censorship fell away" (B Linden and Prybyla 73). Anders Aslund notes that

> The process culminated with the First Congress of Peoples Deputies of the USSR in May and June 1989, whose sessions were televised and attracted huge audiences. For the first time in the Soviet Union anything could be said in public. What could be said was, and none was punished. (B *How Russia* 32)

With *Glasnost,* Russia took the first small steps toward becoming a free society. While Gorbachev hoped that the new openness would make the Soviet system more effective, in fact, it had the effect of exposing all of the evils of the system, and perhaps more importantly, of making it clear that change in fact was possible.

Perestroika was Gorbachev's attempt to reform the economic and governmental system. *Perestroika* began as an attempt to streamline the economy, moved to "a major reformation of the regime's political institutions," and finally became "a *transformation* of the regime itself" (B Linden and Prybyla 73). For example, in June 1988 Gorbachev called for establishing a new parliamentary system in which two-thirds of the parliament would be elected and one-third chosen by the party (B Linden and Prybyla 76).

While Gorbachev wanted *perestroika* to shake up the government system of the Soviet Union, he was not willing to subject himself to the risks posed by free election. Gorbachev took one of the one-third safe seats. Yeltsin, who Gorbachev had brought into the Politburo as an ally in his reform efforts and then kicked out when he became too fervent in supporting reform, ran for a free seat and was elected overwhelmingly. As this example indicates, Gorbachev had let loose the concept of reform but was not personally willing to follow that concept to its logical conclusion: the end of totalitarian party rule and the birth of a liberal democracy.

Gorbachev was trying to save the Soviet Union not destroy it. *Glasnost* and *Perestroika* were his attempt to reform the system, improve economic efficiency, eliminate functionless bureaucracy, and, therefore, narrow the gap to the West. Anders Aslund explains that "To Gorbachev, reforms were a means to an end rather than an end in themselves. His aim was to reinforce and revitalize the USSR so that it could maintain its superpower status" (B *How Russia* 27). What he did not realize was that half-steps could not be enough to fix the system. And his reform efforts pleased no one. "The new regime satisfied neither the defenders of the old party regime nor the new political forces his electoral politics had brought into being" (B Linden and Prybyla 77). By unleashing reform, many believe that Gorbachev doomed the Soviet Union.

On the domestic scene, Gorbachev's efforts opened up a floodgate of reform sentiment. One of the key leaders of that sentiment was Boris Yeltsin, who was forced out of the Politburo in 1987 and quit the Communist Party after his election to Parliament in 1990. Yeltsin was elected President of Russia in 1991, prior to the death of the Soviet Union.

After starting the reform process, Gorbachev received massive aid from the West. One estimate is that in 1990 and 1991, the Soviet Union received $50 billion, far more than Russia would receive after the death of Soviet communism (see P Griffin 226). Of course, Gorbachev had some strong negotiating levers. A great deal of the aid was received as an implicit bargain with the West. In essence, Gorbachev traded allowing the Iron Curtain to come down in Eastern Europe for cash. In particular, West Germany provided substantial aid at the time of the reunification with East Germany.

Gorbachev also implemented a reformist foreign policy. One of the first key steps was to allow for foreign inspectors to carry out visits on Soviet territory. This 1986 agreement quickly led to a treaty in which the United States and the Soviets banned intermediate range nuclear forces (P Sharp 130). In 1990, the Conventional Forces in Europe treaty was signed, which established equal ceilings for NATO and Warsaw Pact forces and created zones in which there also were limitations on force deployment. This treaty led to the "destruction of some 50,000 pieces of treaty-limited equipment during a three-year reduction period between 1992 and 1995" (P Sharp 130–131).

How did the Soviet Union move from superpower to dissolution? The collapse of the Soviet Union after so many decades as a world superpower seemed shocking. One expert argues that the key factor was growing "institutional loss of confidence" that "turned into a self-fulfilling spiral" (P Kotkin). Soviet expert Steven L. Solnick compares this result to "a colossal 'bank' run" (qtd. in P Kotkin 26).

The main factor producing this loss of confidence was reform. Gorbachev's reforms had several significant effects leading to the destruction of the Soviet system. First, the reforms had the effect of demonstrating that change was possible. As early as 1961, internal poll data on members of the Communist youth league found that "only one-quarter of them listed building a Communist society as a goal of their lives" (P Kotkin). Thus, even among those who should have been the most committed communists, there was remarkably little support for the Soviet system. However, the system endured because there did not seem to be any alternative. With *Glasnost* and *Perestroika,* however, it became clear that change could occur. That opened the floodgates to public opposition against the system.

The second key factor was the breakdown of the Communist Party system. In an attempt to facilitate implementation of his reform proposals, Gorbachev granted greater autonomy to the Communist Party structure in individual Soviet republics. In so doing he "also inadvertently placed the republics beyond Moscow's control" (P Kotkin 27).

A third key factor was the terrible status of the Soviet economy. Anders Aslund argues that by 1991, the Soviet economy faced an economic crisis (B *How Russia* 41). Gorbachev's reforms were an attempt to confront that crisis, but they were too little and too late.

While Gorbachev's reforms were not enough to salvage the Russian economy, they were more than enough to outrage traditional hard line communists. On August 21, 1991, these hardline Soviet leaders attempted to take over the Soviet Union and depose Gorbachev. Gorbachev was placed under house arrest, and for a time it appeared that the Soviet Union and the entire world might return to the Cold War era.

But it was too late for the communists. Everyone knew the system had failed and the people had experienced a taste of freedom. In this circumstance, Boris Yeltsin became the key leader of those who opposed the coup. Yeltsin, who had been elected President of Russia in June 1991 elections, led pro-reform forces from the parliament building in Moscow. In the most memorable moment of the coup, Yeltsin climbed up on an army tank outside the parliament building to denounce the coup. Senator Bill Bradley describes this moment:

> On August 19, 1991, Russian president Boris Yeltsin mounted a tank outside the Russian White House and helped to seal the fate of an empire. His act of defiance consigned the Union of Soviet Socialist Republics (USSR) to the dustbin of history and launched his country—and ours—into uncharted waters. (P 81)

When the plotters gave up, Yeltsin was a national hero. Gorbachev attempted to return to power, but his day was done. And so with a whimper, not a bang, the Soviet Union was dissolved on Christmas day 1991. Boris Yeltsin was the first president of a new Russia.

It is important to recognize the magnitude of the problem facing Yeltsin. The death of Soviet communism called for truly radical change. Strobe Talbott, then a *Time* columnist and later a State Department official in the Clinton administration, wrote

> Yeltsin is sometimes said to be presiding over the Second Russian Revolution, but that understates the challenges he faces. Russia is actually in the throes of three transformations at once: from totalitarianism to democracy, from a command economy to a free market and from a multinational empire to a nation-state. (qtd. in P Griffin 220)

And he was doing all of this while sailing off into waters that from the perspective of Russia were completely uncharted.

Russian Political Reform

It is important to recognize that until the end of the Soviet Union, the title "President of Russia" was largely ceremonial. It was Gorbachev who called the shots. But after the failed coup and the death of the Soviet Union, Yeltsin had both the job title and the national credibility to act as the leader of Russia. Yeltsin's first important reform efforts were focused on the economy. In fact, he initiated a major economic reform program in January 1992, only a short time after he took power. I will discuss this program in more depth in the next section.

In relation to reform of the political system, the most important development was the end of what had been essentially a Russian empire, the Soviet Union. The Soviet Union broke up into a loose Confederation of Independent States (CIS). Since several of these new states had been oppressed within the Soviet Union, calling the CIS a loose confederation may overstate the degree of organization. For example, several of the states of the former Soviet Union have expressed interest in joining NATO, in order to get the protection of the American nuclear umbrella in case Russia returns to totalitarianism. In any case, one of Yeltsin's great accomplishments was helping to organize the breakup of the Soviet empire.

The first key event for Russian democracy occurred in October 1993, when Yeltsin ordered the use of force to disband the "Congress of People's Deputies" a legislature dating from the Soviet era. Yeltsin took this step because of strong opposition from holdovers from the Soviet era, including even his Vice President, Aleksandr Rutskoi. Some have viewed this as a necessary step in the democratization process. Others argued that "Democracy in Russia had failed once again" (P McFaul 320). The situation was so serious that it was not even clear if Russia would maintain its power. Paul Goble of the Carnegie Endowment predicted that "Russia is unlikely to survive 1993 in its current borders" (qtd. in P Griffin 228).

In retrospect, Yeltsin's action in crushing opponents of reform can be seen as both antidemocratic and necessary for democracy. The action itself was an attack on what might be called an illegitimate democratic institution. Such an action would not be tolerated in any established democratic society. In the Russia of the time, Yeltsin may have had no choice.

After the military action, significant political reforms were put into place. In December 1993, a new constitution was ratified in a public referendum. The new constitution made a number of important changes in the Russian governmental situation.

First, the constitution guaranteed equal rights for all of the units in the Russian federal system. Only Chechnya rejected it (P McFaul 320). Commentators believe that the balance of power between Moscow and the provinces reflected a move away from central control and toward a more balanced system (see P McFaul 321). In that regard, Strobe Talbott noted recently that "Political power is devolving downward from the Kremlin and outward from Moscow." He added, "overall, the devolution of power has already made government in Russia more accountable to average citizens. It has engendered greater pluralism and more competition of ideas" (P "America and Russia" 537).

Second, the constitution "provided the legal basis for a strong presidential system that has inordinate executive power compared to Western constitutions" (P McFaul 320). The president is the dominant official in the system; there is no vice president. The parliament (Duma) does have the power to draft laws, approve the President's candidate for Prime Minister, and ratify the national budget. However, the specific procedures mandated in all of these cases undercut parliamentary power. For example, "If the Duma rejects the president's candidate for prime minister three times, then the president has the right to dissolve the Duma and call for new elections—a procedure that can also be used during budgetary impasses" (P McFaul 321). It would be fair to say that the principles of separation of power and limited executive power are not adequately represented in the Russian system. In fact, one expert on Russian politics, Steven Cohen of Princeton, argues that "the Parliament has no real powers" (P 5). Moreover, if the president dies or is incapacitated, the prime minister becomes acting president and new elections are held within 90 days (P Fish 329).

The current Russian system, which has been labelled "superpresidentialism" (see P Fish), has some important weaknesses. First, it is not a fully democratic system in that one person, the president, wields extraordinary power. Second, the system can be quite fragile since "Any lapse in the president's command of office automatically creates a vacuum of power" (P Fish 327). Third, since so much rides on presidential elections, the system can be destabilized. M. Steven Fish of the University of California at Berkeley writes:

> After presidential elections, losers are more likely to resort to illegal behavior, since they may feel excluded from the one office that controls most of political life. Where the losers in the contest for the presidency are challengers, they may abandon peaceful competition in favor of mass action or insurgency. Where the losers are the incumbent and his or her supporters, they may be tempted—and have the capabilty—to thwart a peaceful transfer of power. (P 327)

When there is so much riding on a single election, instability will be an inherent part of the system.

Fourth, the system does not adequately incorporate the principle that the powers of the various branches of the government should be separate. One issue relates to the linkage between the executive and the court system. Cohen of Princeton says that Russian appellate courts have "little independence from the presidency" (P 5).

Fifth, the absence of checks and balances in the system increases the risk of corruption. Finally, "The absence of a vice presidency under the current Russian constitution is a glaring institutional flaw that guarantees the persistence of a high level of political uncertainty" (P Fish 329).

On the other hand, it is easy to overestimate the dangers posed by super-presidentialism in the present constitution. Fish himself refers to the present situation as "decaying Caesarism" a phrase he uses to describe a situation in which the president has vast formal power, but is "sharply circumscribed in actual practice" (P 330). In addition, in the immediate aftermath of the death of Soviet communism, there is a powerful argument that a strong leader like Yeltsin was needed to guarantee that there was not a turn back toward totalitarianism. And for all of

Yeltsin's many weaknesses—excessive drinking, health problems, occasionally eccentric behavior, and so forth—he has continued to support democracy and economic reform.

In 1993 and again in 1995, Russians voted in parliamentary elections. The news in the 1993 elections was that Russian nationalist Vladimir Zhirinovsky received 23% of the vote. At the time of the 1993 elections, many in the West decried Russia's move toward nationalism and totalitarianism. It now appears that their fear was overstated. In the 1995 elections, opposition parties, including both nationalists and the communists, did better than the reformers. The communists won the largest percentage of the vote (only 22%) (P Cooper "Russia's Political" 389).

The return of the communists to political prominence probably was tied to voter resentment against the effects of reform. In another sense, however, the success of these opposition groups supported the view that democracy had been entrenched within the Russian system.

In 1996, Yeltsin won re-election as Russian President. At one point, his re-election seemed extremely doubtful.

Yeltsin was extremely unpopular, had been forced to fire the architect of much of the economic reform program, Anatoly Chubais, had suffered from severe health problems, and was rumored to be an alcoholic. It appeared that he had little chance of winning re-election.

However, Yeltsin was successful in winning reelection. The major new capitalist figures in the nation threw their economic resources behind him, an action that many experts think was decisive. And Yeltsin ran a very active campaign, at least through the first ballot, demonstrating that he was strong enough to serve as President of Russia. In the first round of balloting, he held a narrow lead over the communist candidate. In the run-off, Yeltsin won decisively. Many say that Yeltsin's come-from-behind victory can be tied to public opposition to a return to communism. Yeltsin also ran a very strong campaign and was clever in inviting former general Aleksandr Lebed, who ran third in the original balloting, to head his defense team.

What did the election say about Russian democracy? At one level, the election results suggest that Russian democracy is quite strong. Participation in elections has increased from roughly 50% in 1993 to almost 70% in the presidential elections of 1996 (P McFaul 320). This participation rate, which is far higher than in the United States, indicates the existence of a robust democracy. And election observers labelled the 1996 election as generally free and, with the exception of media coverage, fair (see the report of the International Observer Mission in D *Russia's Election* 73-78). Based on such data, Deputy Secretary of State Strobe Talbott recently referred to the 1996 Russian presidential election as "a vote for reform, for the future, and against a candidate representing a party [the communists] whose very name is a synonym for the past" (P "U.S-Russian" 361).

On the other hand, some see the election not as proof that democracy has become entrenched in Russia, but as one more sign of Russian corruption. So, for example, Steven Cohen, professor of politics and Russian studies at Princeton, characterizes the election as "one of the most corrupt in recent European history" (P 5). Daniel Singer argues that "the election was a fraud perpetrated on the Russian public: The Russians would not have voted for Yeltsin had they known he was such an invalid" (P 18). Others argue that Russia is evolving into a political system in which "robber baron" capitalists have major control. In this view, "The combined resources of state and private business produced a campaign whose bias beat all records for a supposedly 'democratic' non-totalitarian country" (P Singer 18).

Some see the election results themselves as disquieting. Richard Pipes of Harvard notes in relation to the first round of the election that "had the anti-liberal opposition combined forces it would have decisively defeated him [Yeltsin]" with 52% of the vote against 35% for Yeltsin (P 69). Pipes concludes that

> The popular base of democracy in the country is thin and brittle; the political climate can change overnight. Countries like Russia, lacking in strong party organizations and loyalties, are capable of swinging wildly from one extreme to another, often in response to a demagogue who promises quick and easy solutions. (P 70)

Michael McFaul of Stanford and the Carnagie Endowment makes a similar point when he notes that "what happens in the absence of those organizing ideologies is that it allows for extremists, populists, people without a set of ideas" to do well in elections. McFaul concludes "That, to me, is a very dangerous sign, and it's dangerous because there's not a party system there to control that kind of movement" (D *Russia's Election* 21).

In addition to the election results and the establishment of a constitution, there has been one other important action in relation to the Russian political system. In 1994, Russia began using troops to quell a rebellion in the breakaway province of Chechnya, which is in southern Russia. It is important to understand that Chechnya was not set up as an independent state at the death of the Soviet Union. Rather, it was a province in Russia, in the same way that Oregon is a state in the United States.

In the first sixteen months of the conflict, more than 30,000 people were killed (P Cooper "Russia's Political" 390). Despite the brutality of the war, the United States did little to criticize Russian actions, a policy that Marshall I. Goldman of Harvard labelled as "inexcusable" (qtd. in P Cooper "Russia's Political 391). Over the course of the conflict between 40,000 and 60,000 people were killed (P Goltz 20). Other sources estimate that more than 100,000 people were killed (P McFaul 321).

The conflict ended in 1996 when Aleksandr Lebed brokered a deal with the leaders of Chechnya. Although the final details have not been worked out, it appears that some form of independence or quasi-independence will be achieved by Chechnya.

What is the status of the Russian political system? The answer is mixed. Clearly, there are major weaknesses in the Russian democratic system. Russia's political institutions are dominated by the presidency, which in the words of *The New York Times* has "lopsided power" in the system (P "The State" WK 14). It is also a political system that is built around the personalities of the leaders of various parties. Walter Connor notes that "In a time of new, shallow-rooted institutions, national-level politics is necessarily personalized" (B 177).

One of the major problems with the system is the total dominance of the president, in this case Yeltsin. He is as Paul Quinn-Judge argues "the pivotal figure in Russian politics" (P 38). Yeltsin "rules by arbitrating among competing factions in his own administration and by intimidating the opposition-controlled Duma when necessary" (P Quinn-Judge 38). In this regard, some claim that the United States may have made a mistake in placing all our bets on Yeltsin. Henry Kissinger argues that Yeltsin is anything but a true democrat. He says, "Yeltsin has shown few signs since that democratic values, including acceptance of dissent, are a central part of his value system" (P 42). Recently, Jane M.O. Sharp of the Institute for Public Policy Research argued that

> The optimists in Washington and Bonn may be correct that Yeltsin will turn out to be a democrat, but there is no evidence of it on the arms control front. There, as in Chechnya, Yeltsin has so far been closer to Leonid Brezhnev than Gorbachev. (P 134)

And David Remnick notes that over time "Yeltsin became more and more isolated and withdrawn from public life" and in that way was behaving "very much like a tsar" (P "How Russia" 10). In this regard, Sergei Kovalev argues that Yeltsin turned away from democratization in 1994 in favor of a "desire to 'establish order in the country'"(P 28). Of course, he also argues that after the defeat in Chechnya, Yeltsin turned back to the reformers (P 30). Many others agree that Yeltsin has moved toward authoritarianism (see testimony of Peter Reddaway in D *Russia's Election* 22–26).

Moreover, Yeltsin sometimes does things that only can be described as odd. In fact, Yeltsin occasionally acts in a manner that some have labelled as "bizarre" and others have attributed to over-medication. One political reporter noted that in some "recent appearances, the 67-year-old president seemed to have little awareness of where he was or why he was there" (P Kaplan A16).

One example of the inherent instability of a system in which so much power is vested in one man is that in mid-spring 1998 Yeltsin fired his entire Cabinet, including Prime Minister Viktor Chernomyrdin (P Kaplan A16). In the aftermath of this act, the *New York Times* worried about a possible "scramble for power" if Yeltsin became incapacitated or died (P "The State" WK 14). Eventually the crisis was resolved when the Duma backed down and agreed to accept Yeltsin's new candidate for Prime Minister after twice rejecting him.

Yeltsin's health is also a serious issue. Katrina vanden Heuvel says simply that Yeltsin "is unlikely ever to return to office as a healthy leader" (P 5). When he is ill "the country stalls in neutral" (P Quinn-Judge 38). This has created a situation in which in the words of David Remnick, "the Kremlin depends on the heart tissue of one man" (P "Can Russia" 46). Some experts believe that Yeltsin may be quite ill. Such a situation could create "uncertainty about the entire nation's immediate and long-term health" (P Quinn-Judge 38).

On the other hand, Yeltsin sometimes acts in a vigorous manner and seems fully in control (P Kaplan A16). And it is easy to overstate what the *New York Times* referred to in the title of an article as "Czar Boris's Madness" (P Gordon "Searching" WK 4). Later in the same article, Michael R. Gordon noted that

> it is important not to overdramatize Mr. Yeltsin's moves. The vast majority of his top aides are being reappointed, including Foreign Minister Yevgeny M. Primakov, Defense Minister Igor D. Sergeyev and a leading pro-reform aide, Boris Y. Nemtsov. The financial markets took the dismissal of the Cabinet calmly. (P "Searching" WK 4)

In sum, the overwhelming power of the president in the Russian system is a definite weakness in their political system. On the other hand, that presidential power may have been needed in the context of Russian reform over the last five years.

In addition to placing excessive power in the hands of the president, the Russian political system has other weaknesses as well. Some argue that Russia has not made a complete transition to democracy. In a recent commentary in the the *New York Times Magazine,* Russian reformer Grigory Yavlinsky argues that Russia has "regressed to a replica of the old Soviet system, with different titles" (P 66). In this view, institutional inertia has prevented truly fundamental change. Yavlinsky claims that "The bureaucracy, the absence of civil society, the existence of the old Soviet monopolies all created obstacles for people who wanted to live differently or start their own businesses" (P 66).

A third point of weakness in the Russian system relates to political parties, which are far weaker than in Western democracies. Parties play a number of crucial functions in a democratic system, including providing an outlet for citizen participation, an on-going structure for picking political leaders, and so forth. Those functions are not currently being fulfilled in Russia. On the other hand, some commentators see signs that parties are growing in strength (P Fish 328).

A fourth weakness is that Russia lacks a strong court system to enforce the law in a fair and impartial fashion (P McFaul 325). As a result "The combination of a weak state and an incompetent judicial system has produced a sense of anarchy in Russia" (P McFaul 325).

Clearly, there are reasons to be pessimistic about the status of Russia's political institutions. Anatol Lieven of the United States Institute of Peace is not optimistic that a progressive democratic society can be created. He concludes that it "seems unlikely that Russia will be able to establish a stable and prosperous democracy, even in the longer term. Public apathy and demoralization, as well as private violence, are so extensive that it will be difficult for a true civil society to emerge" (P 22). Another sign of weakness in the institutions of democracy in Russia is that there already is talk of Yeltin running for a third term in the year 2000, despite the fact that the Russian constitution limits any president to two terms (P Remnick "How Russia" 14). And Lilia Shevtsova and Scott Bruckner of the Carnegie Moscow Center argue that the same political forces that always have controlled the country "have remained intact" and that "government still occupies an inordinately important place in political and economic affairs" (P 33). In this regard, David Remnick says that "Power in Russia is now adrift, unpredictable and corrupt" (P "Can Russia" 35).

Not everyone agrees with the judgment that Russia has failed to evolve toward a democratic political system. Recently, Michael McFaul of the Carnagie Endowment for International Peace and Stanford University, wrote:

> The first five years of the post-Soviet Russian state represented a transitional phase in which the political rules of the game remained uncertain and contested as a new Russian polity emerged from the remnants of a collapsed Soviet regime. This era of polarized, revolutionary politics began to wind down after the adoption of a new constitution in 1993 and ended soon after Russia's 1996 presidential election. The 1996 election demonstrated that all major political actors in Russia had acquiesced to a new, albeit minimal, set of rules of political competition in which popular elections were recognized as the only legitimate means to political power. In other words, Russia had completed its transition to an electoral democracy. (P 319)

And the reliance on elections means that "accountability is now a component of Russian politics" (P Shevtsova and Bruckner 35).

Other advances also have been made, especially in terms of guaranteeing rights and free expression. Lilia Shevtsova and Scott Bruckner of the Carnegie Moscow Center argue that

> strides have even been made in providing increased guarantees for individual liberties. Russians now enjoy freedoms of speech and organization, travel and movement, and access to uncensored mass media, foreign and domestic literature, and science texts. Russian citizens have eagerly seized these new freedoms including the freedom to participate actively in politics. They turn out to vote, for instance, in numbers that put U.S. voters to shame. While the gap between the Russian people and their leaders is still exceedingly wide, popular participation has begun to penetrate elite circles and have an impact on government policies. Strikes by unpaid workers, for instance, are a big reason why the government is seeking ways to avoid its perennial budget shortfalls. . . And the antiwar protests that Yeltsin heard while on the campaign trail undoubtedly played a role in pushing him to see an end to the war in Chechnya. (P 33)

David Remnick also cites the improved situation in regard to civil liberty, noting that "Russians are free to travel. They are free to consume as much foreign journalism, intellectual history, and popular culture as they desire. The authorities encourage foreign influence and business" (P "Can Russia" 44).

Russia is also beginning to develop an independent judicial system. Thomas Dine of the Agency for International Development (AID) cited a recent example in which Microsoft successfully prosecuted two Russian firms that were acting as software pirates. He concludes that the case "shows courts and legal systems taking shape, not just as a patchwork of unenforced laws, but as real cases tried by real lawyers and judges. It shows reform taking root" (D *U.S. Assistance* 7). In addition, there is reason to believe "that basic principles of private ownership and free economic activity have now been accepted by most of the population" (P Lieven 17).

Finally, the move away from central control by Moscow may be quite positive for the long term development of Russia. David Remnick notes that "Russia is a far less centralized country than the Soviet Union" (P "Can Russia" 46). He adds "Now one decree after another is issued, but local authorities adopt what they like and ignore the rest" (P "Can Russia" 46). He also cites encouraging developments in some regions (P "Can Russia" 46).

On balance, Russia has made major progress since the end of the Soviet Union. Remember, Russia has existed as an independent state for less than seven years. In that time, there have been two parliamentary and one presidential election. A new constitution was enacted. The old Soviet empire broke up into constituent states. A free press has developed. And of course, there have been major economic reforms, which I will discuss in a moment. Is the Russian system a stable democracy in the same way as the United States, Canada, or Great Britain? No. But Russia has made enormous strides toward freedom and democracy in a very short period.

One other point about the status of the Russian political system at the end of the 20th century is relevant. The weaknesses in the system create dangers, but they also have one benefit. Russia is not nearly the threat to world peace that the Soviet Union was. For more than four decades NATO planners worried about how to deter Soviet troops from an assault on Western Europe. Today, Russia cannot defeat rebels in Chechnya. Recently, Anatol Lieven argued that Russia was falling behind China in political and military power (P 15). In relation to the United States, Lieven concludes that "the idea that Russia might be a serious direct threat to vital U.S. interests over the next 10 to 15 years is quite simply ludicrous" (P 15).

What is the cause of this weakness? Some might argue that it is simply the result of a difficult transition to democracy. On the other hand, Lieven suggests that Russia is currently an "anarchic quasi-feudalism," a system similar to that found in many nations in Latin America (P 15–16). As such, it is in his view a "weak state" that cannot "enforce the law, raise taxes efficiently and fairly and protect the weaker sections of society" (P 16). On the up side, such a state will be "highly incompetent in projecting power and influence" in the world as a whole (P 16).

Russian Economic Reform

The Russian transition to a market economy began in the aftermath of the failed coup attempt. A radical economic policy labelled "shock therapy" was implemented under the leadership of Yegor Gaidar. The "shock" consisted primarily of eliminating price controls and a privatization effort in which previously state-run organizations were transformed into private businesses. The privatization effort will be discussed in more depth in a moment. In addition, substantial other changes were made in the economy including a 68% cut in military procurement funds in 1992 (B Gaddy 85).

Some argue that "shock therapy" failed because it wasn't really tried (B Sachs 53–54). In this view, the Yeltsin government pulled back from a full commitment to free enterprise under pressure from those who feared that their enterprises might go under.

The effects of this dramatic change in economic policy were perfectly predictable: "hyperinflation and a catastrophic drop-off in output" (P Kotkin 28). One estimate of the inflation rate in this period was 2,200% (P Griffin 219). In 1992, industrial production dropped by roughly 25% and some believe that about 75 million people fell into poverty (P Griffin 219).

An additional problem was capital flight estimated by some sources at from $4 to $15 billion (P Griffin 230) per year. Others suggest the figure is much higher, perhaps "$2 billion a month . . . [a figure that] continues to exceed all foreign investment, aid, credits, and loans, including those of the International Monetary Fund and the World Bank" (P vanden Heuvel and Cohen 25). In total, it may have been as much as $150 to $300 billion (P Singer 18).

Along with inflation, declining domestic product, and capital flight, the Russian people faced grave problems associated with vast social change. As Mary Cooper explains: "But the reforms have also brought wrenching changes. For 75 years, the Soviet state had guaranteed the basics Russians needed to survive—a place to live, adequate food, employment, an orderly society" (P "Russia's Political" 387). The reforms "destroyed those guarantees for" most Russians (P Cooper "Russia's Political" 387).

In response to the economic problems, the West (including the United States) promised significant aid. A plan produced during the Bush administration promised $24 billion in aid. However, many believe that nowhere near this amount of money actually was made available to the Russians. A Rand Corporation expert in the area, John Tedstrom, labelled the aid package as "mostly smoke and mirrors" (qtd. in P Griffin 223).

Economic reform was bound to be difficult. Essentially no one in Russia had any experience with a market economy. In that circumstance, "shock therapy" was indeed a shock to the system. It is understandable that Yeltsin and his advisors pulled back from a full-scale immediate transition to a pure market economy. Also in this period Russian Prime Minister Viktor Chernomyrdin moved to a stricter anti-inflation policy (P Kotkin 28).

Probably the most important single economic reform was the move toward privatization, which occurred in a series of starts and stops. One problem is that much of the valuable property in Russia essentially was stolen at the end of the Soviet era by those who managed it. Stephen Kotkin has referred to this as the "spontaneous appropriation of state-owned industry by managers" (P 28).

Even so, Yeltsin and his advisors put into place an ambitious program. (For a detailed description of the program see B Boycko, Shleifer and Vishny.) The government privatization program was organized by Anatoly Chubais, who wanted to firmly establish a market economy in order to make it impossible to return to a communist system. Under his leadership, local and regional governments were given the responsibility of privatizing small businesses, and the Russian state itself focused on larger enterprises. His goal in working with local governments was "to make them self-interested beneficiaries" (P Kotkin 28) in the privatization process.

In relation to large firms, over 70% chose an option in which management and workers in a firm were granted a 51% controlling interest in the firm. Another 29% of the shares of the firm were sold, with the remaining percentage retained by various levels of government. The 29% that was sold at auction was purchased with stock vouchers that had been distributed to the population by the government (see P Kotkin 28). These vouchers were supposed to reflect the individual value of state-owned enterprises from the communist era. The vouchers could be traded and thus functioned in a way similar to money, except that they could be spent directly only on the newly privatized corporations.

It also should be pointed out that in the period before the June 1996 election, the privatization program "ground almost to a halt" (P Cooper "Russia's Political" 389). And privatization has yet to take hold in agriculture, where "less than 5 percent of the land has been turned over to private family farming" (P Goldman 318). On the other hand, "a recent agricultural land privatization law gives citizens the right to buy and sell land." Already "nearly a thousand parcels of land had been transferred to privatized industrial enterprises throughout Russia by October 1996" (testimony of Thomas Dine of the U.S. Agency for International Development in D *Consideration* 29).

Was economic reform in general and privatization in particular successful? The situation is somewhat mixed. In one way, privatization was quite successful in that it largely broke the dominance of the state in all economic matters. According to Mary Cooper, by July of 1994 "more than 100,000 small businesses, as well as more than 15,000 medium and large firms had shifted to private ownership" resulting in a situation in which 70% of Russian industry and "two thirds of the country's production capacity—had been privatized" (P "Russia's Political" 394). David Remnick claims that "Nearly 80 percent of the Russian economy is in private hands" (P "Can Russia" 48). And Strobe Talbott has referred to the privatization effort as the "largest transfer of assets in history" (P "America and Russia" 537).

Moreover, by creating a new class of the wealthy, privatization also created a constituency that would fight tooth and nail for their economic freedom. That fight might be self-interested, but it would have the effect of protecting Russian reform. Walter Connor notes that one of the main goals of privatization was "to get enough property off the state's books to make the escape from the command economy irreversible" (B 147). As Marshall Goldman has noted, reformers believe that privatization has created a situation in which "it would become considerably more difficult for the Communists to gain support for a return to communism" (P 314). And Anatoly Chubais argues that privatization also will lead to other economic reforms. Writing with Maria Vishnevskaya, he notes that "The increasing influence of Russian private owners in political and legislative processes will make the solution of remaining problems inevitable in the future" (B "Russian Privatization in Mid-1994" 97).

In another way, the effects of privatization have not been so benign. First, privatization eliminated the economic security provided by the socialist system. One result was massive layoffs, creating a situation in which unemployment reached 30% in some areas (P Cooper "Russia's Political" 394). Second, corruption was a major problem. There is little question that many managers essentially stole the resources of their state-run enterprises.

Third, privatization resulted in the concentration of economic power in the hands of a few. This problem became significant in the middle 1990s, when newly formed private Russian banks loaned the government money with the state percentage of privatized industries as collateral. When Russia could not repay the loans, the previously state-owned shares were sold. Kotkin notes that "The upshot was the creation of a small group of billionaires, who repaid the favor by helping procure Boris Yeltsin's reelection in 1996" (P 30). This group of wealthy individuals is concentrated in Moscow where in 1996 "5 percent of the Russian population . . . generated 35 percent of Russia's GDP and controlled 70 to 80 percent of its capital" (P Goldman 316). Steven Cohen notes that "Russia's new private sector is dominated by former but still intact Soviet monopolies seized by ex-Communist officials who have become the core of a semicriminalized business class" (P 5). And Lilia Shevtsova and Scott Bruckner of the Carnegie Moscow Center argue that privatization "mostly entrenched the power of those who already controlled the levers of economic power in the Soviet Union" (P 34).

There is also a strong argument that industrialists and bankers have far too much power in the Russian political system. These groups have massive influence within the Russian government (P McFaul 324). David Remnick argues that "the most powerful men in the country today are seven business barons—'the seven boyars,' 'the Magnificent Seven'—who own nearly the entire news media and a fantastic proportion of the national wealth" (P "How Russia" 14). Remnick refers to this group as "a new class of oligarchs" (P "Can Russia" 36). And Adrian Karatnycky, President of Freedom House, argues that the super-rich in Russia are committed to perpetuating "the dominance of monopolies and oligopolies in key Russian industries" and to stifling "democratic development" (P "Emerging" 41). In this view, Yeltsin is "a prisoner of those powerful interests, which control many of the levers of state power" (P Karatnycky "Emerging" 41).

On the other hand, experience suggests that the Russian system is becoming more competitive. A recent auction for Svyazinvest, a Russian telephone company, set off a furious bidding war, resulting in a price "50 percent more than the government had accepted" (P Remnick "How Russia" 15). This led first deputy premier Boris Nemtsov to comment, "From a bandit-like amassing of capital, the country is moving to a more or less civilized regime" (P "How Russia" 15). His point is that the market is a very powerful instrument and eventually will force reform.

Another problem with privatization relates to obsolete industries. Many Soviet-era enterprises were hopelessly antiquated. As a consequence, they either produced inadequate products or goods that were not cost competitive in the world market. Privatization has not created an incentive to close down obsolete plants. In fact, many of the newly wealthy in Russia have sought a maintenance of the kind of government guarantees that were so prevalent in the Soviet era.

Nor has privatization been accompanied by new business creation to the same extent as it has in other nations that have gone through a similar process. Mashall Goldman notes that in Poland, a nation one-quarter of the size of Russia, 1.8 million new businesses were created in the first five years of reform, as against only 900,000 in a similar period in Russia (P 315). Michael McFaul explains this result by arguing that privatization has not assisted small business adequately which is the key to job creation. He states that: "Exorbitant taxes, inflation, the lack of liberalization at the local level, the mafia, and the consolidation of large financial groups occupying monopoly control over many markets have combined to create an unfriendly environment for small businesses" (P 324).

A general problem with Russian economic policy is that their entire system remains quite bureaucratic. "The post-1991 Russian Republic has more office holders than the Soviet Union had, to serve not much more than half the Soviet Union's population" (P Kotkin 31). In this regard, Anatol Lieven writes of the "mushroom growth" of Russian bureaucracy (P 20).

Some argue that the most basic economic problems facing Russia relate to the power of the state bureaucracy and of large industrial concerns that essentially act as industrial trusts. The combination of the bureaucracy and the trusts restricts the ability of Russians and foreign investors to develop businesses. In this regard, Grigory Yavlinsky argues that contemporary economic theory is of less importance to Russia than an historical analysis of how the United States dealt with trusts in the Progressive Era (P 66).

The next economic problem facing Russia today may be the most important, the threat of organized crime. The general crime rate doubled from 1988 to 1992 and then stagnated (testimony of Anders Aslund D *Newly Independent States* 62). However, organized crime is a particular problem for the economy. According to Lieven, "As in Colombia, Mexico, Pakistan and elsewhere, the state forces are hopelessly out-spent and out-gunned by the criminals, and in any case are largely controlled by them" (P 20).

The effect of organized crime on business development may be quite severe. According to one commentator

> Nearly every small to medium-sized business, as well as several large companies, has its own krysha or roof. A krysha is otherwise know as a criminal organization, which gets 10 to 20 percent of a business's profits in exchange for protecting it from other mafias. This krysha also offers the only real option to resolve disputes with clients who refuse to pay for delivered goods, or with companies that do not pay off their debts. (P Shlapentokh 341)

The mafia is so much a part of Russian life that many "Millions of young boys across the country who have been raised in Russia's new postcommunist society yearn to join these criminal structures" (P Shlapentokh 333).

Organized crime not only threatens economic development but could harm the political stability of Russia as well. Strobe Talbott observed recently that

> Widespread lawlessness in Russia today constitutes a major threat to public confidence in government, a threat to reform, and a threat to the political fortunes of reformers. (P "U.S.-Russian" 362)

He added, "rampant criminality threatens to undermine the Russian people's confidence in reform and in democracy itself and could serve as a pretext for the reimposition of stultifying state controls" (P "Managing" 59). Anatol Lieven's judgment is the harshest. He writes, "To a very real extent, the state itself has been hollowed out, turned into a vessel to be captured and plundered by the piratical forces of a frequently criminalized Russian private enterprise" (P 20).

While the organized crime problem is certainly serious, its importance should not be overstated. In fact, some argue that organized crime will be dealt with over time. Recently, American ambassador Thomas Pickering argued that "Crime very often accompanies reform in its early phases, because old social norms are broken down before they can be replaced by new ones" (P 529). His conclusion is that "some of the crime problem will die away naturally as reform consolidates its position in Russian society" (P 529). He also notes that the United States is "already working closely with the Russian Government on ways to fight organized crime" (P 529).

On the other hand, there may not be much that the United States can do about Russian organized crime. As Ambassador Morningstar noted "In the end, however, efforts to combat corruption will succeed or fail depending on the level of commitment of NIS [newly independent state] leaders and the public" (D *U.S. Assistance* 107).

Another problem has related to the liquidity of Russian currency. Even today, "One-third of the exchange between enterprises is in the form of barter, or the exchange of products in kind instead of money" (P Shlapentokh 332). An economy based on barter is never going to be as efficient as one based on the flow of money.

Russia also faces massive problems in its tax system. Strobe Talbott notes:

> Russia urgently needs a prompt and massive overhaul of its tax-collection system. The Russian Government's failure to collect revenues has jeopardized its eligibility for further lending from the International Monetary Fund. It has scared off badly needed foreign investment and stimulated the flight of Russian capital abroad, which is another impediment to growth. (P "America and Russia" 538)

Closely related to the tax collection problem, Russia faces a grave situation in servicing $130 billion in foreign debt. The economic consequences of this debt-servicing problem are severe. As Senator Bill Bradley notes, "Russia's arrears have excluded it from the international capital markets that it must tap for both the noninflationary financing of its budget deficit and the hundreds of billions of dollars in capital needed to pay for necessary technology" (P 89).

Another source of economic weakness is the bloated defense sector. Marshall Goldman argues that one of the key factors explaining the decline in production was the commitment of the Soviet economy to military production. With the end of the Soviet Union, there was no need for this massive production of military goods. On the other hand, it was not so easy to switch production facilities over to civilian goods. In this view,

> Russia's low civilian productivity today stems from decades of channeling the best human, technological and material resources into defense and related industries, relegating the civilian economy and its infrastructure to partial or complete inefficiency. The backwardness of the civilian industries is proportionate to the funds that were diverted from them into the defense sector. (P Mann "Economic Morass" 70)

(This topic is covered in detail in Clifford Gaddy's book, *The Price of the Past: Russia's Struggle with the Legacy of a Militarized Economy*.) Unfortunately, it will be extremely difficult to convert the defense sector into civilian production (see B Gansler 44-45). Many experts agree with this judgment (see B Balzer).

Given the problems afflicting the Russian economic situation, it is reasonable to consider whether a more rapid transition to an efficient market economy would have been possible. On this point, there is grave disagreement. Some say that many problems would have been avoided had Russia followed through on the shock therapy. On the other hand, it is important to note that there has been substantial backlash against free market advocates such as Anatoly Chubais. Polls in Russia suggest that 80% of the population strongly dislikes Chubais for the effects that his policies have had on their lives (P Reddaway C1).

Russian Economic Development on the Eve of a New Millennium

What then is the status of Russian economic development in 1998? Recently, Marshall Goldman, one of the foremost experts on Russia, said simply that "almost six years after Boris Yeltsin's reforms were set in motion, the results have been meager at best" (P 313). According to Goldman, the Gross Domestic Product of Russia in 1996 was between 50 and 66% of what it had been in 1991. He cited a 20% decline in electricity generation as proof that economic production had declined substantially (P 313). Since production of goods requires energy, so precipitous a decline in electricity production would seem to indicate major economic problems.

The decline in production reflects a trend going back to the end of communist rule. According to Goldman, in no year since 1991 has the Russian economy grown. The economy in 1992 was only 81% as big as in 1991. In 1993, the economy was only 88% as big as in 1992. In 1994, it was only 87% as big as the previous year. Even in 1995 and 1996, the economy shrank slightly.

The economic shrinking occurred at a time when inflation also was quite rapid: 2,600% in 1992, 940% in 1993, 315% in 1994, 120% in 1995 and 22% in 1996 (see a chart in P Goldman 315). One gets an idea of the terrible status of the Russian economy when 1996 is almost a boom year, because inflation was only 22% and the economy only shrank by about 5%. To make matters worse, by 1996, real interest rates reached 200% and many workers went without pay "for three to four months at a time" (P Goldman 317). Malcolm Gray noted recently that "Millions of Russians in the state sector, among them soldiers, coal miners, schoolteachers and nuclear plant workers, go without wages for up to six months at a time" (P 27). Bill Powell drew a particularly negative assessment of the Russian economy at the time of the Helsinki summit, when he said that "The country's economy bears more than a passing resemblance to a corrupt, Third World kleptocracy" (P 32).

It is also important to recognize that economic growth has been much faster in Moscow than elsewhere in Russia. Katrina vanden Heuvel and Steven Cohen note that

> The rest of Russia remains in the throes of the twentieth century's greatest depression—even according to the government's own statistics. The fall in production, down nearly 50 percent since 1991, continues, and unemployment is expected to exceed at least 10 percent by next year. Capital investment dropped 18 percent last year and 8 percent in the first quarter of this year. (P "The Other" 25)

Citizens in the "provinces" refer to Russia as a "'dying nation'" (P vanden Heuvel and Cohen "The Other" 25).

It is also instructive to compare the Russian economic experience with that of other nations of the "Soviet bloc." It is interesting that "the Russian economy has not experienced the kind of turnaround that has occurred in most of the countries of Central Europe" (P Karatnycky 40).

Even apparent points of strength may not actually reflect economic power. For example, while there is a large export sector in the economy, exports mainly have been confined to military products and natural resources. In fact, a high percentage of consumer goods are imported into Russia, many by the so-called "shuttlers." Vladimiri Shlapentokh explains that

> About 10 million young and middle-aged people regularly visit neighboring countries (mainly China, Turkey, and Poland) in order to bring back in their personal luggage goods they can sell on the Russian market. It is as if Russia now still lives in a feudalistic society, or even earlier when professional merchants who didn't carry their goods on their backs were unknown. (P 332)

Clearly, there has been massive economic regression.

The various economic problems have created, according to some, a situation in which "the country totters on the brink of chaos" (P Singer 20). One recent review of the Russian economy referred to the status of economic reform as a "Transition to Nowhere" (P "Russia: Transition to Nowhere" 139).

On the other hand, some see substantial progress in Russia's program of economic development. As early as 1994, "the private sector produced 62 per cent of officially recorded gross domestic product" (P Bradley 87). Moreover, economic decline was inevitable until the infrastructure supporting a strong economy could be created. In that regard, Strobe Talbott notes that "The rudiments of retail commerce, market mechanisms, and a financial infrastructure are now in place" (P "America and Russia" 537). And U.S. Ambassador Thomas Pickering argues that downswing in defense and other sectors has created the preconditions for economic development that is already beginning to show up in the service sector.

In the view of some, the Russian economy is about to take off. A recent *Business Week* column cited efforts by Yeltsin to integrate Russia into the world economy and concluded that "*bizness* is Russia's guiding light" (P Kranz "The Business" 143). It is certainly encouraging that Russia had a $28 billion trade surplus in 1995 (P Pickering 529).

Some believe that economic progress has occurred outside the export sector of the economy as well. Talbott predicted recently that Russia's economy finally has stabilized and "may be registering a real upturn" (P "The End" 23). Some data backs up his judgment. A review of the economic situation cites data indicating that "average real consumption has been consistently higher than in early 1992, when the marketization reforms were introduced" (Duke economist Jim Leitze qtd. in P "Russia: Transition to Nowhere" 140). Moreover, the poverty rate in Russia declined from about 35% in 1995 to 22% in 1996 (P Goldmann 316). This decline would seem to indicate that the Russian economy is getting stronger.

There is also an argument that Russia is actually doing better than many economists believe because "Much of this [growth] is not fully captured in the official statistics, but is evident in the construction and new retail trade outlets that are visible not just in Moscow and St. Petersburg, but out in the provinces" (P Pickering 529). Rob North agrees with this judgment. He argues that "some of the best evidence filtering out of Russia today, in fact, indicates that capitalism is doing far better than we've been led to believe" (P 32).

Another sign of Russian economic development is that the nation has been invited to join the group of leading industrial nations that formerly had been known as the G-7 and now will be the G-8 (P Kranz "The Business" 143).

In addition to the evidence of economic progress, there are also signs that the Russian government is beginning to work on problems such as tax collection and reform of the energy industry (P Goldmann 318). And major advances have been made in the organization of Russian capital markets (Ambassador Morningstar in D *U.S. Assistance* 123).

Moreover, there is something decidedly unfair in judging Russia a failure based on the experience of less than a decade. Recently, Deputy Secretary of State Talbott argued that full reform of Russia "will take a generation or more" (P "American and Russia" 537). Certainly, there are problems. And Russia has not made the transformation to democracy and a market economy as rapidly as some of the nations of Eastern Europe. On the other hand, Russia faced greater problems than those nations and had no history of either democratic government or a truly free and open capitalist economy. Judged from that perspective, it could be argued that Russia has made rapid progress.

Optimists also argue that economic (and political) progress will be more rapid as the new generation takes over institutions within Russia. Talbott cites data that speaks to this point: "Although 65% of those Russians over the age of 65 think things got worse over the last year, 60% of those under 35 think things got better. So among the positive trends underway in Russia is perhaps the most basic one of all, the one represented by the actuarial tables" (P "The End" 26).

In sum, the Russian economy went into free fall after the end of the Soviet Union. Economic reforms were implemented in fits and starts. In many cases, the reforms were used by the modern-day Russian equivalent of the American capitalist "robber barons" of the 19th century to create (or steal) massive wealth. The Russian people have suffered with massive inflation and declining GDP. There also are substantial barriers to achieving more rapid economic growth.

And yet with all of these problems, it is clear that Russia is making economic progress. There are signs that growth is beginning to occur. But most of all, economic reform eliminated the state monopoly on economic power. It now would be very difficult to return to a communist system.

Russian Foreign Policy

What is the status of Russian foreign policy? Any number of observers have noted Russian attempts to carve out space for an independent foreign policy. In this view, Russia wants to regain some of the influence that it possessed during the Cold War, while not offending the United States or other donor nations. Russian attempts to mediate the recent crisis between UN arms inspectors and Iraq are signs of this effort.

Russia's desire for independence also was reflected in recent remarks of Boris Yeltsin at a summit meeting with Jiang Zemin of China. Yeltsin commented on the need for "the world to be multipolar" (qtd. in P Filipov A2), an obvious reference to the current dominance of the United States. In order to counteract the power of the United States, Yeltsin has embarked on a "rapidly developing Russo-Chinese *entente*" (P Blank 71).

In relation to foreign policy, Russia's top aim is to solidify their position in areas of historic strength. Sherman Garnett argues that

> This consensus sees Russia's top foreign policy priority as deepening integrative trends in the territory of the former Soviet Union. The policy's advocates intend not to mire Russia close to home but rather to solidify Russia's place in the former U.S.S.R. and, in so doing, build a foundation for restoring Russia as a great power beyond the "near abroad." (P 66)

If Russia's primary aim is to solidify its own position in its own backyard, then, despite the talk of multipolarity and close relations with China, it seems unlikely that Russia will pose much of a threat to the United States.

However, it should be noted that the policy of building closer ties among the states of the Commonwealth of Independent States (CIS) faces problems. As Sherman Garnett notes, "The desire for sovereignty is a stronger force than many observers in Moscow appreciate" (P 71). As a consequence, "There can be no talk of burden-sharing nor of anything like an Eastern European equivalent of NATO or the European Union. Russia must come to terms with diversity in its own backyard" (P Garnett 71). In other words, the Soviet Union is not coming back, not even as a weak alliance, if nations like Ukraine and the Baltic states have anything to say about it.

The fact that Russia faces severe problems in carrying out foreign policy objectives with the CIS also indicates that Russia lacks the power base to oppose the United States.

One worrisome trend is that "the Russian foreign policy community has become increasingly skeptical about a productive partnership with Western countries" (P Garnett 66). This reflects frank paranoia among some that the West wants to destroy Russia. As I will discuss in Chapter Four, the decision to expand NATO greatly has exacerbated those feelings. On the other hand, the Russian attitude also reflects the reality that the West promised massive amounts of aid in making the transition to democracy and capitalism and to a large extent did not fulfill those promises.

While Russian foreign policy has moved away from what almost might be labelled the "love affair" with the West that defined the relationship in the early days following the death of the Soviet Union, there is little reason to fear Russia. A number of commentators argue that Russia is unlikely to oppose the United States directly on issues of great import. As Andrei Kortunov of the Russian Research Foundation recently observed, "Russia is likely to deviate from the United States only on the margins" (qtd. in P Daniel Williams A47).

Thus, Russian foreign policy today is defined by a desire to preserve independence and a sense that the CIS exists in an area where Russia naturally should be dominant. This attitude is similar to the American perception that the Caribbean is our own private lake. Russia will oppose the United States at times, notably in supporting former Soviet allies such as Iraq, but is unlikely to constitute a major threat to this nation.

United States Foreign Policy Toward Russia

United States foreign policy toward Russia has gone through a dramatic evolution over the last ten years. Only a little over a decade ago, Ronald Reagan was referring to the Soviet Union as "the evil empire." At the end of the Reagan administration, the relationship between the United States and the Soviet Union/Russia began a period of very rapid change. In his farewell address, Reagan himself said that Gorbachev, at least up to that point, had been different than other Soviet leaders. In retrospect, Reagan clearly was right.

The most radical changes in U.S. policy occurred during the Bush administration. In 1989, in the Malta accord, the Soviet Union and the United States agreed that they "would not regard each other as 'enemies'" (P Garthoff 307). This accord was followed in 1992 by an agreement at Camp David that the United States and Russia would no longer see themselves as even "'potential' enemies," which in turn led to the signing of a new charter on relations between the two nations (P Garthoff 307).

There also was major progress on arms control and defense issues. The Strategic Arms Reduction Treaty (START) II agreement, which I will discuss in some detail in Chapter Four, was signed in January 1993. In the Bush years, a number of other arms control and military agreements were established. It is also important to note that Russia did not actively oppose the U.S.-led coalition in the Gulf War.

The Clinton years have been characterized by what Raymond Garthoff characterizes as "growing normalcy in the relationship" between Russia and the United States (P 307). Clinton and Yeltsin have met more than a dozen times, and a joint commission chaired by Vice President Gore and Russian Prime Minister Viktor Chernomyrdin has met even more often (P Garthoff 307). The "normalcy" in the relationship is reflected in the more than 100 agreements signed between Russia and the United States between 1992 and 1996 (P Garthoff 307).

Another sign of normalcy in the relations between Russia and the United States is found in the defense sphere, where joint exercises, including a war game, were held starting in 1994 (P Garthoff 310). President Clinton has expressed special pride in an agreement that the United States and Russia would no longer target the territory of the other nation with their remaining nuclear weapons. It must be admitted, however, that some of these agreements are more important for their symbolism than the specific policies they contain. The agreement on targeting, for instance, symbolizes the fact that Russia and the United

States are no longer enemies, but it does not alter the fact that either nation could retarget its weapons in a matter of minutes or even seconds.

In general, United States foreign policy toward Russia over the last five years has emphasized three themes: assistance for making the transition to a stable democracy, support for the development of a market economy, and a focus on restricting or destroying weapons of mass destruction. All of these policies have been tied to the perception that a stable democratic Russia plays a crucial role in U.S. national self-interest. Anthony Lake explained in 1996

> A stable democratic, market-oriented Russia would be far less likely to threaten America's security and far more likely to work with us to solve global problems. It can be an important partner in prosperity, with 150 million new consumers for American products. It can be a strong ally against the forces of destruction, whether they take the form of rogue nations or ethnic hatreds or terrorists trafficking in nuclear materials. And it could be a force for stability on a continent long wracked by division. (P 181)

In other words, United States policy has not primarily been altruistic, but aimed at serving the interests of this nation.

What are the specific goals of U.S. foreign policy toward Russia? Former U.S. Ambassador to Russia Jack Matlock provides a clear list of our objectives:

> Among its most important interests in Russia, the United States counts the maintenance of responsible control over the arsenal of weapons of mass destruction, a rapid and substantial reduction in nuclear warheads and delivery systems, and the elimination of chemical and biological weapons. It would like to see Russia participate in a European or Eurasian security system that included the United States as well as western Europe. It wants Russia integrated into the world economy as a full-fledged member. Finally, it would like Russian cooperation in resolving regional disputes, and working partnership in addressing global problems such as international terrorism, crime, and damage to the environment. (P 39)

It is important to keep Matlock's list of goals in mind because his list is also organized in rough order of importance. Far more important than anything else, the United States has focused on the dangers associated with Russian nuclear weapons.

Three specific aspects of U.S. foreign policy deserve note. Since the early 1990s, the United States has maintained a strong commitment to the government of Boris Yeltsin. This policy is similar to that of the Bush administration, which remained committed to working with Gorbachev long after there was strong evidence that Gorbachev's approach could not be successful. Some argue that in hitching our wagon behind Yeltsin, the United States is making the same mistake that we made with Gorbachev (see P Yavlinsky). Senator Bill Bradley characterizes the policy of personal commitment to a given leader as "the romantic impulse" (P 82). He argues that "American policy was blinded by the complexity of events in Russia, and support for reform became inextricably bound with support for leaders" (P 82).

The U.S. policy also has worked to integrate Russia into partnership with the rest of the developed world. Strobe Talbott describes this effort:

> We are doing what we can to ensure that the international community is as open as possible to Russia. That's why we pushed in Denver for the expansion of the G-7 agenda to become the Summit of the Eight. That's also why, in Helsinki, President Clinton and President Yeltsin set a joint goal toward Russian accession in 1998 to the World Trade Organization and to launch a dialogue in Paris that will accelerate Russia's admission to the OECD. (P "The End" 24)

The push for integration into the world community serves the function of tying Russia to other democratic and capitalist nations.

Finally, the United States has worked with Russia in a number of specific areas, such as space development, which I will discuss in Chapter Four. The United States also has worked with Russia in Bosnia, an effort that U.S. Ambassador Pickering says is an "excellent example of how the U.S. can work closely and cooperatively with our former adversary" (P 530).

In carrying out these policy aims, the United States has used three primary mechanisms. One of these mechanisms is diplomacy aimed at producing agreements between the two nations. The second is U.S. monetary assistance. The third is the threat of retaliation, usually in the form of trade sanctions against a particular Russian company or the entire nation. In some cases, cutoff of aid also may be threatened. Sanctions may be threatened by the administration in private, or Congress may act to require sanctions. Before discussing the efficacy of these three mechanisms for changing U.S. policy, it is important to consider the evolution of U.S. assistance to Russia.

U.S. Foreign Assistance to Russia

United States aid to Russia skyrocketed after the death of the Soviet Union. Obviously, the United States did not provide significant assistance to the nation that generations of Americans thought of as the "evil empire." With the birth of a new Russian state, that situation changed dramatically.

United States aid for Russia expanded from a mere $10 million in fiscal year 1991 to over a billion dollars in 1992 and 1993. Of that figure in 1992, the United States provided roughly a quarter of a billion dollars in technical assistance grants for economic development, about $120 million in medical assistance, over $300 million in food assistance, and a half billion dollars in aid from the Department of Defense. The figures for 1993 were similar, although the expenditures came from somewhat different accounts. In addition to direct aid, the United States provided roughly $2 billion a year from 1991–1993 in various loan programs. (The information I have cited is summarized from a useful chart in P Griffin 220.)

U.S. aid and loans continued to expand in 1994. In that year, the United States provided slightly more than $1.6 billion in credits and $2.8 billion in grants to all of the nations of the former Soviet Union. These figures fell sharply in 1995 to $1.3 billion in credits and $1.35 billion in aid. In 1996, the figures fell again (see P Cooper "Russia's Political" 397).

In addition to the aid and loan programs, the United States also provided revenue to the International Monetary Fund (IMF) to assist Russian economic development and stabilize the Russian currency (see P Griffin 221). The IMF has not only provided assistance to Russia but also set conditions on that assistance. In fall 1996 the IMF denied Russia a $350 million loan installment (P "Russia in Turmoil" 9) when it did not meet the standards.

Other nations also provided assistance to the new Russian state. It is, however, easy to overestimate the quantity of assistance that actually was provided to Russia. Some experts believe that the majority of the total of perhaps $12 billion received by the Russians in the early 1990s took the form of deferred payments on debt owed by the Soviet Union (see P Griffin 223). Of course, deferral of this debt was useful for Russia, but in another sense those payments were not aid at all.

What programs did the United States provide assistance for in Russia? The U.S. government has funded a wide variety of programs in order to support Russian economic and political reforms. For example, the United States Agency for International Development (AID) funded a program that assisted in the design of the privatization program in Russia (P Kotkin 28). And the United States has supported "Freedom Support Act" initiatives that

> have done everything from . . . [training Russians] in how to conduct an election and how parties organize and work, poll watching and so forth, on up through the efforts to institutionalize trial by jury and many aspects of human rights and civil liberties. (Ambassador James Collins in D Russia's Election 9)

The United States also supported a number of specific grant programs. For example, the United States provided aid in areas such as housing for soldiers in the Russian army, assistance in developing a justice system and other means of supporting the development of democratic institutions in Russia. (For a good discussion of U.S. aid see D *U.S. Assistance*.) The United States is also funding programs to improve the tax system and enforcement of antitrust laws (Dine in D *U.S. Assistance* 10). There also is an anticorruption program (Dine in D *U.S. Assistance* 11).

Under the bipartisan Nunn-Lugar, "Cooperative Threat Reduction Program," which was passed in 1991, the United States provided funds for "the dismantlement of Russia's nuclear weapons and the purchase of bomb-grade materials for permanent disposal in the United States" (P Cooper "Russia's Political" 397). That included $400 million to facilitate disarmament and reduce the likelihood of proliferation involving Russian nuclear materials. Of that $400 million, $230 million already has been spent and another $60 million was allocated for fiscal year 1997 (P Mann "Helsinki" 25). Under the initiative, the United States has provided assistance to improve security at nuclear sites. The Nunn-Lugar program later "was expanded to assist in creating new scientific research opportunities for former Soviet nuclear weapons specialists" (P Garthoff 306).

There have been other deals related to defense issues. An agreement "in February 1993, provided for the United States purchase of some 500 metric tons of highly enriched uranium (for use as reactor fuel) over a 20-year period for about $12 billion" (P Garthoff 306).

While the United States provided substantial aid in the early 1990s, the amount of assistance decreased rapidly by the middle 1990s. For example, in 1996, the United States provided only about $95 million in aid directly to Russia (see P Miller A1+). In fiscal year 1997, the United States provided about $625 million in aid to all of the nations of the former Soviet Union (P Doherty "Senate Passes" 1718). Of that, about $100 million was for nondefense related foreign assistance to Russia (see a chart in D *Consideration* 15). For Fiscal Year 1998 the Clinton administration requested $242 million in aid for Russia (P Doherty "Clinton Wins" 1085).

The recent developments in U.S. aid to Russia reflect three trends. First, the total quantity of aid has shrunk dramatically since the middle 1990s. The $242 million requested for 1998 represented only 15% of the aid provided in 1994 (Morningstar in D *U.S. Assistance* 6). Second, the point of continuity in U.S. aid to Russia is the Nunn-Lugar act. Since that program was designed to reduce the threat that Russia poses to the United States, it seems quite sensible that Congress has funded it year after year.

Third, there is a trend toward shifting funding away from aid to the government of Russia and toward assistance to specific groups or pilot programs run by private organizations in Russia. This aid has been aimed at building the institutions that are needed in a market system and a democratic society. Representatives of the Clinton administration made clear in testimony that most of the requested assistance was for programs "designed to work with the private sector" and not with the Russian government (testimony of Richard Morningstar in D *Consideration* 3). In fact, over 90% of the funding will not go to the Russian government (Morningstar in D *Consideration* 51). One major focus is to aid the development of small business (Morningstar in D *Consideration* 4). Ambassador Morningstar reports that the United States has "ended large enterprise restructuring programs that were funded in 1994 and 1995 and . . . redirected private enterprise training resources to small and medium-sized enterprises" (D *U.S. Assistance* 80). Others programs focused on improving law enforcement in Russia and the creation of stable democratic institutions (Morningstar in D *Consideration* 8). The administration calls the new program the Partnership for Freedom.

In addition to aid, loans, and loan guarantees from the United States government, Russia has received a considerable amount of private assistance from the United States. The most important source of that aid has been billionaire George Soros, who has invested more than $2 billion in Russia and given hundreds of millions of dollars. It recently has been estimated that Soros personally provided more assistance to Russia in 1997 than did the United States Government (see P Wickham A15). It is an odd situation when the richest nation on the planet believes that it cannot afford to give as much aid to a former enemy as can a single rich person. For the three year period beginning in 1997, Soros has promised Russia over $500 million (P Deane A9). Soros labels his approach as aid to "open societies" and he has been primarily concerned with supporting various aspects of a free and open society, especially a free press (see P Miller A1+).

The Effectiveness of U.S. Foreign Policy Toward Russia

To what degree has United States foreign policy toward Russia been successful since the death of the Soviet Union? Many experts argue that U.S. foreign policy has not been effective at all. For example, some argue that the United States lacks any clear policy in dealing with Russia (P McMillan and Massie A29). Bill Bradley says that the policy "sounds suspiciously like ad hocism" (P 84). And Michael Mandelbaum of Johns Hopkins argues that U.S. policy of almost blind support for Yeltsin has failed (P "Our Outdated" 39).

On the other hand, it should be kept in mind that the situation involving Russia has evolved quite rapidly. In such a situation, it may be important that the United States show what Deputy Secretary of State Talbott has called "strategic patience," which he defines as "a policy not just for coping with the issue or the crisis of the moment or the week or even of the season, or for getting through the next summit meeting; rather, it means a policy for the next century" (P "The End" 26).

Judged from the perspective provided by Deputy Secretary Talbott, there is much to praise in U.S. policy. The focus of the United States has been on controlling weapons of mass destruction. That emphasis is quite, sensible, and, as I will indicate in Chapter Four, the Nunn-Lugar program has been quite successful. In other ways, the United States has adapted to a changing situation, both in Russia and in the U.S. Congress. In the period immediately after the death of the Soviet Union, technical assistance and emergency relief programs took precedence. Over time, the focus has shifted to building institutions and supporting the free market via aid to Russian organizations and targeted pilot programs. It would seem that our aid policies have adapted to the situation in Russia.

Primary Methods of Changing U.S. Foreign Policy Toward Russia

As I noted earlier, there are only three main ways that the United States can change its foreign policy toward Russia. We can alter policies that directly relate to Russia or negotiate over those policies. We can cut or expand aid. Or we can threaten Russia with some sort of sanction if they do not comply with some policy request. In the next three sections, I will discuss the pros and cons of each of these approaches.

Direct Policy Action and Negotiation

There are a number of areas where the United States simply can act or negotiate with Russia about some action. There is, however, an important distinction in relation to policy advocacy between direct action and policy negotiation.

There are some areas where the United States can act and does not need any response from Russia. For example, the United States could change refugee policy and admit more Russians who claim to have suffered religious discrimination. That action does not require a corresponding response from Russia, although a totalitarian government could block the refugees. Similarly, the United States could unilaterally change aspects of its military policy that relate to Russia. Russian agreement is not needed.

There are, however, relatively few examples where such direct action is possible because, as the saying goes, "it takes two to tango." In almost every context of U.S.-Russian relations, action is required by both parties to achieve useful objectives.

The second type of direct action involves negotiation and agreement with the Russians. Programs to increase cooperation with the Russian military fall into this category. Former Ambassador Jack Matlock argues that

> The United States should engage the Russian military in as many cooperative efforts as are feasible. The joint peacekeeping operation in Bosnia, if successful, can have great symbolic meaning, and Washington should support a vigorous program of joint training and consultation under NATO's Partnership for Peace initiative for Warsaw pact nations. (P 50)

In an example such as this, the United States can propose the action, but a Russian response is required. Thus, negotiation is necessary.

Another example of direct action involving negotiation relates to U.S. human rights policy. One possible change in U.S. policy toward Russia would be for the United States to more strongly criticize the human rights policies of Russia in public settings. In an important hearing (D *Russia's Election*), a number of the experts who testified and several elected representatives, argued for such action. They noted an example in which Vice President Gore compared the war in Chechnya to the American Civil War (Blair Ruble in D *Russia's Election* 32) as a case where the United States failed to put pressure on the Yeltsin government. The point was that the comparison reduced pressure on Yeltsin by seeming to justify Russian action. In contrast, they argued that the United States should have strongly and publicly criticized the war in the same kind of manner that President Reagan criticized the Soviet Union as the "evil empire." Michael McFaul argues simply that "the United States government must vocally criticize undemocratic policies and practices by the Russian government such as the Chechen war or antisemitism" (D Russia's Election 67).

It is important to recognize, however, that merely changing U.S. policy on criticizing Russia is not enough. The second step of negotiating with Russia is needed. For a tougher human rights policy to work, the United States must say the same things in private that we say in public. We must continually push the Russians on the issue and be willing to threaten various negative outcomes if they do not comply. In other words, it takes more than a single policy action to effectively change our policy on criticizing human rights abuses in Russia. It requires on-going policy change and consistent negotiation.

This example illustrates the difficulty associated with many of the possible changes in U.S. foreign policy toward Russia that could be implemented via direct action and negotiation. In many cases, direct action would implement a general policy change that then must be carried out on a day to day basis. The problem is that this carrying out process will not be successful unless the attitudes of those implementing the policy also have changed. Why did the Reagan administration consistently use public pressure to criticize the Soviet Union? The simple answer is that they believed what they were saying. On the other hand, the Clinton and Bush administrations obviously have believed that public pressure on Russia could be counterproductive. In this view, it is better to speak in private about problems to Yeltsin and his advisors. Right or wrong, that is the attitude.

Now consider what happens if a sense of the Congress resolution directs the administration to use public settings to criticize human rights abuses in Russia. The administration easily can "technically" meet that resolution, while in fact changing nothing. They can criticize human rights abuses in such a way that they signal to Yeltsin that nothing has changed. Or the administration can undercut public criticism with private comments. All of this suggests that direct action proposals are likely to be effective, only if they can be implemented as a specific public policy change. Later I will discuss a proposal that the United States should move away from what is called a "launch-on-warning" policy as an example of such a direct action policy. Under this approach, the United States would not respond to a nuclear attack, until any missiles actually had landed on our shores. Such a change in policy can be implemented via a presidential directive. On the other hand, it would not be so easy to change the general arms control approach of the administration because that policy requires on-going negotiation and is tied to the attitudes of the negotiators.

Another way of making this point is to consider the necessary ingredients in successfully changing any policy. There are two such ingredients: the ability to specify exactly how the new policy is different from the old one and the capacity to mandate how the new policy will be carried out. If an on-going process of negotiation is required, it will be difficult for the advocate of change to successfully include either ingredient.

This means that direct action proposals are most likely to be effective if it is possible to specify precisely the change in policy and no ongoing negotiation with Russia is necessary or if it is possible to specify the first step in the process and prove that Russia is likely to respond favorably to this step.

Aid to Russia

One of the hallmarks of U.S. foreign policy toward Russia has been the use of foreign assistance. A good case can be made that an expanded program could be useful today. I will discuss the specific case to be made for more aid when I consider individual issues in Chapters Three and Four.

The general case for expanded aid might be justified as follows. Some claim that the West in general and the United States in particular have not done enough to help Russia. Anders Aslund argues that "foreign nations have not been particularly forthcoming in offering assistance to Russia" (B *How Russia* 314). Others point to the promises that were made in the early days after the end of the Soviet Union and say that the West has not done their part.

In addition to the moral argument, advocates of expanded aid say that more funds could make an enormous difference. Recently David Gordon of the Overseas Development Council testified to the efficacy of foreign aid in assisting economic development (D *Economic Freedom* 53-55). And former National Security Advisor Brent Scowcroft noted that "Foreign assistance is one of the most valuable levers we have to fill that gap and to influence countries in directions that we wish them to go" (D *Newly Independent States* 50).

Expanded aid might be justified in the manner indicated by Scowcroft as a well-defined means of achieving some specific objective. Alternatively, more aid could be defended as a means of responding to dangerous social conditions in Russia. On that ground, Maxim Boycko and Andrei Shleifer argue that foreign assistance can and should be used to "support the social safety net" (B 116) in Russia. They cite a proposed program to fund day care centers and conclude that "a reasonably small amount of aid, properly designed and administered, can go a considerable way towards addressing a major social problem in Russia, encourage enterprise restructuring, and perhaps even reform local government finance" (B 117).

While a good general case can be made for more aid, there are strong arguments against aid as well. First, there are good reasons to believe that expanded aid by itself can do little. In the middle 1990s, former Ambassador to the United Nations, Jeane Kirkpatrick, argued that foreign aid doesn't work effectively:

> One lesson is clear from our experience with economic aid in Africa, Central America and parts of Asia. . . . You cannot necessarily produce economic growth or democracy with resource transfers. In fact, there is no sure recipe for jump-starting economic development from the outside. Development occurs as people change. (qtd. in P Griffin 222)

Nicholas Eberstadt, of the American Enterprise Institute, agrees with Kirkpatrick. He concludes that "there is little in the record to suggest that these programs contribute to economic liberalization or development, while there is considerable evidence to the contrary" (D *Economic Freedom* 15). Bryan Johnson of the Heritage Foundation draws a similar conclusion: "Over the past

50 years the U.S. government has conducted a costly experiment in loans, grants, and development expertise. This experiment has failed miserably" (D *Economic Freedom* 40).

Second, the opponents of expanded aid argue that foreign assistance is rarely spent on the projects that are designated by Congress. In this view, the idea that foreign aid is "targeted" is specious. Recently, Boris Fedorov, former Russian finance minister, claimed that further assistance could do little for Russia because the money would not be spent for the "common good" of the Russian people (see P Reddaway C1). Jonas Bernstein emphasizes this same point, essentially arguing that money appropriated in the United States is unlikely to actually be spent on the particular issue for which it was appropriated. He cites an example to prove this point:

> According to the Accounting Chamber, the government's quixotically persistant-but-toothless watchdog agency, half of the budget money earmarked last year for improving work conditions in regional tax offices was 'lost somewhere between the Finance Ministry and the State Tax Service.'" (P 64)

If the Russians cannot target their own expenditures on a particular problem, how can the United States do so?

If the money doesn't reach the people who need it, where does it go? Bill Bradley explains the answer to that question when he says that "Billions of dollars are promised to Russia, hundreds of millions go into the pockets of American consultants, and only pennies reach Russians" (P 95). In that situation, our aid makes things worse. We promise a lot and then fail to deliver, which "creates anti-American backlashing erupting from disappointed expectations" (P 95).

Third, there is an argument that general U.S. foreign assistance historically has been counterproductive because it creates dependence on aid. Nicholas Eberstadt, of the American Enterprise Institute, testified recently

> The fact is that American development-assistance policies, for many years, have been more likely to lead a prospective beneficiary toward an Eastern Europe-style economic morass than to help it escape from one toward economic health and self-sufficiency. (D *Economic Freedom* 14)

In this view, Russia will have to stand on its own at some point and putting off that time only makes things worse. While emergency food assistance and other aid may have been needed at the birth of the Russian state, seven years later there is no longer a justification for such assistance. Advocates of this perspective believe in the words of Ted Galen Carpenter that "Washington should pursue a policy of trade not aid. The United States should open its markets to the products of Russia and other embryonic democracies of the former Soviet bloc without restriction." He adds "Beyond taking such steps, there is little that the United States can or should do" (P 233).

One note is important here. Since Russia already has Most Favored Nation status, there is little that we can do to increase trade, without providing some sort of assistance in the form of aid, loans, or some sort of special financing.

Against the view that aid generally fails, it could be argued that there are many problems in Russia that, in theory at least, could be solved via a targeted U.S. assistance program. So, for example, the United States might provide aid to a particular region to protect a given species. Or the United States might invest a few tens of millions of dollars in cleaning up mercury pollution in a given river. Alternatively, the United States might essentially hire a nongovernmental group in Russia to carry out a particular mandate.

While such targeted aid seems reasonable at first analysis, it is important to recognize that such proposals are regarded by policy makers as completely unrealistic. In late 1995, Ambassador Richard Morningstar testified before Congress on the future of U.S. aid programs. In essence, he presented his wish list:

> In Russia, for example, I envision our program will increasingly focus on areas where we must have continuing interest and impact: Weapons, security and nuclear material safety, macroeconomic reform, especially in the tax area, training and changes, democracy and development of non-governmental organizations and independent media and trade and investment, especially through the development of small business . . . (D *Newly Independent States* 6)

There is no mention of the kinds of specific programs that I described earlier. Rather, Morningstar focuses upon aid programs that serve core functions for Russia and, therefore, the United States as well. In fact, Morningstar added that "We must be engaged at an appropriate level when our own national interests continue to be very much at stake" (D *Newly Independent States* 7).

The upshot of Morningstar's testimony is that U.S. aid programs should be aimed at crucial problems in Russia that are directly tied to United States national interests. Former National Security Advisor Brent Scowcroft makes a similar point: "I believe that our foreign bilateral assistance should be used only in direct support of our own national interests and not for altruistic purposes, no matter how noble they may be" (D *Newly Independent States* 50). This does not mean that it would be illegitimate for an advocate to argue for a major change in U.S. aid policy to provide assistance on specific projects that are not tied to our national interest. But it does mean that there are serious reasons to doubt the efficacy of such targeted aid programs since they haven't been used to any significant degree before in Russia. And it also suggests the importance of considering political reasons why targeted aid programs haven't been provided in the past.

The obvious reason is that Americans will support aid to Russia (or any other state) only if the aid either is required for humanitarian reasons or serves our own interests. That in turn means that congressional backlash or a fund cutoff should be seen as a very real possibility in response to the micro-targeted programs I described. I will discuss these issues in detail in the final chapter.

Sanctions and Threats

·   The third possible general means of altering U.S. foreign policy toward Russia would be to threaten or actually impose some sanction against Russia in order to force them to change a policy. In theory, any number of sanctions or threats could be made, up to the threat of war. In practice, there are two main sanctions open to U.S. policy makers: the threat of a cutoff of aid or loan programs and the threat to impose trade sanctions.

Before considering the case for and against sanctions, it is important to recognize that threats are an implicit aspect of many foreign policy negotiations. Under current law, the president has the right in numerous situations to impose trade sanctions on a company that violates a U.S. policy. And the Secretary of State may threaten to take specified or unspecified action unless a policy is changed. To meet the resolution, it would seem that the advocate of change would have to defend mandating a specific sanction. It would not be enough to call on the President to consider applying a given sanction. In the present system, critics of current U.S. policy already make such requests. Thus, to meet the resolution, the affirmative will need to impose a given sanction, although they may include standards for defining when Russian action merits removal of the sanction.

What case can be made for imposing strict sanctions on Russia? Some make a strong moral argument about sanctions. They argue that U.S. aid is just that, aid, and that we should cut it off when the country receiving that assistance violates our standards of morality. Recently, Senator Hatch commented in relation to legislation calling for a cutoff of support to Russia because of a law restricting religious liberty:

> U.S. assistance is not an entitlement. It is a demonstration of our support for the emergence of democracy in a land cursed by communism for most of this decade [he probably meant century]. If Russia turns back to the night of authoritarianism, we should not squander our resources. (CR "Foreign Operations Export" S7521)

Thus, the United States should impose trade sanctions or cut off aid when Russia violates fundamental moral principles.

There is also an argument that failure to act against a violation of some sort sends precisely the wrong signal. Failure to act indicates U.S. acceptance of the behavior and, in this view, reduces our ability to negotiate in the future.

Finally, the advocates of tough policies argue that sanctions often work. In this view, the threat of punishment can force the Russians to mend their ways. The power of the United States in the current world situation is so great, according to those who advocate this view, that sanctions are likely to be effective.

The opponents of tougher sanctions against Russia deny that such a policy is likely to be effective. It should be noted that Congress has tried to influence Russian policy with the threat of sanctions in any number of cases. According to Raymond Garthoff, Congress has threatened to cut off funds unless Russia changed its policies in many areas, including the following:

- withdrawal of Russian troops from Latvia and Estonia by a designated date;
- withdrawal of troops from Moldova by a designated date;
- demilitarization of the Kaliningrad area in Russia;
- a deal to sell space technology to India;
- a deal to sell nuclear reactors to Iran;
- a deal to sell missiles to China;
- a deal to build a nuclear reactor in Cuba. (P 311)

The point is that sanctions have been threatened in so many cases that, according to some, they have lost any effectiveness.

Opponents of sanctions also cite a variety of types of evidence indicating the general ineffectiveness of the policy. For example, in the early 1990s, the United States applied sanctions to a Russian export firm for selling rocket engines to India. After the Clinton administration took office, a deal was brokered in which the sanctions would be waived, Russia would receive $400 million in space project funding from the United States, and Russia would stop providing the technology to India. Apparently, Russia accepted the money and then "quietly transferred much of the production technology to India anyway—in violation of its high-level promises" (P Cloud 12). This example is suggestive of how little power the United States has over Russia, at least in cases where we are unwilling to cut off all trade/aid.

There is also evidence from U.S. relations with other nations indicating that the use of sanctions is generally ineffective. A recent study of the effect of American sanctions on Iran indicates that sanctions were not effective. The study found that sanctions have not succeeded in isolating Iran from the rest of the world but instead have pushed Iran to closer contacts with nations such as Russia (P Slavin A12). Three year's ago, in the analysis of U.S. policy toward the People's Republic of China, I cited similar evidence that sanctions have not been effective in changing Chinese behavior.

A second key problem with sanctions as a policy is that they undercut the ability of the President to negotiate a solution to any issue. Sanctions publicly enforce a given policy. In that way they eliminate all discretion on the part of the President. In fact, many of the issues upon which sanctions have been threatened are also "issues that the United States government has taken up with Russia and in many cases resolved" (P Garthoff 311). It may be more sensible for the President to threaten action in private, as opposed to public action by Congress. Representative Hamilton of Indiana got at this point in discussion of a resolution dealing with Russian and Chinese arms sales to Iran. He said

> What bothers me is that I think the resolution is not going to be helpful to the diplomatic process. This problem is going to be solved eventually through diplomacy I think, I hope, and our goal should be to help the President and not make his job more difficult on the very tough questions of nonproliferation, where we all share the same goals. (CR "General Leave" H10126)

Hamilton went on to characterize the threat of sanctions as "counterproductive" to the negotiations process (CR "General Leave" H10126). Senator Jeff Bingaman made a similar point when he argued against a call for sanctions against Russia based on religious discrimination:

> To tie our Nation's foreign aid decisions too closely to legislative outcomes in other countries—even absolutely egregious ones like the Russian law . . . can have serious unintended consequences and disrupt national security objectives of our Nation. Through legislative actions such as this one . . . we can actually trigger the enactment of outrageous laws in other nations, which could seriously damage the existing freedoms that citizens in other nations have. (CR "Foreign Operations Export" S7521)

In this view, it makes more sense to give the President the discretion to negotiate on issues of concern to the United States. Of course, that policy defines the present system.

A third point relates to the need for a stable policy toward Russia. There is a strong argument that U.S. policy toward Russia should be consistent. James Collins of the State Department has testified: "A stable and steady policy in the face of less steady direction on the part of the new states will remain a constructive and key source of support to those who seek to take these states in the direction of reform" (D *Newly Independent States* 4). In a different hearing, Ambassador Collins said that

> "Steady as she goes" should be our watchword now. We can afford to remain patient, assuring the Russians that our doors remain open to cooperation on the full range of security, economic, and political issues, while at the same time neither ignoring nor condoning Russian policies and actions which are destructive. (D *Russia's Election* 5)

Ambassador Collins also defended the present policy process, which he labelled one of "engagement" (D *Russia's Election* 5). Under that process "We will continue to address these issues [where we disagree] frankly" (D *Russia's Election* 5). He then referred to the policy of Secretary of State Warren Christopher, which was that "we will cooperate with the Russians where we can and we will manage our differences where necessary" (D *Russia's Election* 5).

Collins builds a strong argument for consistency and stability. In essence, he says that it is more important to maintain a strong relationship with the newly democratic Russia than it is to confront specific problems with sanctions. Moreover, because they represent policy shifts, sanctions could undermine the stability of our relations with Russia and, therefore, prove counterproductive.

A fourth general problem with sanctions is that using them often alienates the nation we are sanctioning (see P Sanger "Two-Edged" A12). Sanctions policies are in the words of Raymond Garthoff of the Brookings Institution, "always resented" (P 311). Former U.S. Ambassador to Russia Jack Matlock commented about the counterproductivity of threats in relation to calls for sanctions because of the Russian war in Chechnya: "Political sanctions are even more inappropriate since they reinforce the false image many Russian 'super-patriots' have of the United States as an enemy power" (in D *Crisis in Chechnya* 7). He went on to suggest that sanctions could "strengthen the hand of chauvinist forces in Russia" (D *Crisis in Chechnya* 7). Anatol Lieven, a Russian journalist, echoed Matlock's point, noting that "even Russian liberal public opinion . . .[is] not very receptive to Western influence" (D *Crisis in Chechnya* 15).

All of this means that sanctions are unlikely to influence Russian behavior (see Lieven in D Crisis in Chechnya 16), but likely to cause a Russian backlash against the West. Sanctions may be a particularly risky policy because of Russian paranoia about the actions of the United States. Recently, Deputy Secretary of State Strobe Talbott noted the potential problem:

> If too many Russians overindulge their misplaced suspicions that we want to keep them down, then words such as partnership and cooperation will become synonyms for appeasement, subservience, and humiliation at the hands of the West. The result then could be that we will indeed cooperate less and compete more on precisely those issues where it is in our common interest to cooperate more and compete less: arms control, environmental degradation, terrorism, regional conflict, and proliferation of weapons of mass destruction. (P "America and Russia" 540)

If sanctions produce backlash, that result could make the problem at which the sanctions were aimed worse. Or sanctions could even harm general U.S. relations with Russia. Or, worst of all, sanctions could play into the hands of Russian hardliners who hate the West and want to return to something like the Cold War. Given these risks, defenders of present policy argue that it is sensible to use sanctions and other threats only on crucial issues and generally in a negotiation process carried on in private.

It also is important to have a wide perspective on the proper policy goals of the United States in dealing with Russia. The most important goal, as Senator Bill Bradley has noted, must be "to prevent that [nuclear] capability from being used against us or anyone else. We must build on the fact that our core national interests do not conflict and that working together will make the world a safer place for both our countries" (P 90). How does Bradley's comment relate to the use of sanctions against Russia? The implication is that the United States should use sanctions only on issues that are essential to our national security. We should not risk offending the Russians on other issues because of the continued danger of nuclear war. In this view, to risk offending Russia or even pushing it toward strident nationalism over arms sales or some other issue of lesser concern is quite foolish.

In sum, there is no doubt that sanctions have great appeal when Russia (or any other nation) enacts some dangerous policy. And Russia clearly has no moral right to our assistance or aid. On the other hand, there are significant risks associated with threats or sanctions of any kind. Those risks suggest that the policy should be utilized only in the most serious of situations and only after an attempt has been made to find a diplomatic solution to the problem.

Conclusion

The focus of this chapter has been on outlining the evolution of political and economic policy in Russia since the end of the Soviet empire. I also have described American foreign policy toward Russia from the Bush through the Clinton years. In the last section, I considered the three main methods of substantially changing U.S. foreign policy: direct policy action, increases or decreases in aid, and the use of sanctions. In the following two chapters, I consider specific problem areas in U.S.-Russian relations and the actions that might be taken to alleviate those problems.

3 Economic, Political, and Social Issues in U.S. Foreign Policy Toward Russia

In this chapter, I will discuss the main proposals for assisting the Russians in strengthening their economic and political systems and dealing with any number of social ills afflicting the Russian state. My focus will be on the problems that the United States might confront through a changed foreign policy.

Economic Reform

In the previous chapter I described the status of the Russian economy and the process of reform that has occurred so far. Clearly, one goal of current U.S. foreign policy toward Russia is to support economic reform efforts and, therefore, strengthen the Russian economy. As I mentioned, the United States has aid programs that are designed to assist small business, help in the development of a tax system, improve crime-fighting to combat the Russian mafia, and accomplish other aims as well. Given the breadth of the assistance programs already in place, it is important to ask what else could the United States do to assist Russian reform?

In answering this question, the first step is to recognize the importance of Russian economic reform. The United States has not spent billions of dollars on economic reform efforts merely because we care about the Russian people. The programs have been motivated by genuine concern, but also by the fear that if reform programs fail and the economy declines further, the result may be a return to communism or a move toward totalitarianism of some other kind. I will discuss the likelihood of such results in the section on Russian political reform.

Thus, the United States might change foreign policy in order to facilitate the reform process and protect our national interest. There are three main approaches that could be taken. First, the United States could reduce or eliminate traditional foreign aid based on the reasoning that such assistance creates dependence and impedes long-term growth. Clearly, this idea, while supported by some conservative ideologues, lacks merit. Initially, U.S. economic aid is so small that it is hard to see how any dependence could be created. Second, because current aid is distributed to non-governmental organizations, including some businesses, its primary function is to provide key information and assistance to facilitate adaptation to the new economic situation. Third, there are key problems in the Russian economy on which U.S. aid programs can provide vitally needed assistance.

The second main approach would be for the United States to substantially expand general economic assistance to the Russian government in order to speed up the reform process. While there is a strong argument that the United States has not fulfilled our moral responsibility to the Russian people in providing sufficient aid, it would not be sensible to support a general expansion of economic assistance. First, the Russian government is not efficient. Expanded assistance is quite likely to be wasted or not reach the people or institutions it was designed to help. That certainly was true of the aid programs established in the early 1990s. Second, expanded aid programs are subject to all of the arguments that I discussed in the previous chapter. Aid is often ineffective and may create dependence on the aid giver. Third, the barriers to economic reform are not mainly tied to lack of funding. For example, one of the key problems holding back Russian economic development is the lack of a strong court system to enforce contractual rights. General economic aid does not confront that problem (and many others) and, thus, will do little to remove the bottlenecks that are holding back economic development.

Finally, a call for general expansion of economic assistance to Russia would exacerbate antiaid attitudes in Congress, possibly producing a backlash that could have extremely negative effects. In the present system, some in Congress complain about aid spent on dismantling Russian nuclear weapons and providing housing for soldiers returning to Russia from the Baltic states. If such obviously justifiable programs produce controversy, it is easy to see the enormous reaction that a proposal to dramatically expand aid to Russia would produce. And that public response could lead to curtailment of other essential aid to Russia or some other nation, an argument that I will focus upon in the final chapter.

The third main approach would be for the United States to selectively expand programs aimed directly at removing the roadblocks that are limiting Russian economic development. In this view, the primary factors limiting the development of an efficient market economy in Russia are barriers that are tied to the economic system in the Soviet Union. Obvious barriers to Russian economic development include a weak judicial system that is ineffective in fighting crime and often fails to enforce contractual responsibilities, an inadequate tax collection system, inefficient former defense producers, and of course the mafia.

If these barriers could be overcome then, in this view, Russian economic development would move rapidly. That rapid development would lessen the chance of instability or a return to Cold War policies.

While the policy of targeting economic assistance at key blockages in the Russian system seems sensible, there are some major problems. First, it is not clear that such a proposal meets the requirements of the resolution. Current U.S. policy is to use targeted aid programs to assist Russian economic development. It is unclear how the proposed plan in any way changes U.S. policy. Of course, the advocate of the program will claim that expanded funding is a substantial change in policy. On the other hand, it could be argued that the same policy would be in effect in both situations and that the only difference is the increased support.

Second, it is not so easy to target aid programs at specific blockages in the Russian system. Take the case of organized crime as a relevant example of this point. What can the United States do about the Russian mafia. In truth, the answer is not much. The United States could provide training programs for Russian police, pay for seminars, provide specific technical equipment, and so forth. But the real problem of the mafia relates to a lack of will of the police and an acceptance of the situation among the general public. Absent changes in those two perspectives, no program will accomplish much. Moreover, the idea of the United States paying for anti-mafia training programs seems absurd. I quoted Senator Bradley in the previous chapter, who argued that such programs do much more for American consultants than they do for the people of Russia.

Third, the experience with targeted programs in the present system is not especially encouraging. Clearly, the programs that have been utilized over the last seven years have not succeeded in altering the economic situation facing the Russian people. While many of those programs could be defined as general economic assistance, there also were some programs aimed at specific problems.

Fourth, a proposal to expand targeted programs arguably could be counterproductive. As I noted earlier, there is some risk that such programs lead to dependence not development. Moreover, such programs may cause a backlash within Russia. The problem is that many targeted programs set firm requirements on the actions of the Russians. Like any nation, the leaders of Russia tend to respond very negatively to aid proposals that tell them how to run their country. Thus, there is substantial danger that even targeted programs could prove counterproductive. A similar point could be made about the potential that an expanded aid program might produce backlash in the United States Congress. Such backlash could lead to cuts in other vitally needed programs.

The opponent of expanded economic assistance also might argue that the United States government is not the appropriate vehicle to spur economic reform. In this regard, Michael Mandelbaum argues that pressure for economic reform

is most appropriately and effectively conveyed not by the American State Department but by the International Monetary Fund, which is lending Russia billions of dollars and is therefore in a position to tell the Russians that if they do not follow sensible economic policies, they will not receive Western loans. Moreover, it is better that Russian anger at that message be directed at an international financial institution than at the U.S. (P "Our Outdated" 39)

Mandelbaum's perspective is consistent with the arguments for a stable U.S. policy focusing on essential U.S. security interests that I discussed in the previous chapter. In this view, the United States should do nothing that could impede efforts to reduce the number of Russian nuclear weapons and make them safer. A targeted aid program could produce backlash in either Russia or the United States that could impede those crucial objectives.

The best way to advocate expanded aid for economic reform is to identify a very specific proposal for what the United States should do and argue that general indictments of U.S. aid do not apply to this specific plan. At this point, however, the affirmative faces an inherent tradeoff. Detailed specific proposals are more likely to be implemented effectively. But these same proposals may not meet the resolution because they arguably do not change general U.S. policy at all. One other point is important about advocating such detailed proposals. It may be hard to find defensible real-world specific proposals. In my review of extensive literature on Russia I did not find a host of such proposals.

Trade Reform

As I noted earlier, some conservative economists argue that the most important need is to increase trade with Russia. In this view, increased access to markets in the United States and the West is the key to Russian economic development.

Trade policy will play a crucial role on this resolution. In particular, there are important trade issues relating to Russia's export of arms and other technology to a number of nations. On the other hand, I don't think that changes in U.S. trade policy is likely to play an important role in encouraging Russian economic reform. First, there are no significant barriers to expanded trade with the United States. Russia has received Most Favored Nation (MFN) status and can sell as many products as it wants. Second, Russia already has a healthy balance of payments surplus. The export sector has been doing very well. Third, while Russia has a strong record of exporting natural gas, minerals, other raw materials, and arms, it is not clear that there are other goods that could be sold in an expanded export program. Currently, Russian domestic products are not perceived as of high quality, a perception that is apparently all too accurate. What would they sell to the United States if some kind of expanded export program could be created? It seems doubtful that Russian industry has the products needed to support more trade with the West.

On the other hand, the advocate of changing U.S. foreign policy toward Russia could argue that the United States should provide loan guarantees or some other subsidy to support Russian exports to the United States. Again, such a proposed policy seems foolish. Subsidies for export promotion would have the effect of supporting inefficient Russian industries. It is unclear why the United States government should provide incentives to keep such inefficient producers in business. To the contrary, a strong argument can be made that these inefficient industries need to fail in order to clear the deadwood from the Russian system.

Moreover, a program of export subsidies for Russian firms would be subject to the general arguments against economic assistance that I discussed earlier. In particular, such a program would risk producing a domestic backlash against U.S. relations with Russia or more broadly against all U.S. foreign aid programs. Clearly, many would be outraged by the Federal Government spending large sums of money to subsidize inefficient Russian industries, at the same time that American workers are being displaced from their jobs by cheaper competition from abroad.

For the reasons I have identified, alterations in trade policy are not a viable means of supporting Russian economic reform. The key point is that trade only occurs when you have a product that is valued by your trade partner. If you have that product and there are few restrictions on trade, then you will be able to build a market. On the other hand, if you do not have a product that is valued, then support for trade will do little. An example may make this point. Imagine that the United States government provided substantial subsidies to encourage Russia to export 1950s electronics based on vacuum tubes. Would anyone buy a radio containing vacuum tubes, even if it were dirt cheap? Clearly, the answer is no.

Currently, the only products that Russia has that people want are natural resources and arms. They do not need any help in selling these products and, in the case of arms, it may be in U.S. interest to discourage, rather than encourage, exports.

Energy Policy

One particular economic issue, energy policy, deserves specific analysis. There are two aspects of the energy policy that merit attention, the situation in the Caspian basin and a deal between Russia and Iran.

The situation in the Caspian is probably the more important of these two issues. As I noted last year in the analysis of the potential of renewable energy policy, there are substantial oil reserves within the former Soviet Union. Glen Howard of the Strategic Assessment Center of Science Applications International states that "The Caspian Sea region is poised to become one of the most important energy producing areas of the world" (P A22).

While Russia borders the Caspian, the most important oil resources apparently are in Azerbaijan to the south (P Howard A22). U.S. energy companies already have made major investments both in Azerbaijan and also Kazakhstan (P Morgan and Ottaway A1+). This region is likely to be particularly important to the United States since "during the coming years American dependence on imported oil will only increase from the current level of 50 percent" (P Ebel 344).

In relation to U.S. foreign policy toward Russia and our increasing oil dependence, the most important single fact is that Russian oil reserves are important only at "the margin" (P Ebel 344). The crucial oil reserves are in the former Soviet Union, but not Russia. Even so, there is an argument that a change "toward" Russia is warranted.

Recently, an aide on the National Security Council testified that U.S. policy has been to support the independence of the former Soviet republics possessing large oil reserves in order to break a Russian monopoly on oil production in the region (see P Morgan and Ottaway A1+). This testimony would seem to indicate that in relation to the republics of the former Soviet Union, a change in policy aimed at them also functions as a change in foreign policy toward Russia. At the same time, this definition of *toward* is not overly expansive because of the inherent relationship between Russia and the various republics.

How could the United States change its foreign policy toward Russia in relation to oil exports? One option would be for the United States to stop attempting
to isolate Russia. The government could encourage joint agreements between
Russian companies and U.S. energy concerns. Alternatively, the United States
could encourage the development of a pipeline through Russian territory to trans-
port the oil from the Caspian basis to the nations of the world.

None of these proposals make sense. The United States has attempted to isolate Russia in relation to energy exports because it is clearly in our interest that
there be a number of energy suppliers in the world. If Russia had more market
power, that would inevitably lead to higher prices and give Russia greater capacity to threaten the United States with an oil cutoff. Second, joint agreements with
Russian companies or support for a pipeline are merely handouts. The Russian
economy will never prosper until Russian firms can compete on the world market. It does not help Russia for the United States to subsidize inefficient firms.

It makes no sense for the United States to work with Russian companies in
developing oil fields in Azerbaijan. U.S. firms should attempt to maximize their
own profits. And a quick look at a map of the region immediately reveals that
building a pipeline through Russia would go far out of the way.

There is a possible alteration in U.S. foreign policy in relation to oil and the
former Soviet Union that might be sensible. One particular danger to future oil
production in the region is the on-going conflict between Azerbaijan and
Armenia. How does this relate to U.S. foreign policy toward Russia? The answer
is that Russia actively has supported Armenia in the conflict with Azerbaijan. It
is estimated that Russia sent more than a billion dollars worth of arms, including
32 Scud missiles to Armenia between 1994 and 1996 (P Howard A22). Howard
notes that the Scuds "could potentially hit Azerbaijan's capital, Baku, [or] the oil
fields," and concludes that "Armenia's acquisition of the missiles may be the single most destabilizing development to occur in the Caucasus since the breakup of
the Soviet Union" (P A22). Since Baku is "littered with exposed oil pools and sur-
rounded by a network of oil-storage facilities" a Scud attack "could ignite a hor-
rific series of fires" and "force an exodus of Western oil representatives and cause
significant economic damage" (P Howard A22).

Of still greater importance, a future war between Armenia and Azerbaijan
could cause oil exports from the region to be stopped. In that situation, there
could be substantial effects on the world. In last year's analysis, I described the
effects that the two oil shocks of the 1970s had on the United States and world
economies. In both cases, there were very substantial negative effects. An oil
shock in the future brought on by conflict between Armenia and Azerbaijan might
produce a world recession or even depression with horrible effects, one of which
would be increased risk of military conflict.

Given this situation, some argue that the United States should put pressure on
Russia to stop supporting Armenia and to work toward resolution of the conflict.
In this view, U.S. foreign policy could reduce the risk of conflict in the region

and, consequently, reduce the chance of a catastrophic oil shock occurring at some point in the next century.

Against the proposal for the United States to pressure Russia on Armenia, there are a number of strong arguments. First, it is current U.S. policy to encourage peaceful resolution of disputes and to discourage Russian arms sales that could lead to conflict among the states of the former Soviet Union. In other words, the proposal for "change" in U.S. policy would seem to describe current U.S. foreign policy in the region.

Second, the cat is already out of the bag. Armenia has received the arms and has very little incentive to return them. The Russian arms provide Armenia with both defense and leverage in their dispute with Azerbaijan. It is hard to see how the United States could force removal of the weapons.

Third, it will be decades before the Caspian basin plays a crucial role in world energy production. For the foreseeable future, the Persian Gulf in general, and Saudi Arabia in particular, are the keys to world oil reserves. Thus, it is incredibly speculative to identify specific risks to energy production in the Caspian basin at this point.

Fourth, Russia has armed Armenia, against the protests of the United States and others, because it is in Russia's perceived self interest to do so. It is hard to see how the United States can do much about that. The United States could threaten major trade sanctions or to stop all aid, unless the action was taken. However, given our other priorities in dealing with Russia, either of those actions would seem to be foolish. Again the problem with threats is that they may make the situation worse or aid hardliners in Russia who, in turn, could threaten our national interest. Perhaps we should take such risks if Russia appeared to be providing nuclear weapons technology to Iraq or Iran. On the other hand, the risk hardly seems worth taking in relation to Armenian arms sales.

Unlike the Armenian issue, which is really a long-term problem, the Iran oil deal is a significant concern today. In September 1997, Gazprom, a Russian energy conglomerate agreed to participate in a $2 billion plan to develop oil off the Iranian coast (see P Kramer). In taking this action, Gazprom would be in violation of the Iran and Libya Sanctions Act of 1996. It is U.S. policy to isolate Iran from the world community because Iran is a terrorist state. The United States believes that continuing economic isolation can force change in Iranian policy over a period of years. Thus, we strongly oppose deals that break the economic isolation of the country, especially in regard to oil production, because of the massive amounts of money that are potentially involved.

How does U.S. policy relate to a private deal between a Russian company and Iran? The answer is that Gazprom has received substantial assistance from the U.S. Export-Import bank. In 1994, Gazprom and the Ex-Im bank committed themselves to an agreement under which the Ex-Im bank could provide "loan guarantees" for up to $750 million worth of purchases by Gazprom of U.S. equipment (see P Kramer). Over a hundred million dollars already has been guaranteed

(P Kramer A19). Thus, because it has received this U.S. aid, Gazprom is subject to U.S. law concerning Iran.

The existence of the agreement between Gazprom and the Ex-Im bank gives the United States considerable leverage for dealing with the oil deal. Some argue that the United States should impose sanctions in order to force the Russians out of the energy deal (see Senator D'Amato in CR "The Gazprom Deal" S10915–S10917).

What are the arguments against sanctions? First, it could be argued that the Gazprom deal is not very important. In this view, Iran is going to develop the oil fields at some point. France also has expressed interest in a joint deal. Second, the deal might actually push the liberalization process in Iran. The deal would bring in money for Iran and also increase contact with other nations, both of which might lead Iran back to the world community. Since the new Iranian President has made statements indicating slight movement in this regard, now might be the perfect time for economic cooperation with the nation. Third, the deal brings vitally needed foreign exchange into Russia. It would seem counterproductive to cut it off.

Fourth, the Clinton administration argues that the best way to handle such a situation is with diplomacy, not sanctions imposed by Congress. In this view, it is better to let the administration negotiate than require that sanctions be imposed. Negotiations may be more effective and, at worst, the deal might be part of a trade-off on some more critical issue. Finally, the proposed imposition of sanctions means that the policy is subject to all of the general objections to sanctions that I have discussed previously.

Russian Political Reform

Most commentators on U.S.-Russian relations believe there are three critical priorities for the United States in dealing with Russia: control of nuclear weapons, economic reform, and political reform. In this view, the security of the United States depends upon Russia retaining tight control of nuclear weapons and remaining a stable government. That stability best can be guaranteed if Russia develops a dynamic capitalist economy and creates strong democratic institutions. In this section, I will focus on political institutions in Russia, especially the various risks that democracy might fail.

There are four main scenarios in which Russian democracy would fail and the interests of the United States would be threatened: return to communism, military dictatorship, Russian nationalism, and break-up of the Russian Federation. Why are American politicians and experts on Russia so concerned with these issues? Some fear that Russia could in the words of one commentator slide "back toward political and economic instability" (P Griffin 219). Lilia Shevtsova and Scott Bruckner note that "many others have forecast long-term catastrophic social and political upheavals resulting from Russia's transition" (P 32).

If such a "catastrophic upheaval" occurred, the ultimate results could be terrible for Russia, the United States, and the world. Boris Nemtsov, governor of the third largest city in Russia, Nizhniy Novgorod, and a well-known reformer, says that in that circumstance Russia could become "a monster armed with missiles." (qtd. in P Griffin 219). Recently, Alexei Arbatov, the deputy chairman of the Defense Committee of the Russian Duma, noted that

> The Cold War is not likely to be resurrected, but Russia's relations with the West regarding the regions of Central and Eastern Europe, the Balkans, the Black Sea-Caspian basin, Central Asia and the Far East could again become confrontation. Regional rivalries between Russia and the West would be greatly exacerbated by a disintegration of the regional and global arms control regime and nuclear non-proliferation efforts. (P "Eurasia Letter" 103)

Obviously, the risk of a move not to a Cold War, but to a Cool Conflict, would be exacerbated in the situation outlined by Nemtsov.

Thus, it is very important to weigh the risk of serious instability in Russia. Therefore, I will consider each of the scenarios in turn and then briefly discuss possible means of strengthening Russian democracy.

Return to Communism

To many in the United States, especially conservatives, the nightmare scenario is that Russia might return to communism. Advocates of this view note that the Communist Party did very well in the 1995 parliamentary elections, in fact winning more seats than any other party. They also note that the leader of the party, Gennady Zyuganov, led Yeltsin in the polls at one point and might have won the 1996 election if it had not been for the arguably illegal spending blitz on behalf of Yeltsin. Thus, according to some, there is a real risk that Russia could return to communism.

If that happened, according to conservatives, the great victory in the Cold War would mean nothing. They fear that Russia again could become a totalitarian aggressive state, oppressing the Russian people and threatening Eastern Europe with reimposition of Soviet rule.

Those who argue that there is a serious risk of return to communism note that "Russian communists have remained traditional and repressive, championing a nostalgic vision of the past rather than alternative program for the future" (P McFaul 322). This indicates that for the communists nothing has changed.

Moreover, the platform of the Communist Party "calls for the reintegration of the Soviet Union" (P Matlock 44). Former U.S. Ambassador to Russia Jack Matlock notes that "the proviso that it [reintegration] be accomplished by peaceful means is not terribly reassuring, considering the Orwellian twist that communists give words like 'peaceful'" (P 44). It seems clear that the new nations of the former Soviet Union would not accept such reintegration. The likely result would be war in which the United States and NATO could be involved.

While it is impossible to rule out the chance that the communists might return to power and remilitarize Russia, the best evidence indicates that this result is extremely unlikely. First, the data do not suggest that return to communist rule is likely. It is important to remember that almost all power in Russia is in the hands of the president and in the presidential election Yeltsin won decisively. Yes, Zyuganov was ahead of Yeltsin in the polls, but the ultimate outcome shows a decisive vote against communism. This situation led Strobe Talbott to comment "With Boris Yeltsin's victory over Gennady Zyuganov, the communist electoral tide began to recede from its high-water mark" (P "The End" 23). U.S. Ambassador Thomas Pickering makes a similar argument. He claims simply that "Soviet communism is dead" (P 529) and cites the 1996 presidential election as proof of that point.

From this perspective, the successes of the communists at the polls do not reflect real support for a return to the policies of the Soviet Union. Rather, the pro-communist sentiment reflects merely a nostalgia among "the older part of the population . . . for the peace, order, stability, and above all economic security of Soviet days" (P Lieven 17). It would seem unlikely that this nostalgia could be translated into a return to communist rule. Pickering supports this thinking when he notes that the failures of communism are well known to all and "there is no all-encompassing alternative to the path toward democracy and a market economy" (P 529).

Were the Russian people angry about the failures of reform? Yes. Were they angry at Yeltsin for his various sins? Yes. But when push came to shove, did they want a return to Soviet communism? The answer was an emphatic NO!

One other point about the risk of a communist victory is important. The aging of the electorate means that the chance of a communist victory will diminish further in the future. A very high percentage of the supporters of Zyuganov are the elderly. This means in the words of one expert that "Communism in Russia is fading fast" (P Lieven 17).

Finally, it should be noted that the risks of a return to communist rule may have been overstated. Some experts argue that the Communist Party in Russia today is nothing like the Communist Party of the Soviet era. In this view, today's communists are in the words of one high official "typical classical social democrats" (qtd. in P Cooper "Russia's Political" 392). It also should be noted that there have been cases in Eastern Europe, notably Poland, in which the communists were returned to power without producing a reversion to aggressive totalitarianism.

Moreover, Russia simply lacks the power of the Soviet Union. Even if there were a mass tide to re-create a Stalinist state (a very unlikely scenario), Russia in the 1990s could not be the same danger to the world as was the Soviet Union. The nations of the former Warsaw Pact are out of the Russian orbit and they are not going back if they have anything to say about it. Remember that even Ukraine wants to join NATO. And at least some of the new nations of the former Soviet republics would fight against Russia, if necessary.

Yes, Russia has many nuclear weapons. But nuclear weapons, as the United States found out in Vietnam and the Soviets in Afghanistan, do you little good in a conventional war. And the nations of Europe are still protected by the American nuclear umbrella. And Russia is a very weak conventional power. NATO's conventional forces are far more powerful than the Russian army today.

Military Dictatorship

An alternative scenario leading to instability and the threat of war is the risk of "revival of authoritarianism" (P Griffin 221). After centuries of totalitarian rule under the Czars and the communists, democracy is a very new experience. In this regard, U.S. Ambassador Thomas Pickering admits that "The democratic virtues of tolerance and compromise, as well as the democratic separation of the public and private spheres, have shallow roots in Russia" (P 530). Those shallow roots create a situation in which an authoritarian group could take power.

Another factor is the risk of massive economic failure. As I noted earlier, the Russian economy suffers from major problems and is quite unstable. If there were a major downturn, that could increase the chance of a return to totalitarianism. Boris Yeltsin himself argues that "If Russia fails in its reforms, especially of the economy, a dictator will appear" (qtd. in P Griffin 230). Experts such as vanden Heuvel and Cohen agree. They conclude that "the fabled patience of the Russian people has limits, and when they are reached the result could be beyond anyone's control" (P "The Other" 26). Their point is that economic and political conditions are so bad that a coup of some type could occur, which would be the end of democratic rule.

One possible scenario is a military mutiny or coup. Recently, "Workers at a nuclear submarine facility sealed off the yard and took the managing director hostage until wages were flown in from Moscow" (P vanden Heuvel and Cohen "The Other" 25). Another sign of danger is that General Lev Rokhlin, a former high commander and now a member of the Duma, wrote an open letter in which he "accused Yeltsin of surrounding himself with brazenly corrupt advisors, willfully destroying the army and the defense industries, betraying Russian national interests" (P vanden Heuvel and Cohen "The Other" 25). Yeltsin responded by attacking Rokhlin, but also promising that military salaries would be paid.

Clearly, the situation is unstable. Perhaps that is why

> In a recent survey, 60 percent of Russian experts on military affairs responded that coup, mutiny or complete disintegration of the army is likely within eighteen months. Indeed, several ranking political figures remarked privately that by comparative political science criteria, the Russian military should have taken power two or three years ago. (P vanden Heuvel and Cohen "The Other" 25)

In historical terms, countries suffering through political and economic instability often turn to military leaders.

Another factor that could increase the chance of a military coup relates to the military reform program. That program has not been successful so far. Paul Mann writes that the program is "near a dead end" and that "without major reform, the military will become the number one threat to the nation's security" (P "Russians Sound" 64). In fact, some believe that the Soviet defense establishment is "at risk of disintegrating within 24 months if its decline is not reversed" (P Mann "Russians Sound" 64).

The key failure is in the demilitarization program. Up to now, there has not been extensive privatization in the area of military production. Since defense contracts have fallen by over 80%, that has precipitated a crisis in the military/economic system (P Mann "Russians Sound" 64). Nor has there been anything like adequate investment in conversion to civilian production (P Mann "Russians Sound 64). Another problem is, according to Alexei Arbatov, that "political control of the military 'is extremely weak'" (P "Russians Sound" 67). Additionally, a number of state-funded paramilitary organizations have emerged that conduct surveillance and carry out other acts. These organizations are quasimilitary in nature and spend a significant amount of money. Jacob Kipp of the United States Army Foreign Military Studies program, notes that "In a crisis, the multiple militaries are likely to be a source of political maneuvering" (P Mann "Russians Sound" 69).

In summary, there is grave economic and political instability. The Russian defense system is disintegrating. The Russian military establishment is angry. In such an unstable situation, a coup does seem possible.

It is also possible that a dictatorship might be set up by someone other than the current military. On that subject, there is great fear that former general Alexander Lebed could become a dictator. Lebed is "rated the country's most popular politician, with a 26% support, nearly double Yeltsin's" (P Kranz "What's Bringing" 59). With this popularity, Lebed is viewed as the most likely successor to Yeltsin. Some commentators particularly worry that Lebed might take control if Yeltsin were to die or be forced out of the presidency in the near term. At that point, Lebed could win the presidency and "use vast presidential powers to wreak revenge on enemies in the Kremlin, dismiss the legislature and re-distribute wealth" (P Kranz "What's Bringing" 59).

It is important to recognize that a military coup might have particularly negative consequences for the United States. Richard Pipes of Harvard notes that "Anyone who spends an hour with Russian generals cannot but feel the intensity of their resentment against the West as well as against their own democratic government for reducing to the status of a negligible force the army that defeated Nazi Germany and was acknowledged by the U.S. military as a peer" (P 72). And Hall Gardner cites the opinion of former Russian Foreign Minister Andrei Kozyrev that one possible scenario for United States-Russian relations is "return to confrontation" (B 224).

What needs to be done to lessen the risk of military or other dictatorship? First, the army needs to be dramatically cut in size from perhaps 1.7 million to 500,000 crack troops (P Mann "Russians Sound" 64). Second, there needs to be adequate investment in the conversion of defense industries to civilian uses.

Third, more funding needs to be provided for the military, especially in the areas of maintenance and pay for soldiers (P Mann "Russians Sound" 65).

What barrier exists to military reform? The key is money. While military reform would save money in the long term, it would cost money in the short term and that money simply isn't available (P Mann "Russians Sound" 67).

Thus, a strong argument could be made that in addition to supporting programs to strengthen democratic institutions in Russia, the United States should do more to assist military reform. The United States might provide assistance to carry out defense conversion more rapidly. We also might support expanded programs to provide housing and other services for the military. Military exchange and joint training programs might be implemented in an attempt to inculcate the Russian military with democratic values. Such efforts would not eliminate the risk of military coup, but they might substantially reduce that risk.

On the other hand, there are strong arguments that the risk of coup has been overstated and that current U.S. policy is on track. First, some argue that the risk of return to totalitarianism has been overstated. For example, Ambassador Pickering argues that the journey away from totalitarianism is irreversible (P Pickering 530). Similarly, Anatol Lieven argues that there is little chance of a revolutionary political movement reimposing a dictatorship on the Russian people. He writes that

> the apathy of the population and the ability of the state to guarantee certain basic living standards mean that these [political] troubles will not spill over into mass civic violence or new mass revolutionary movements. (P 21)

He concludes that even if an authoritarian regime were to take power in Moscow "it is highly unlikely that such a government would be able to impose effective authoritarian rule across the whole country, let alone mobilize the country to project strong Russian influence in the outside world, or in the last resort to go to war" (P 21).

There is also a strong argument that Russian democratic institutions are growing stronger. The successful 1996 election is one sign of that increasing strength. And at least so far, the Russian military as a whole has remained loyal to democracy. Recall that the military refused to intervene to support the attempted coup against Gorbachev.

What about the need for military reform? There are really two issues here: defense conversion and reform of the military directly. Defense conversion is an important economic issue, but failures in the area are not the key factor in risk of military coup. Moreover, without providing a massive assistance program, there is little that the United States can do to facilitate defense conversion. The basic problem is that Russian factories that formerly produced defense products cannot currently produce high quality consumer goods at competitive prices. In the conversion to civilian production, some will make it and most probably won't. That is unfortunate, but the United States cannot repeal the laws of economics. The defense factories are not modern and they aren't efficient. Unless we pumped in billions of dollars of targeted aid, that won't change.

The military reform issue is more complex. The Russian military needs to be leaner, but also adequately supported. One of the most serious problems in Russia today is failure to pay troops for months at a time. But again, U.S. options are limited. In theory, the United States could use foreign assistance to pay a portion of the salaries of the Russian military. However, such an action would set an unfortunate precedent and could produce political backlash in both the United States and Russia.

If the United States started paying Russian troops or dramatically expanded support for housing or other services for Russia, that would reduce the incentive of the government of Russia to confront these problems. Moreover, as noted earlier, there is no guarantee that the aid would be used effectively. In addition, such a program undoubtedly would anger the Russian military, who might feel that they were being bought off by the nation that formerly was their greatest enemy. And the reaction in the Congress would be incredible anger. Members of Congress would argue that at a time when the United States has had to cut back on military spending, it is absurd that we are acting as the pay clerk for the Russian military. Backlash against Russian and other aid programs would be the likely result.

The one thing that we should do is continue to support joint exercises and exchange programs with the Russian military. Such programs can be used to bolster a democratic ethic in the military.

Finally, it is important to remember that the Russian military is very weak. As one commentator has noted it is "decimated, divided, and demoralized" (P Fish 329). Given that situation, it is not clear that a military coup would be successful, especially if the military establishment were not united and the paramilitary groups remained loyal to their leaders.

Russian Nationalism

Russia is technically known as the Russian Federation, which refers to the various regions that are federated together as part of the Russian state. And Russia still maintains armed forces in all of the states of the former Soviet Union, except the three Baltic states and Azerbaijan (P Pipes 72). These troops serve, according to Richard Pipes of Harvard, as "the vanguard of Russia's imperial drive" (P 72). Given the motive of many in Russia to "regain not only the empire but the status of superpower" (P Pipes 74), there clearly is risk that a new "Evil Empire" could be created.

One sign of the danger posed by Russian nationalism was the vote of the Duma under communist leadership to "nullify the Soviet Union's dissolution" (P Cooper "Russia's Political" 392). This non-binding action certainly indicates an expansionist mentality that could lead to serious problems if an antireform government were to be elected. In that regard, some experts think that the revitalized

Communist Party really reflects nationalism more than it reflects support for communist ideology (see P Matlock 42).

Signs of nationalism can be found even in the policies of the Yeltsin government. According to Henry Kissinger, Russia has claimed a "right of military intervention in all countries containing Russian minorities" (P 43). Kissinger also notes that

> Two Russian divisions are being maintained on the territory of Georgia, where Russian intervention in a civil war made that country ungovernable until Russian conditions were met. Russia's encouragement of the conflict between Azerbaijan and Armenia has given Moscow a voice in both countries and blackmail potential over Azerbaijan's vast oil reserves. Russian troops participate in the civil war in Tajikistan. (P 43)

Thus, signs of rising Russian nationalism are present in Russia today.

There is potential for the creation of an aggressive expansionist nationalist state. The perilous economic situation, combined with corruption, the power of the mafia, and a weak political system make possible the rise of Russian nationalism. A possible scenario is that

> The opposition would try to gain the upper hand by ousting the Westernizers from the Kremlin. Then, with a strong dose of xenophobia and anti-Semitism, and with the television services under their control, it would be possible to restore the extremist nationalist ideology to the Russian mind, exploiting feelings of inferiority, feelings that are very strong in postcommunist Russia and that many Russians are trying to overcome with the new upsurge of anti-Western invective. (P Shlapentokh 335)

In that manner a powerful nationalist regime could take control of Russia.

The impact of such a result could be disastrous. One possible result of this scenario would be "a civil war" (P Shlapentokh 335). Another risk flowing from Russian nationalism is the danger of remilitarization. Recently, Richard Rose noted that

> demoralization may also encourage an irrational yearning to recapture great-power status. Vladimir Zhirinovsky has voiced conspiracy theories about the threat of the West to Russia's security, and Solzhenitsyn has warned of the West's threat to the Russian soul. Potentially, such rhetoric is a call to arms for the Third Rome to defend itself against Western barbarians. (P 43)

Henry Kissinger is cognizant of this danger:

> If Ukraine were to share the fate of Belarus and return to Russian satellite status, tremors would be felt all over Europe. A militarization of diplomacy would be nearly inevitable. A Russian stranglehold on Central Asian oil would provide dangerous blackmail potential during the predictable energy crises of the next century. (P 43)

If an expansionist nationalist government were in power in Russia, there could be substantial dangers for the region, world peace, and the United States.

Clearly, it is in the interest of the United States to do everything possible to make certain that such a nationalist regime does not take power. The problem, as I will indicate in a moment, is that U.S. action to prevent the rise of nationalism easily could be counterproductive and actually lead to that result.

There are good reasons to oppose an alteration in U.S. policy to fight Russian nationalism. First, there is strong evidence indicating that nationalism is not as strong a threat as some believe. Recently, Strobe Talbott argued that there were good reasons to believe that Russian nationalists were losing ground to those who take a more open approach to government (P "The Struggle" A22). For example, perhaps the foremost Russian nationalist, Vladimir Zhirinovsky, received 23% of the vote in parliamentary elections in 1993, 11% in 1995, and only 6% in the presidential election in 1996 (Representative Smith in D *Russia's Election* 2). At the time of the 1993 elections, many in the West decried Russia's move toward nationalism and totalitarianism. It now appears that their fear was overstated.

Other information backs up Talbott's observation. Richard Rose cites public opinion data from Russia indicating that "There is no strong demand to regain the 'lost' republics of the Soviet Union" (emphasis in original P 43). Nor are Russians willing to use war as a means of protecting ethnic Russians now living outside of the Russian Federation. While 92% favored use of negotiation to protect Russians living in former Soviet republics, only 16% favored military action (P Rose 43).

It also seems doubtful that an aggressive regime could be created. Anatol Lieven argues that regardless of who leads Russia in the future, that person is likely to be a pragmatist who "will realize that they have to operate under the most severe economic, military, social, and international constraints on Russia's behavior" (P 17).

There also seems to be little evidence indicating the danger that Russian nationalism could lead to the re-creation of a Soviet-style empire. As Garthoff explains

> the Russian government has consistently reaffirmed the territorial integrity of all of these states [of the former Soviet Union], rejecting opportunities to accept incorporation of actual or would-be separatists in Ukraine (Crimea), Moldova, and Georgia. (P 310)

David Remnick agrees, arguing that "there is no imminent threat of renewed imperialism, even within the borders of the old Soviet Union" (P "Can Russia" 44).

One of the foremost experts on contemporary Russia, Jack Matlock, supports this position:

> the Russian government has steadfastly repeated its pledge to respect the independence and territorial integrity of its neighbors. It gave no comfort to separatists in the Crimea and has not questioned Kazakhstan's right to retain its northern provinces, populated predominantly by Slavs, despite public appeals to create a Slavic commonwealth. It withdrew its troops from Estonia and Latvia even though it was dissatisfied with the status ethnic Russians had been granted in those countries. (P 48)

Matlock also notes that "Most of the successor states have proved proficient at resisting Russian pressure to compromise their sovereignty" (P 48).

In addition, there is an argument that Russian influence on the states of the former Soviet Union and in Eastern Europe as well is only the natural result of the importance of Russia in the region. This influence could be compared to the U.S. policy under the Monroe Doctrine of acting as the dominant power in the Western Hemisphere.

Finally in relation to the risk of nationalism, there is a strong argument that the decay of the Russian military machine has progressed to the point that Russia could not pose much threat to the peace and security of the world.

The other major problem with the argument that Russian nationalism is a threat to regional stability and world peace is the difficulty of effectively acting against it. One method would be to implement a program to support basic democratic institutions, teach Russians about the political process, support party building, and so forth. Of course that is all being done to one degree or another in the present system.

And there is also a risk associated with any major expansion of U.S. programs aimed at suppressing nationalism. One prime cause of nationalist response is backlash against Western influence in Russia. If it is perceived that the United States is trying to dictate the policies of the Russian government, the result could be to increase the power of the nationalist movement.

Breakup of the Russian Federation

The final source of political instability is the potential that the Russian Federation might be torn apart. This risk is in essence the opposite of the danger posed by Russian nationalism. Rather than Russian nationalism leading to the creation of a new Russian Empire, it is argued that nationalism could rise among nationalities across Russia, leading eventually to the break-up of Russia.

There is a sizable population within Russia of nonethnic Russians. Senator Bill Bradley notes:

> The rise of ethnic consciousness has challenged Russia's integrity and its development. While the dissolution of the Soviet Union unraveled Russia's outer empire, the Russian Federation remains a multiethnic state. More than 100 non-Russian ethnic groups, while accounting for one-fifth of the population, control wide swathes of mineral-rich territory. The end of communist ideology and the weakening of the central government have opened the way for a resurgence of ethnic assertiveness that has forced Moscow to develop a formula to reconcile local autonomy with a unified Russian Federation. (P 89)

Given this situation, it could be argued that there is a significant chance that Russia could face internal conflict, even civil war. If that is the case, then the war in Chechnya might be the first of many internal conflicts.

Of all the threats to Russian political stability, the breakdown of the Russian state seems the least serious. For example, Thomas Pickering, United States Ambassador to Russia, argues that Chechnya is the exception rather than the rule and that there is no significant separatist sentiment in Russia. According to Pickering

> My extensive travels over Russia—I have visited two-thirds of the Russian Federation's 89 federal units—have unearthed no strong separatist urges. Rather, the regional leaders I have met all stress one point: The need to develop a durable federal system based on an equitable division of responsibility between central and regional authorities. (P 528)

In this view, the risks posed by nationalities in Russia dramatically have been overstated. In many areas the "dominant nationality" is actually a minority in the area and the region is still economically dependent on the central government of Russia (P Lieven 18).

Methods of Strengthening the Russian Political System

In the preceding section, I discussed a number of scenarios in which the Russian government could face serious instability. Of these scenarios, probably the most threatening is the danger of a military coup. But regardless of which scenario is emphasized, the most difficult issue is to identify methods of strengthening the Russian political system.

What can the United States do to strengthen democratic institutions in Russia? There are two basic options. The first would be to argue that a major expansion of aid would provide the resources to strengthen the Russian economy and also help the Russians deal with any number of political or social problems. In this view, the primary problem with current aid is that there isn't enough of it.

The trouble here is that it is not at all clear what the United States would accomplish if we provided an extra billion dollars or two every year. Would that money strengthen the Russian political system or would it be funnelled to Russian elites and American researchers? All of the arguments against aid that I discussed previously apply here and indicate that more aid might not make that big a difference.

There is also an argument that expanded aid for democracy might be counterproductive. The argument here is that any major aid package risks irritating nationalists, who want the United States out of Russia. In that way a major package could make things worse. In addition, a major package might create a precedent, which would lead the Russians to believe that the United States simply owed it to them to pay for x or y or z program. That in turn might discourage the Russians from taking steps to fix the problem themselves. A major expansion in aid for democratic institutions or to fix economic problems could create dependence which would be counterproductive in the long term.

The second option would be to target U.S. assistance programs at building the infrastructure of democracy. The program might be aimed at solving some of the specific problems that I discussed in the previous chapter. For example, a program might try to provide assistance to the various political parties in Russia in building party organizations. Or a program might assist the Russian police in combatting the Russian mafia.

Again, there are problems with this approach. First, it is essentially a restatement of current U.S. policy, which is designed to strengthen democratic institutions in Russia. It is arguable that the policy option I have discussed does not represent a substantial change in U.S. foreign policy. Second, any expanded program could be threatened with all of the problems which I discussed earlier. In particular, there is a strong argument that the process of building strong democratic institutions must be left to the Russians themselves. It is pretty arrogant on the part of the United States to believe that only we know how to live in a democracy. Over the last seven years, we have provided them with aid and programs explaining the democratic process. Now, it is up to them. In fact, expanding aid in this area could either create dependence or lead to backlash against the program.

In sum, there is a strong argument that the threats to democracy and stability in Russia have been overstated. There also are good reasons to believe that current policy is well designed and that a major expansion of aid would not be useful.

Social Conditions in Russia

In the previous sections of this chapter, I have focused on proposals for improving the Russian economy and strengthening the political system. In the final major section, I focus on possible U.S. actions that could alleviate major social problems in Russia. The first of these social problems is an environmental crisis.

The Environment

Russia faces a number of significant environmental problems. According to a study prepared by the International Monetary Fund and several other world organizations, "many of the industrial and agricultural regions (of the former USSR) are on the verge of ecological breakdown, posing an imminent threat to the health of present and future generations" (qtd. in B Hill 3). Hill summarizes the effects of pollution according to the IMF report as "significant deleterious effects on life expectancy, morbidity of adults and children, and genetic mutations" (B 4)

Other research confirms these conclusions. A Soviet report on the status of the environment found 20% of the population lived in "unfavorable environmental conditions" and that there were sixteen "zones of ecological calamity" (qtd. in B Jancar-Webster 119).

Some argue that a growing environmental crisis lies behind a catastrophic decline in life expectancy for Russians. Bill Bradley writes that

> Russia may be a nuclear superpower, but all its missiles cannot defend against looming environmental calamity. The Environmental and Health Atlas of Russia, edited by Georgetown University's Murray Feschbach, reports that the life expectancy of a Russian male has dropped from 64.9 years in 1987 to 58.3 in 1993—and even lower to 57.3 in 1994. In some areas it is as low as 45. The 1993 and 1994 figures are on a par with countries like Egypt and Bangladesh. Unlike those countries, however, Russia's trend is downward. (P 89)

According to Bradley, one major reason for these horrendous statistics is massive pollution. He notes that over 40 million people "in 86 cities breathe air that holds more than 10 times the maximum allowable concentration of various pollutants" (P 95). Such statistics lead Bradley to conclude that "Russia's most pressing problem is environmental degradation" (P 95).

Why is the environment in Russia in such a terrible state? One reason is that environmental protection never received the support in the Soviet Union that it has in the West. To make matters worse, Russia's commitment to environmental protection has declined because of other enormous domestic problems (B Jancar-Webster 121). In particular, "monitoring, and control, [of pollution] has decreased" (B Jancar-Webster 121).

What can be done about this situation? In answering this question, it is important to recognize that the United States and Russia have cooperated on environmental protection in the past. Jancar-Webster notes that "U.S.-Russian cooperation remains at the heart of Russia's international environmental activities" (B 126). She adds that "Environmental concerns rank high on the U.S. list of government-proposed initiatives for democratic and economic reform in Russia" (B 126).

Given this past cooperation, the obvious solution would seem to be expanding aid to deal with specific environmental problems. I have focused on a general discussion of the environment, but the aid could be targeted to any specific environmental problem. For example, the aid could be aimed at reducing water or air pollution, solid waste disposal, reduction in greenhouse gases, minimizing hazardous wastes, or even protection of endangered species.

Or the money could be spent more broadly on pollution control in general. In this regard, Bradley suggests targeting "a large portion of U.S. assistance toward making Russians healthier" (P 95) especially in the area of air pollution. He advocates spending money on monitoring and clean air scrubbers and concludes "For anywhere from thousands of dollars to millions per plant, American aid could lead directly to Russian children breathing cleaner air" (P 96).

Some believe that this is one of the most crucial aspects of U.S.-Russian relations. Barbara Jancar-Webster notes that "In a very real sense, the environmental future of the whole world hangs on the progress of this revitalized relationship [between Russia and the United States]" (B 132-133).

While there is no doubt that Russia faces a number of pollution problems, there is a case to be made opposing a major expansion of U.S. aid. First, while the Russian mortality crisis is undeniable, many experts do not think that the root cause is environmental degradation. For example, Judith Shapiro argues that "the key new factor pushing up death rates, arguably, is increased stress" (B 149). That only makes sense. Pollution has not skyrocketed since the end of the Soviet Union. In fact, because economic growth has plummeted, pollution is down significantly since the Gorbachev era (B Jancar-Webster 121). Since pollution has fallen at the same time that the death rates have soared, it seems clear that pollution is not the primary cause of the death rate increase.

Second, there are signs indicating that Russia is making progress in relation to pollution control. Recently, Thomas Dine testified that

> Modern economic tools are being incorporated into environmental policy making, e.g., introduction of user fees and regional forestry codes. Environmental NGOs [Non Government Organizations] are vigorously pursuing public education, clean-up projects, and legal and legislative efforts. (D *U.S. Assistance* 66)

Moreover, "In December 1991, the Russian Parliament passed a comprehensive environmental law that established a legal basis for natural resource use and stipulated that environmental protection in the Russian Federation was regulated by law" (B Jancar-Webster 121).

There also seems to be a growing trend toward stricter enforcement of the law. According to Jancar-Webster, "Arbitration courts at the local and regional levels are becoming very active in the enforcement of environmental laws. In 1992 these courts reviewed about 6,000 cases, and violators were charged 2.8 billion rubles" (B 125-126). And the "main monitoring agency" at the national level "reviewed more than 55,000 projects, approving without change only 40% of them" in 1992 (B Jancar-Webster 126).

Business groups also are getting involved:

> In 1993, the Russian Chamber of Commerce and Industry developed an Environmental Activities Strategy that included, among other things, the promotion of an ecologically oriented national economy, the promotion of ecological enterprise entrepreneurship, the creation of a market of ecological equipment and services, and expansion of environmental-economic, and environmental-technological contacts between Russian entrepreneurs with foreign businesses. (B Jancar-Webster 124)

The Chamber is considering "creating its own ecological fund" which "would complement the existing system of financing environmental protection" (B Jancar-Webster 125). The Chamber also may raise funds "through international cooperation" (B Jancar-Webster 125).

Third, the opponent of change should argue that the United States has a program to share information and provide technical assistance in environmental control, but that we should not take the next step of actually funding or directing the pollution control program. It is important to recognize that there is a long tradition of cooperation between the Soviet Union and the United States in relation to the environment. According to Barbara Jancar-Webster, "American-Soviet cooperation in the field of the environment is one of the most successful stories in the history of U.S.-Soviet relations" (B 113). There was, for example, a joint statement on climate change included in the final summit statement after Gorbachev's visit to the United States in December 1987 (B Jancar-Webster 118).

In the early period of U.S. assistance to Russia, there were a few projects relating directly to the environment. In fact, of $4.1 billion in aid that was promised in 1992 and 1993 to all of the newly independent states, about $75 million was designated for environmental concerns (B Jancar-Webster 127). The cooperative effort and the early projects, it could be argued, have provided the Russians with the tools they need to enact policies to control pollution.

The existence of a history of cooperation does not, in this view, justify expanding the environmental support effort. Initially, it is important to note that the aid provided in the present system has been relatively small. Of the total aid figure I mentioned earlier, only about two percent was designated for the environment. And

> the United States is not, and has no plans to be, directly involved in environmental remediation. The Freedom Support Act specifically states that the U.S. taxpayer is not responsible for cleaning up the environment of the former Soviet Union. (B Jancar-Webster 127)

Clearly, no precedent for paying for environmental protection has been set.

Fourth, the opponent of expanded aid should argue that the assistance programs which have been funded have not been especially successful. A General Accounting Office review of all U.S. aid considered one of the environmental projects and found that it "met few or none of . . . [the] objectives" (testimony of Harold Johnson D *Newly Independent States* 146).

Fifth, expanded aid on the environment could set a terrible precedent that would create problems for the United States in dealing with Russia and other nations. If the United States steps in to clean up the worst environmental sites in Russia, that sets a precedent for Russia and potentially other nations to ignore environmental problems until they become true crises in the hope that Uncle Sam then will pay the bill. The limited U.S. environmental aid to Russia that has occurred over the last decade has been aimed primarily at building environmental institutions. Demonstration projects, even when focused on particular pollution sites, serve that function. A shift in policy toward direct funding of antipollution programs arguably would send decidedly the wrong signal.

Sixth, expanded environmental aid could create a backlash in Russia. Barbara Jancar-Webster notes that

> Russians have always had a fear of Western technological hegemony. If their place as joint decision makers in the international community is not given its due weight, the old Russian turn east toward Asia becomes increasingly more likely,

as the hope for Russian democracy, and with it a cleaner global environment, diminishes. (B 132)

Here, the United States is caught between the proverbial rock and a hard place. To make an environmental assistance effort effective, the United States would have to set specific standards and target funding. Otherwise, Russia simply would take U.S. funds, say thank you and spend them where they wanted. Moreover, Congress certainly would insist upon controlling how U.S. money is spent. On the other hand, if tight controls are applied, there is a substantial risk that Russian decision makers might react negatively against the arrogance of the West.

Seventh, a program of environmental assistance to Russia certainly would produce a backlash in Congress. Some in Congress already have expressed anger that the United States is spending too much money on Russia. If Congress reacts in that manner to spending to reduce the risk of nuclear war, how will they react to major spending to clean up Siberia? In that circumstance, it would seem almost certain that other aid to Russia would be cut or that there might even be a backlash against all U.S. foreign aid.

Finally, it is important to recognize that any specific program of aid is subject to arguments applying directly to the type of pollution control being implemented. Issues relating to specific forms of pollution have been discussed in two volumes in this series, *United States Policy on Renewable Energy Use* and *U.S. Policy and the Global Environment*.

Given the wide variety of environmental problems that could be discussed, it is not feasible to consider each in turn. To illustrate how a program of targeted aid might be aimed at a single pollution problem, I will consider the state of air pollution control in Russia.

The advocate of expanded U.S. aid to Russia to deal with air pollution would begin by arguing that there is a significant air pollution problem in Russia. According to the World Bank, "Russian enterprises alone discharge more SO_2 than Belgium, France, Holland, the United Kingdom and West Germany combined" (qtd. in B Hill 4). As I noted earlier, these discharges have produced a pollution problem so severe that tens of millions of Russians breathe highly polluted air.

The advocate of expanded U.S. assistance programs also would argue that the market will not be sufficient in Russia to produce strong control of air pollution. One problem is access to technology. According to Hill, "there are various business barriers which prevent these transfers [of needed technology] from taking place" (B Hill 225) in the present system.

The solution would be to encourage Russia to shift to alternative energy production technologies in order to improve efficiency and reduce pollution. Malcolm Hill has identified a number of technologies that might be applied in Russia (B Hill, see especially a chart on 94–95). Another approach would be for the United States to encourage the use of pollution control technologies, such as flue-gas scrubbers which remove harmful sulfur oxides from the exhaust. Hill notes that "it is apparent that a demand exists for the transfer of technology related to reduced environmental pollution" (B 151). The barrier is "a shortage of domestic investment funds" (B Hill 151), a problem that could be solved with a targeted U.S. aid.

The objections against a targeted program to control air pollution are similar to the general objections against any U.S.-funded environmental effort. First, it could be argued that present Russian efforts are sufficient. In relation to air pollution, for instance, increased use of natural gas in Russia has had a very positive effect in leading to reductions in sulfur and nitrogen oxides (B Hill 238). Additionally, standards for air pollution have been established in Europe, including a set of national targets for production of sulfur oxides (B Hill 7). The standards were set by the United Nations Economic Commission for Europe and the Long Range Transboundary Air Pollution Convention. At least into the early 1990s, Russia "was apparently on target to meet the 1985 Helsinki Protocol requirements for SOx reduction" (B Hill 205). Hill adds that Russia also was making progress on the NOx standards (B 205).

Moreover, the marketplace may act to encourage effective Russian pollution control. Hill writes, "There are clear international economic advantages to be gained by the former USSR from the reduction of atmospheric emissions of SOx and NOx into the atmosphere, with associated production of acid rain and deleterious effects on woodlands and forests" (B Hill 213). In addition, Russia has set new standards for emissions of sulfur oxides and nitrogen oxides from new coal-fired plants (B Hill 35).

Finally, all of the general arguments against U.S. environmental aid to Russia would apply to a proposal to focus such aid on air pollution.

It is also important to briefly comment on the possibility of targeting U.S. foreign assistance to help the Russians control their production of greenhouse gases. I will not discuss the debate about global warming itself at this point. That debate was considered in depth in *United States Policy on Renewable Energy Use*. There are, however, two key points to be made about a program aiding the Russians in dealing with the problem.

First, helping Russia decrease production of greenhouse gases will, by itself, not make much difference in world production of CO_2 and other greenhouse gases. Second, such a proposal is subject to all of the general objections to U.S. environmental assistance. In particular, the argument that expanded aid might produce backlash in either Russia itself or in the United States is a powerful one. Control of greenhouse gases will require tight regulations. If it appears that the United States is behind the policy, the result easily could be major public outcry. In this country, a program funding Russian greenhouse control efforts would cause substantial conservative backlash. Conservatives don't believe in global warming, don't like Russia, and despise foreign aid. They in all likelihood would be outraged if the United States spent any significant amount of money to aid Russian control efforts.

In summary, while Russia is threatened by a variety of pollution problems, a strong case can be made against expansion of U.S. assistance to confront those problems.

Nuclear Power

A second social problem in Russia where a changed U.S. foreign policy might make a difference relates to nuclear power. The essential idea is that the United States should expand efforts to assist Russia in implementing safety systems in their nuclear power plants. This approach would be justified as needed to prevent future accidents like Chernobyl.

The first step in justifying U.S. assistance for nuclear power aid is to consider the devastating effects of the accident at Chernobyl. According to Representative Christopher Smith, the accident "released 200 times more radioactivity than was released by the atomic bombs at Hiroshima and Nagasaki combined" (D *The Legacy* 1). All of the health effects of the accident are not yet known because of the long latency periods associated with injuries from excessive radiation exposure, but it is clear that the impact was substantial. For example, the thyroid cancer rate of children in Belarus is 200 times the normal rate (Representative Smith in D *The Legacy* 1). Recently, Dr. Murray Feschbach of Georgetown testified that the health effects of the accident on the people of Russia, Ukraine, and Belarus were truly horrendous (in D *The Legacy* 9–12).

Of course, nothing can be done about the radiation released at Chernobyl, which in any case is not in Russia. The justification for expanded aid to Russia is that the Russians still operate reactors with designs similar to that of Chernobyl. In other words, there is an ongoing risk of another accident like Chernobyl. If that were to happen, the impact would dwarf what happened previously. According to Senator Lugar:

> Another nuclear accident [like Chernobyl] could well destabilize political and economic conditions in the nascent democracies of the former Soviet Union and Eastern Europe and cost the United States vast sums in relief assistance. (CR "National Defense Authorization" 7 July 1997 S6879)

Given this risk, it is arguable that the United States should target substantial assistance to upgrading safety systems at the nuclear power plants of the nations of the former Soviet Union, including Russia.

It is important to note that a strong argument can be made distinguishing a nuclear power safety program from other sorts of aid to Russia. A program to decrease water pollution, for instance, aids only Russia (and perhaps a few tourists). But a program to improve the safety at Russian nuclear reactors has the potential to help the United States directly, by reducing the chance that a nuclear accident could occur that would produce fallout worldwide.

While a good case can be made for U.S. assistance to Russia on nuclear power safety, there are counterarguments. First, the negative should argue that the

United States already supports the "International Nuclear Safety Program," which provides adequate assistance to Russia and other nations. According to Senator Lugar:

> The program's focus is on projects that improve the operation, physical condition, and safety culture at nuclear power plants; the establishment of nuclear safety centers in the United States and countries of the former Soviet Union; and technical leadership to promote sound management of nuclear materials and facilities. (CR "National Defense Authorization" 7 July 1997 S6879)

This program already has accomplished a lot, including the implementation of "more than 150 plant-specific safety projects, involving 17 plant sites," the creation of "eight design and scientific institutes," and "nuclear safety training centers in Russia and Ukraine" (Senator Lugar in CR "National Defense Authorization" 7 July 1997 S6879). The ultimate goal is to help Russia and the other states of the former Soviet Union "implement self-sustaining nuclear safety programs and . . . achieve international nuclear reactor safety norms" (Senator Lugar in CR "National Defense Authorization" 7 July 1997 S6879). The negative should use this program to argue that the problem is already being confronted and to suggest that an expanded effort would not represent a substantial change in U.S. policy, but only an increase in funding levels.

Second, the opponent of a changed policy should argue that any expansion in funding would be ineffective and possibly counterproductive. The current program provides U.S. technical assistance. Expanding the program might create a situation in which the Russians simply expected the United States to clean up all of their problems. Moreover, an expanded program could result in the internal Russian or the external American backlash that I have mentioned.

While strong arguments can be made against providing additional assistance for nuclear safety to Russia, the problem is a serious one and the potential for radioactive fallout provides a justification for U.S. action that is not present in relation to most other social issues.

Freedom of Religion

A third social problem on which the United States might take action relates to a threat to freedom of religion. In this instance, the United States would threaten or actually apply sanctions or an aid cutoff in order to force the Russian government to rescind a law that is widely believed to threaten religious liberty in Russia.

The issue arose because of legislation passed into law in 1997 that appears to favor the Orthodox church and sharply restrict the rights of other religions. Under the law, special status is granted to any religion that was recognized by the former Soviet Union in the early 1980s. Michael R. Gordon notes that "By that definition the traditional Orthodox Church qualifies, as do Judaism, Islam and Buddhism. But Catholics, evangelical Christians and dissident Orthodox sects have questionable status" (P "Russians Pass" A1). There is something decidedly odd in labeling Catholics and Methodists, for example, as members of "new" religious groups.

The recognized religions may "own property, control radio and television stations and receive tax exemptions" (P Gordon "Russians Pass" A1). In contrast, those religious groups that are not recognized must go through a "time-consuming annual registration with the government and would be prevented from some activities, including running schools and distributing religious literature" (P Gordon "Russians Pass" A1).

Many believe that this legislation threatens religious liberty in Russia. Senator Hutchinson identifies several problems in the legislation:

> Among the provisions in this bill that are most alarming is the requirement that religious groups list all of their numbers, their names, their addresses, a requirement that a commission be established—a commission of state experts—to review the doctrines and practices of groups applying for registration. It is unimaginable in this country, in which we have so enshrined the concept of religious freedom. (CR "Foreign Operations Export" S7520)

Given these provisions, it is understandable that passage of this bill led to howls of protest from religious groups throughout the world.

Was that outcry really justified? Does the legislation really threaten religious liberty to a significant degree? Apparently, the answers are yes the outcry was justified and yes it threatens religious liberty. Lawrence Uzzell, of the Keston Institute, says "it represents a deliberate decision to favor the police state and restrict the free marketplace of ideas" (P C1). Uzzell lays out some of the problems in the bill:

> Church congregations founded in Russia less than 15 years ago—which means the great majority of local congregations—now have no guaranteed right to possess or distribute religious literature. Nor can they invite clergy from abroad, though the suppression of divinity schools during the Soviet era left them with a shortage of qualified Russian pastors. (P C1)

The difficulty is not only the restrictions that will be applied to groups that are forced to go through the registration process. There is also the risk that some groups will be denied registration altogether. Uzzell notes that "The new law gives them [state officials] ample discretionary powers to withhold state registration altogether on the basis of a long list of vague criteria" (P C5). Without registration, the group "will not even have the legal status that would allow it to open a bank account, buy or rent real estate or perform organized acts of charity" (P Uzzell C5).

Uzzell and others also argue that the law restricts religious advocacy to those already within groups. In this view, the law limits the ability of religious groups to seek converts (P Uzzell C5). Another danger is that local governments will apply the law in a capricious fashion. Uzzell cites an example in which a Catholic priest was stopped as he was entering the city of Belgorod, which is 400 miles south of Moscow "and told that he would not be allowed to lead worship services even in his private apartment" (P C5). Despite this example, Catholics may be less subject to discrimination than other religious groups because of the size and power of the church worldwide. In particular, small Protestant churches may face "bureaucratic harassment" and be told that in order to carry out their mission "they must get permission from the local Orthodox priest" (P Uzzell C5). It certainly seems likely that such actions could chill the exercise of religious speech.

It is because of all these difficulties that the law has been characterized as a "huge setback for Russia, back into Stalinist times" (Senator Smith in CR "Freedom of Religion" S9914). Senator Abraham noted that "tens of thousands of people in the former Soviet Union cannot practice their religion without encountering hostility from the government." He went on to cite data indicating that approximately 25% of regional governments in Russia already restrict religious activity (CR "Protecting Religious" S10180).

The legislation also violates international law. Representative Hutchinson notes that "The new law violates not only the Russian Constitution but also the U.N. Universal Declaration of Human Rights and the 1989 Concluding Document of the Conference on Security and Cooperation in Europe" (CR Hutchinson E2082).

Given these problems, what should be done? The obvious alternative is for the United States to threaten trade sanctions and/or an aid cutoff if Russia does not rescind or substantially modify the law. In this regard, the U.S. Senate already has passed a resolution criticizing Russia's action and calling on President Clinton to explain to Yeltsin that the law could "seriously harm U.S.-Russian relations" (P "Senate Resolution" 2865). The House of Representatives endorsed stronger action, which would cut off all aid unless Russia rescinded the law (P "Senate Resolution" 2865). While these tough responses have been debated and even passed by the House, they have not been implemented.

There is some reason to believe that U.S. pressure could make a difference. A somewhat harsher bill was passed by the parliament earlier in 1997, but then vetoed by Yeltsin when the United States threatened to cut off $200 million in aid (P Gordon "Russians Pass" A5). U.S. action still could make a difference. One approach would be to tie U.S. aid to conditions concerning the enforcement of the law. If that were done, Russia might be forced to eliminate the dangerous provisions in the law.

Another possible action would be for the United States to accept more refugees from Russia in order to protect people from religious persecution. Several senators have suggested that 30,000 people from Russia could be accepted as refugees, as opposed to the 21,000 under current law (Senator Abraham in CR "Protecting Religious" S10180).

While a strong argument can be made that the new law threatens religious liberty to some degree in Russia, there are also good arguments against imposing sanctions on Russia over the new law. Initially, it is important to understand the Russian perspective on the law. Russians have defended the law in two ways. First, they have noted that a number of the nations of Western Europe have state religions, but the result is not religious discrimination. They also claim that "the new law is needed to safeguard Russians against fanatical groups and dangerous sects" such as the Heaven's Gate group that committed suicide in California (P Gordon "Irking" A5).

Second, the defender of present policy should argue that sanctions will not be effective in this instance. Of course, pressure from the United States was to no avail following the passage of the second bill, which Yeltsin signed on September 25, 1997. Moreover, it is not clear that pressure on the central government of Russia could do much in any case, since the new law will be enforced primarily by local authorities (P Gordon "Irking" A1). The fact that local authorities, rather than the national government, will be enforcing the law makes it more difficult to use the threat of aid cutoff to force action.

Finally, the general arguments against sanctions apply in this case. There is one difference, however. Since the Duma passed the law overwhelmingly and Yeltsin signed it, U.S. pressure almost certainly would be seen as unjust intervention into the domestic affairs of Russia. This situation makes the risk of Russian backlash very significant indeed.

Health Policy

A final major social problem where U.S. action could make a difference is health policy. Clearly, Russia faces a number of health crises. While the birth rate has been declining, death rates have been rising sharply (P Lieven 19). Judith Shapiro notes that "There were nearly 328,000 more deaths in Russia in 1993 than in the previous year," a situation which she labels as "virtually unprecedented in modern times in the absence of war or famine" (B 151). In fact, in Russia, the "death rate exceeds the birth rate" (P Pipes 75). In addition, the "percentage of babies with genetic defects is well above normal" (P Pipes 75).

Russia faces a number of specific health problems as well. For example, Russia is one of the nations of the world that confronts a growing problem with drug-resistant tuberculosis (see P "Drug-Resistant" A13). In addition, recent reports indicate that AIDS cases are increasing to near epidemic proportions in Russia (P Specter A1+). The danger is that increased drug abuse and sexual activity could lead to exponential growth in the disease. Given the problems afflicting the Russian health system, such a growing crisis could have very severe consequences for Russia as a society.

Moreover, the Russian health care system is in crisis. Recently a reporter for *L'Express* reported that the system was extremely bureaucratic and that a bribe often was necessary in order to schedule a vitally needed operation (in P "Russia in Turmoil" 30).

Given the existence of these problems, a strong case could be made that the United States should expand programs providing humanitarian assistance for medical care and also provide technical assistance support in order to help the Russian health care system deal with the variety of problems I have described.

At the same time, there is a case to be made that the United States should not expand assistance to Russian health care providers. It is unclear, for instance, why Russia is more deserving of health assistance than are many of the nations in Africa that face far worse health crises.

First, some aspects of the health crises may not be solvable with better health care. For example, Judith Shapiro argues that stress, not a problem in the health care system, is the probable cause of the increased death rate. She notes that "The failure of cancer rates to rise . . . is another indicator that declining health care service is probably not the major issue" (B 163).

Second, there is reason to believe that progress in health care is being made. According to Thomas Dine of the United States Agency for International Development (AID), "Health reform has produced new policies, laws, and models that are helping Russia improve the quality, organization, and financing of its health care system. Health care is no longer always controlled from the center, and is becoming more efficient and responsive to patient needs" (D *U.S. Assistance* 65). Dine added that

> U.S.-Russian hospital partnerships have taught Russian health professionals state-of-the-art practices in several specializations, including women's clinical services, and contributed to improved hospital management. Modern contraceptive use is increasing and abortions are decreasing. (D *U.S. Assistance* 65)

In this view, current programs, some of them nongovernmental, are sufficient. No major expansion of aid is needed.

Third, the general arguments against increased assistance to Russia apply to the health care case as well. In fact, there are two reasons that these general arguments apply particularly well to calls for expanded U.S. health assistance. First, there is no good reason that health care reform in Russia should be the responsibility of the U.S. government. Again there is danger in setting a precedent that creates dependence on U.S. assistance. If we do it for Russia, why shouldn't we do it for any number of other nations? Second, major assistance to Russia for health care would be quite likely to create backlash in the United States, where more than forty million people lack health insurance. Imagine the outcry when the government tells the American people that we cannot afford to take care of your health insurance, but can afford to pay for the health needs of Russians.

Other Social Problems

In the final major section of this chapter, I have focused on the major issues in U.S.-Russian relations that fall into the broad category of social problems. It should be recognized that there are a few other minor issues as well.

Some argue that the United States should expand exchange programs with Russia. According to Jack Matlock, former U.S. Ambassador to the Soviet Union,

> The greatest long-term payoff from limited funds will come from educational and cultural exchanges. Russians still need more exposure to the outside world if they are to understand how democratic societies and market systems work. (P 50)

Others agree with Matlock. For example, Ambassador Richard Morningstar testified to Congress in 1997

> In the area of building civil society, the question is how can we best stay engaged? One of our proposals is to endow foundations on a cost-sharing basis to create sustainable programs in the NIS [newly independent states]. A second is to expand professional and academic exchange programs. I know for any of you who have met some of the people who have been here on exchanges, you can recognize the tremendous multiplier effect that they have and the effect that it can have on the long-term transformation. (D *U.S. Assistance* 5)

In this view, if the Russians see how our system works and Americans see Russia, there will be more understanding and less risk of conflict.

On the other hand, there is a strong argument that the United States is already taking sufficient steps in the areas of citizen exchange programs. According to Anne Sigmund of the U.S. Information Agency, "since 1993 using funding under the Freedom Support Act and resources from its own appropriation, USIA has brought over 20,000 NIS [newly independent states] leaders to the United States for programs" (D *Newly Independent States* 10). Under one program, "over 1,000 budding Russian entrepreneurs [have been provided] internships in American businesses" (Sigmund D *Newly Independent States* 11). Of course, it is difficult to lay out the precise benefits of expanded exchange programs, and it is hard to see how such a proposal could be interpreted as a substantial change in U.S. foreign policy toward Russia.

Prisons

A final social problem that has received some attention is prison conditions in Russia. Olivia Ward recently reported in the *Toronto Star* on terrible conditions that exist in Russian prisons. Overcrowding is so bad that three times as many inmates as the prison was designed for are often crowded into a given area. In addition, conditions are filthy, insects are prevalent, and inmates must purchase food (in P "Russia in Turmoil" 10). One cause of the prison problem is the vast rise in crime, which has reached the point where the murder rate is now roughly twice that of the United States (P "Russia: Transition to Nowhere?" 139).

The United States could help Russia deal with this problem by providing assistance for model crime control or prison reform programs.

While the crime and prison problems in Russia may well be quite serious, it is hard to justify a substantial change in U.S. foreign policy toward Russia based on that issue. It is not the responsibility of the United States to alleviate all problems that afflict the people of Russia. For that reason, all of the general arguments that I have sketched against expanding aid to Russia apply in this case as well.

Conclusion

In this chapter, I have described economic, political, and social problems in Russia that might be solved if the United States substantially changed its foreign policy. The primary difficulty for the advocate of change will be identifying a targeted program for dealing with a particular problem and providing a justification for a substantial increase in funding.

4 Defense Issues in U.S.-Russian Relations

The focus of this chapter is on defense issues involved in U.S. foreign policy toward Russia. There are six major topics in this area. I will discuss the pros and cons of NATO expansion, various aspects of Russian arms sales, nuclear weapons policy, the threat provided by chemical and biological weapons, the U.S. response to the Russian war in Chechnya, and conclude by considering space policy, which although not quite a defense issue, fits in this chapter better than in the previous one.

Russia and NATO

The North Atlantic Treaty Organization (NATO) has been labelled the "most successful military alliance in history" (P Cooper "Expanding NATO" 435). Still, with elimination of the Warsaw Pact and the death of the Soviet Union, some doubted whether the alliance any longer served a function. In a sense, NATO has been in search of a mission since that point in time.

After the end of the Cold War, an organization called the "Partnership for Peace" was created which allowed joint military training missions and peace-keeping involving the nations of NATO and the former Warsaw Pact. The Partnership included Russia. According to Cooper, "By the end of 1996, 27 countries had joined the partnership and engaged in 27 joint military exercises. Thirteen partner states had contributed to the NATO-led peace keeping operations in the Balkans" (P Cooper "Expanding NATO" 445-446).

While the Partnership has been a successful organization, membership in it did not satisfy nations of Eastern and Central Europe, who formerly had been unwilling members of the Warsaw Pact. These nations continued to fear Russia based on a half century of Soviet domination and, consequently, wanted to join NATO in order to participate in the collective defense pact and protect themselves under the American nuclear shield that is part of it.

The desire of these nations to join NATO forced a reexamination of the function of NATO. It was in this situation that the United States and the other members of NATO established a process through which new members could apply for admission. In the first stage of that process, Poland, the Czech Republic, and Hungary were invited to join the alliance.

For a time this result had been in doubt because of strong Russian opposition to NATO expansion. However, the obstacle was eliminated when Russia agreed to drop its opposition to the plan. In return, the Russians would be included in a permanent council to discuss NATO policies (P Doherty "Pact With" 1149). This relationship was formalized in a NATO-Russian Charter, which in the words of

Secretary Albright "would give Russia a voice in key decisions that affect its security interests in Europe" (P "Speaking to Russian" 16). In this view, the "Founding Act on Mutual Relations, Cooperation and Security . . . will take the sting out of Russian anger that NATO expansion was going to happen whether Moscow liked it or not" (P Ogden 51).

The organization of foreign ministers of NATO and Russia (known as the permanent joint council) met for the first time in September 1997 in New York City and agreed to certain modifications in arms control treaties in an effort to reassure Russia about the motives of the United States and NATO (see P Myers). After the conference, the Russian Foreign Minister commented that "we had a practical exchange of views on very important matters" (qtd. in P Myers A5). Strobe Talbott of the State Department argues that this organization has "real promise. It can help ensure that Europe is never again divided and that a democratic Russia plays its rightful role in that new Europe" (P "The End" 25).

However, there is one potential problem with the permanent joint council. While the U.S. position is that Russia will in the words of President Clinton have "'a voice, not a veto'" (qtd. in P "Helsinki Illusions" 17), advisors to President Yeltsin claim that Russia "'will have the right to block decisions that are unacceptable to it'" (P "Helsinki Illusions" 17). Some conservatives in the United States agree with this analysis and consequently opposed the agreement. Former Secretary of Defense Caspar Weinberger put it this way: "If Russia is against something, there will not be any action taken; that is what used to be called a veto" (P "The Helsinki" 37). Clearly, these two interpretations are inconsistent, a situation that could lead to conflict in the future.

One other action at the Helsinki summit is relevant as background to the debate over NATO expansion. At the summit, the Soviets were assured that NATO had no plans to put significant forces or nuclear weapons into the new member states, although this promise was not formalized as a treaty or agreement (see P Cooper "Expanding NATO" 447).

The initiative expanding NATO has been labelled one of the most important foreign policy acts of the United States after the end of the Soviet Union (see P Apple). On the other hand, Alexei Arbatov, deputy chairman of the Defense Committee of the Russian Duma, labelled it as "the key problem in U.S.-Russian security relations" (P "Eurasia Letter" 103).

And the process of NATO expansion stands at a crossroads. There certainly is potential for further enlargement since nine additional nations, besides the three that have been admitted, have applied to join the alliance. Moreover, the Clinton Administration has said that NATO expansion is a process and that the process is not complete. Currently, it is planned that there will be a second round of invitations, possibly in 1999. This second round could include the Baltic states and Romania. There is strong support in Congress for further expansion. For example, the "European Security Act of 1997," which was proposed in the House of Representatives, expressed "the sense of Congress that Romania, Estonia, Latvia, and Lithuania should be invited to join NATO as soon as they can satisfy all of the relevant criteria" (Representative Gilman in CR "European Security Act of 1997" H3708).

NATO can move in one of two directions. The alliance can continue to expand perhaps up to the border of Russia itself. Alternatively, the alliance could make gestures to reassure Russia, by stopping the expansion process or including Russia to a greater degree in the councils of NATO. It is arguable that either policy choice would represent a substantial change in U.S. foreign policy.

One other point is important. It probably is not sensible to dictate a decision about the future admission of any particular country to NATO. Certainly there are strong arguments for admitting the Baltics to NATO. But those arguments depend upon the Baltic states meeting the standards for NATO admission. Would it be sensible to admit Latvia to NATO if the Latvian parliament passed legislation forbidding any expenditure of funds on meeting NATO standards for communications, training, and so forth? Obviously, the answer is no. Moreover, mandating in advance the admission of any nation reduces the leverage that the United States and other NATO countries have in negotiations with that country. This means that the most sensible way to proceed in expanding NATO is to retain selectivity.

In the following sections, I will sketch the pros and cons of two possible policies: further rapid expansion of NATO and maintenance of the present alliance or even increased consultation with Russia.

The Case for Further NATO Expansion

Proponents of NATO expansion make a number of strong arguments for further expansion of the alliance. First, they claim that the future is uncertain and that there could be any number of situations in which the United States would be better off because NATO had expanded to include democratic nations of Central and Eastern Europe. (The Clinton administration developed its position on NATO enlargement in a Congressional hearing in April 1997, where Secretary of State Albright and Secretary of Defense Cohen both testified. (See D *The Administration's*. For the most complete presentation of competing perspectives on NATO expansion see D *The Debate on NATO Enlargement*.) Madeleine Albright explained this position as follows:

> We do not know what other dangers may arise 10, 20 or even 50 years from now.
> . . . We do know that . . . it will be in our interest to have a vigorous and larger alliance with those European democracies that share our values and our determination to defend them. (qtd. in P Towell "Albright" 2495)

Although advocates of NATO expansion do not like to state it this way in public, one possible benefit of the action is deterrence of an aggressive Russian state in the future. In this view, there is some risk that Russia could again threaten nations in Central and Eastern Europe. After all, Russian influence in the region was not limited to the Soviet era. Given that threat, some, including former Secretary of State Henry Kissinger, believe it is better to set up a strong defense now (see P Apple). Adam Garfinkle cogently explained this "realist" position on NATO:

> The central argument made by realists who favor enlargement is that, in the nature of things, given its size and historical ambitions, a resurgent Russia is likely again in due course to threaten Central and Eastern Europe. . . . It is therefore best to seize the moment of opportunity and to move the line of confrontation east while Russia is weak. We should consolidate the historic outcome of 1989–91 while we can, permanently erasing the unnatural division of Europe represented by the Cold War. (P 23)

Garfinkle also notes that there is a risk that failure to expand NATO would be interpreted by the Russians as a sign that we accepted their dominance in Central Europe (P 23).

Second, advocates of further expansion argue that such action reduces the risk of conflict involving the new nations of the former Soviet bloc. The argument here is that "By guaranteeing their security against external threats on condition of good domestic and international behavior. . . NATO will discourage both domestic extremism and military rivalries in Eastern Europe, which, in turn, could foster international tension over a wider area involving more powerful states to the east and west" (P Towell "NATO Expansion Forges" 652).

In addition, NATO expansion could be used to expand democracy in the nations of the former Warsaw Pact. Some claim that the desire to be admitted to NATO has "already spurred reform in most of Eastern Europe" (P Cooper "Expanding NATO" 441). And Strobe Talbott argues that "The very prospect of admission to NATO for a number of central European states has already induced them to accelerate their internal reforms and improve relations with their neighbors" (P "America and Russia" 539).

In fact, the carrot of NATO expansion can be a major factor in producing regional stability. Adrian Karatnycky, President of Freedom House, argues that nations of Central and Eastern Europe have been taking important actions resolving "longstanding border issues and ethnic disputes that were the source of instability and tension, and that could have led to armed conflict" (P "NATO Weal" 43). Senator Biden agrees with the position that NATO expansion could increase the stability of Central Europe. He explains:

> The enlargement of NATO can now serve to move the zone of stability eastward to central Europe and thereby both prevent ethnic conflicts from escalating and forestall a scramble for new bilateral and multilateral pacts along the lines of the 1930s from occurring. (CR "NATO Enlargement" S5591)

Thus, NATO expansion may be as important for supporting the democratic transition in Eastern Europe and guaranteeing stability in the region as it is for deterring future Russian aggression.

Third, advocates of further expansion argue that the policy can influence Russian behavior in a positive way. According to Karatnycky, Russian "conduct toward its neighbors is improving" (P "NATO Weal" 44). He cites a treaty between Russia and Ukraine which solved the dispute over division of the Black Sea Fleet and confirmed borders. The President of Ukraine, Leonid Kuchma, "who has strongly supported NATO enlargement, declared that the treaty with Russia had been influenced by the climate of 'favorable changes under way in Europe'" (P "NATO Weal" 44).

A related argument is that these nations strongly desire membership and deserve it. Charles Gati of the Foreign Policy Institute at Johns Hopkins writes that "these governments are pursuing very painful and unpopular economic reforms that their political rivals on the Right often oppose. Hospitable to Western investors, they are also determined and enthusiastic applicants to NATO, accepting its rules, including civilian control of the military" (P 28).

Fourth, there is also an argument that NATO expansion is a key to preventing Germany from returning to a nationalist and aggressive foreign policy. From this perspective, without NATO expansion Germany would be on the border of NATO and inevitably involved in a rivalry with Russia for domination in Eastern Europe. On the other hand, if NATO is expanded, then Germany remains part of an Atlantic Alliance and the focus of German politics is on the policy of that alliance. In addition, NATO expansion allows the United States to continue to play a strong role in influencing German defense and foreign policy (see P Garfinkle 24-25). Or as *The New Republic* somewhat sarcastically put it, "the purpose of NATO was to keep the Russians out, the Americans in and the Germans down" (P "Go East" 7). In geopolitical terms, the expansion of the alliance "might just make another European war politically and militarily unthinkable" (P "Go East" 7).

Fifth, NATO expansion is justified as a policy that actually might benefit Russia by helping resolve "ethnic and border disputes in central Europe" (P Albright "Speaking to Russian" 17).

In addition to isolating the possible benefits of NATO expansion, proponents of the policy also argue that Russian opposition has been overstated. Former Russian Foreign Minister Andre Kozyrev says that the West should ignore the anti-NATO rhetoric of some Russians. In his view, "the truth is that NATO is not the enemy" (P 31). Rather, the opposition is "led by an old guard that grew up with NATO as the common enemy" (P 31). He also argues that to give in to those who oppose NATO expansion "would play into the hands of the enemies of democracy" (P 31).

Advocates of expansion also go out of their way to argue that the program will not harm Russia. Recently, Secretary of State Albright explained several reasons why Russia should not feel threatened by NATO expansion. She argued that

a new and enlarged NATO will not pose an enlarged threat to Russia. On the contrary, since 1991, NATO members' defense budgets have decreased by 30%. NATO's land forces are down by 25%. U.S. nuclear weapons in Europe have been cut by 90% and no NATO nuclear forces are on alert today. The building at NATO headquarters where we once planned our response to a Soviet attack on Berlin now houses a Russian general and staff helping to plan our effort in Bosnia. (P "Speaking to Russian" 16)

She went on to promise that "In the foreseeable security environment NATO has no intention, no plan, and no reason to deploy nuclear weapons on the territory of any new state" (P "Speaking to Russian" 16).

Defenders of NATO expansion also argue that the result will not be to strengthen antidemocracy forces in Russia. Former Ambassador to Russia Thomas Pickering commented in recent hearings that the "track record does not support the hypothesis that Russian reform or reformers and security cooperation will inevitably suffer as a result of NATO enlargement" (qtd. in P Towell "Panel Gauges" 2696). Pickering based his judgment on several prodemocracy actions taken by Yeltsin following the decision to admit Poland, Hungary, and the Czech Republic to NATO. Some even argue that NATO expansion "would boost the prospects of Russia's democrats by eliminating the temptation for Moscow to strong-arm erstwhile client states and thus keep the country's political leaders focused on the need for internal reform" (P Towell "Panel Gauges" 2696).

Proponents of NATO enlargement also defend the program by claiming that the cost will not be high. They cite internal estimates of the Clinton administration, a study by the Congressional Budget Office, and a report by the Rand Corporation as indicating that the annual cost should be under a half billion dollars. The Clinton estimate places the figure at between $150 and $200 million per year. On the other hand, Rand estimates that under certain scenarios the cost could be as much as $1.4 billion a year (P Towell "Arms Modernization" 650).

Finally, proponents of NATO expansion suggest that a commitment to an expanded NATO already has been made. To move away from that commitment at this late date would have extremely negative effects upon U.S. security. Moving away from the commitment to an expanded NATO would make the United States look weak and draw into question our commitment to the Atlantic Alliance. Charles Kupchan of Georgetown writes that "Shooting enlargement down in the U.S. Senate would not just scuttle the admission of new members . . . but also call into question the political viability of NATO and of America's military engagement in Europe" (P 24). And Jonathan Dean notes that "once adopted, a big multi-lateral project like NATO enlargement tends to take on a life of its own; it is tough to stop because doing so would be very costly to the prestige of the governments that have supported it" (P 35). Of course, this final argument is a double-edged sword for the advocate of further expansion. It provides a justification for the expansion, but at the cost of explicitly labeling support for expansion as part of the foreign policy of the United States. Such a claim draws into question whether further expansion would be a substantial change in our policy.

The Case Against Further NATO Expansion

Critics of NATO expansion argue that such a policy is unnecessary, potentially costly, sure to produce a Russian backlash, and risky in a variety of partially
unpredictable ways. They also argue that it is motivated by a Cold War ideology
that is no longer applicable and represents backward thinking in foreign policy.
In the memorable words of Michael Mandelbaum of Johns Hopkins, it represents
"A Bridge to the 19th Century" (D *The Debate* 72).

First, opponents of NATO expansion argue that there is no need for an
enlarged NATO. In regard to a possible Russian threat, they note that "there is
simply no Russian military threat in sight, and that there will be plenty of time to
respond if one begins to emerge" (P Garfinkle 25). Charles Kupchan puts it most
simply, "Russia today poses no threat whatsoever to Central Europe" (P 25).

Moreover, even if Russia wanted to threaten Eastern Europe, it couldn't do
so. On this point, Richard Rose has predicted "that if Russia launched an aggressive war a once great military force would be destroyed. The Russian Army
would implode through demoralization and desertion" (P 56). And Sherman
Garnett says simply that "the Soviet Union's ability to project great conventional
power is in ruins"(P 63). The British newspaper *The Guardian* reported that "of
its 78 divisions the Russian army could now field and supply only one in full battle order" (in P "Russia in Turmoil" 11). Perhaps the most telling data is the failure of the Russian army in Chechnya.

In this view, Russia has been transformed from a threatening to "an inward-
looking state. . . . Its military has conducted the largest strategic withdrawal in
history" (P Sherman Garnett 62).

Opponents of NATO expansion also argue that Russian domination of Eastern
Europe occurred at a special time and place, when all of the institutions (and
armies) of Eastern Europe were in tatters and the Red Army was all powerful.
Since this situation is unlikely to recur, there is little reason to expand NATO.

Second, the opponents of NATO expansion argue that the security of Central
Europe is already protected by a "floor-to-ceiling array of arms control agreements" (P Garfinkle 25), which place restrictions on the forces that Russia may
have in the region and, because the United States is a signatory, involve this
nation in the security of the region. In that sense, Central Europe is already part
of the security system in Europe. Some go so far as to argue that NATO expansion "might well lead to the collapse of these existing military-strategic under-
standings" (P Garfinkle 25) and thus would be counterproductive. Moreover, if
there were a need for a new security system, it is argued that a better alternative
would be to "strengthen the Organization for Security and Cooperation in Europe
(OSCE)" (P Geyer 567).

Third, opponents of NATO expansion dispute the "political" benefits of
expansion. For example, Garfinkle argues that there is little risk of a revitalized
German nationalism and that Germany shows no desire to go it alone in Europe
(P 25). Others note that the movement toward reform in Eastern Europe predated

the discussion of NATO expansion. And Alan Geyer argues that NATO expansion could undermine "democratic prospects in Russia" (P 566).

Fourth, some argue that the monetary cost of expansion could be a significant problem. According to the Congressional Budget Office, the total cost could amount to as much as $125 billion (cited in P Cooper "Expanding NATO" 438). Of that figure, the cost to the United States up to the year 2010 could be almost $20 billion (P Cortright 21). And some experts believe that the cost estimates that have been cited may substantially underestimate the eventual figure. For example, Dr. Ivan Eland of the Cato Institute, and formerly of the Congressional Budget Office, criticizes Clinton administration estimates on cost and notes that "The vast majority of government initiatives cost significantly more than their initial optimistic cost targets" (D *The Debate* 169).

Moreover, the costs of expansion apply not just to the United States, but also to other members of NATO and the new members as well. This expense could detract from the ability of the applicant states to modernize their economies and create democratic institutions (see P Schwenninger).

There is also another risk in relation to cost. The risk is that the money will not be found and the new NATO members will not be fully integrated into the alliance. Sherle Schwenninger argues that "It is highly unlikely that the Europeans will come through with their share of the added costs at a time when they are desperately cutting budgets to qualify for European Monetary Union" (P 24). Given this problem, it seems possible that there could be a major problem in achieving integration of the new nations into the NATO structure. The result could be a weakened NATO system.

Fifth, opponents of NATO expansion argue that there will be political as well as monetary costs to expansion. For example, Sherle Schwenninger claims that "the United States has had to use up precious political capital with the Europeans to get them fully on board [in support of NATO expansion]" (P 30). In her view, "NATO expansion gives the United States little or no leverage over the Europeans" and "represents a major misallocation of U.S. diplomatic resources" (P 30). Schwenninger cites the Middle East peace process and the development of market economies in Eastern Europe as two foreign policy areas that might be shortchanged (P 30).

There could be other costs as well. In this regard, Michael Mandelbaum claims that NATO expansion is "a dangerous idea because it will certainly have costs and, although those costs are unpredictable, they may be very steep" (qtd. in P Cooper "Expanding NATO" 440). For example, there could be a cost in relation to U.S. policy toward China. Representative Rohrabacher argues that

> By focusing on Europe, we are taking away our focus from Asia, where a belligerent, totalitarian, expansionist China is fast becoming a threat to our national security and a threat to world peace. Let us focus our efforts on strengthening our alliances in Asia, spending our money so that we can deter war on Asia rather than wasting it on NATO, which is a thing of the past. (CR "European Security Act of 1997" H3712)

There are other potential political costs as well. Schwenninger writes

> the focus on NATO, with its emphasis on military modernization, may divert attention and resources away from other more important dimensions of economic modernization. NATO expansion . . . will not be cheap. Consequently, aspiring NATO members may be forced to shortchange new social and industrial investment. (P 28–29)

Opponents of further NATO expansion emphasize the unpredictable negative effects of such action.

Sixth, some claim that NATO enlargement "works against reconciliation [in Europe] by creating some potentially worrisome divisions in Europe" (P Schwenninger 26). In this view,

> as a result of NATO expansion, the countries excluded will be put at an even greater disadvantage in attracting sizable Western investment, further slowing their economic progress and increasing the gap that already exists between the better-off prospective Central European members of NATO and their neighbors to the east. (P Schwenninger 26-27)

The result might be to create a situation in which longstanding problems fester and are not resolved. Schwenninger concludes that "NATO expansion hinders strategic reconciliation by excluding Russia from full participation in a future European community" (P 27). In fact, NATO expansion opens the door for future geopolitical rivalry by in effect legitimizing Moscow's efforts to create its own alliance" (P Schwenninger 27).

Moreover, there is an argument that focusing on NATO expansion distracts attention from more crucial issues. Sherle Schwenninger writes that NATO expansion "diverts attention and resources from other security-related challenges, from ethnic conflicts in the Balkans to consolidating democracy and market economies in other countries" (P 28).

Another potential cost relates to military doctrine. Critics of NATO expansion argue that it is unclear whether current NATO policies will be applicable to an expanded alliance. If they are not applicable, then NATO expansion could make the alliance less effective. It is decidedly odd, for example, that Hungary is being admitted to NATO, when the nation lacks a border with any other member of the alliance (P Garfinkle 27).

There is also an argument that expansion of NATO is foolish because the United States desperately needs Russia as a counter to the growing influence of China. One result of further expansion could be to "prompt Moscow to reassess its foreign policy and possibly boost its ties with China, Iran, and India" (*Asiaweek* in P "Russia's Smoldering" 10). Michael Lind writes, "If, as is arguably the case, the United States needs an intact and moderately strong Russian republic to serve as a potential counterweight to China, then it makes no sense to alienate Russia and drive it toward China by making Russia the unnamed enemy of the NATO alliance" (P 10). Writing in the *National Review*, Ira Straus argues that such an action "would shape Russia's identity in an anti-Western way—perhaps for generations" (P 39). He concludes that the result could be "a realignment of Russia with China—the one and only development that could threaten the West's global leadership" (P 40). Straus notes that there already have been steps toward such a realignment (P 40).

In relation to the previous argument, it should be noted that China has very strong reasons to work for good relations with the United States, namely access to the U.S. market. And the *Economic Review* of Hong Kong noted that "Many argue that the two sides' mutual distrust is too deep to allow Beijing and Moscow to form a strategic alliance" (in P "China's Buying" 11).

Another potential problem is that NATO enlargement might force the Russians to greater reliance on nuclear weapons for defense. The result could be a situation in which Russian nuclear weapons were operated under the proverbial hair-trigger (see P Steinbrunner B5). Arbatov noted recently that "Russians increasingly feel that NATO expansion is unavoidable." He added that "The official Russian doctrine of nuclear first-use and extended nuclear deterrence approved in November 1993 is largely motivated by this expectation" (P 105). Moreover, Russia already has threatened that they might respond to NATO enlargement by "forward deploying their tactical nuclear weapons, which number some 10,000, plus as many as 10,000 more in storage" (P Mann "Yeltsin" 27). Forward deployment would mean that the Russians would move tactical nuclear weapons into areas near NATO forces. Such an act obviously would reduce the security under which the nuclear weapons are maintained, increasing the risk of theft or unauthorized use. In addition, forward deployment could lead to use of nuclear weapons in a crisis.

The final argument against NATO expansion is the most important. Some claim that NATO enlargement could alienate Russian leaders and make it harder for the United States to negotiate agreements in defense and other areas. This threat is particularly salient since "Virtually every member of Russia's parliament and political elite opposes NATO's expansion" (P Mann "Yeltsin" 27). Raymond Garthoff explains that "To many Russians, the renewal of the cold war Western military alliance by absorbing former members of the defunct Warsaw Pact when there is no threat from Russia can only be seen as creating a new threat to Russia. Why else should NATO, now enjoying enormous conventional as well as nuclear superiority, feel it necessary to advance to the very borders of Russia itself?" (P 311)

The results of alienating the Russians could be catastrophic. If the United States continues to push for further expansion, "It is going to become increasingly difficult to obtain Russian cooperation" (former American Ambassador Jack Matlock in P Towell "Panel Gauges" 2696).

A second possible consequence would be to inflame Russian nationalism. According to Representative David Obey:

> I think that we run a grave risk that future Russian nationalists, under worse economic and political conditions than we have in Russia today, will be able to

exploit any Russian government decision to accept a movement east of the military borders of NATO. And I think that could have profoundly negative consequences long-term. (P Obey 449)

Similarly, *Asiaweek* recently reported that "NATO enlargement may well strengthen the hand of hard-liners in the Kremlin" (in P "Russia's Smoldering" 10). The risk of alienating Russia should not be understated. It is important to recognize the level of fear and even paranoia in Russia today. Even advocates of NATO expansion, like Strobe Talbott of the State Department, understand that this is a problem. Talbott recently commented that "Quite a few Russians have made clear that they believe America's real strategy—indeed this Administration's real strategy—is actually to weaken Russia, even to divide it" (P "America and Russia" 540).

George F. Kennan, who played a crucial role in crafting the policies that first contained and eventually defeated the Soviet Union, is especially sensitive to the danger of Russian nationalism. Consequently, he claims that expanding "NATO would be the most fateful error of American policy in the entire post-Cold War era" (qtd. in P Cooper "Expanding NATO" 435). There is even some danger of conflict, since Russia has unequivocally stated that it would not accept membership of the Baltic nations of Estonia, Latvia, and Lithuania or of Ukraine in NATO (see P Cooper "Expanding NATO" 441-442).

Proponents of NATO expansion sometimes dispute the Russian backlash argument by noting that the expansion of NATO actually would be good for Russia. Opponents of NATO expansion suggest that this argument is irrelevant; it is only the perception that matters. So, for example, Alexei Arbatov, argues that

> it is no longer important whether or not the prospect of NATO expansion actually represents a threat to Russia. What is important is that there is now a broad political consensus in Russia that expansion would not only be against Russian foreign and security interests but would also violate some accepted rules by which the Cold War was ended with the voluntary consent of the USSR. (P "Eurasia Letter" 104)

Arbatov also notes that some see NATO expansion "as the consummation of a 'grand design' to destroy Russia as a European power once and for all" (P 105).

What about the consultation agreement established between NATO and Russia? Opponents of NATO expansion argue that real consultation would create a situation in which expansion would not occur. The current system, in this view, was designed merely to provide Yeltsin with some political cover. But the current consultation system will not eliminate Russian anger over the expansion of NATO. Over time, the situation will worsen, since "the real threshold of conflict with NATO, and thus the United States, lies ahead" (P vanden Heuvel and Cohen "The Other Russia" 24). Thus, consultation will not be adequate to deal with Russian opposition to NATO expansion when the real crisis occurs.

Rapprochement Between NATO and Russia

One means of changing U.S. foreign policy toward Russia would be for the United States to publicly reject further expansion of NATO. Since U.S. policy is currently to consider other nations for membership, this arguably would be a substantial change in our foreign policy. On the other hand, it could be argued that current U.S. policy is to accept only Poland, Hungary, and the Czech Republic into NATO and that no other nations will be admitted for the foreseeable future.

Rejection of further expansion might be sensible given the risks associated with further expansion. Among the nations that desperately want to joint NATO are the three Baltic states and Ukraine. Russia, quite understandably, believes that these states lie directly within its sphere of influence and should not be part of any alternative military alliance. In Aviation Week & Space Technology, Paul Mann reported that "Duma members who were in Helsinki during the summit asserted that Baltic countries that dared to join NATO in the next century would face harsh consequences" (P "Yeltsin" 27).

A policy of publicly rejecting further expansion could have the benefit of reassuring the Russians and improving relations with that nation. Recently, Alexei Arbatov, a member of the Russian Duma, argued that

> The issue [NATO expansion] is affecting the fate of two major packages of arms control concerns: the STARTII/ABM complex and the CFE/Open Skies combination. If Russia and the West were able to come to a compromise on NATO expansion, the way would be opened for a deal on the first and then the second of the above packages. (P "Eurasia Letter" 103)

Arbatov adds that if there were "a reasonable compromise. . . a number of major breakthroughs in East-West relations may be achieved including in the areas of security and arms control" (P 105). He says that the threat of NATO expansion "is politically a much stronger lever than Western credits" (P 107). In this view, a change in U.S. policy over NATO could produce major benefits in other aspects of United States-Russian foreign relations.

On the other hand, what the Russians see as a "reasonable compromise" and what the West would accept may be two different things. After calling for compromise, Arbatov suggested that Poland, Hungary, the Czech Republic, and other states should be admitted into the European Union and the Western European Union, but not NATO. They would then assume a status similar to "Austria, Finland and Sweden" (P 106). Clearly, this would not be acceptable to the Poles, the Czechs and the Hungarians. All three of these nations have good reasons to fear the Russians. They want to be part of NATO in order to be placed under the security umbrella that NATO provides.

A second alternative NATO policy would be for the United States and our European allies to seek an "Alliance with Russia." Michael Lind argued recently that rather than expansion of NATO to contain Russia, "Every European state, including Russia, should be admitted to NATO" (P 10). Several important

Russian leaders, including Yeltsin himself, have called for including Russia within NATO (P Straus 40).

Why would it be sensible to include Russia within the NATO alliance? One result of adding Russia to NATO might be to "add to NATO's power" (P Straus 40). In addition, the step would be a way of building a strong security system all across Europe. Charles Kupchan, of Georgetown University, suggests that "a historic opportunity exists to build a peaceful, united Europe. NATO enlargement could be a vehicle for doing so" (P 24) if Russia is allowed to join (P Kupchan 24).

The primary advantages of allowing Russia to join NATO would be to include Russia within the western alliance and to prevent Russia from moving into alliance with China. This latter benefit is seen as particularly important because it might prevent the creation of a multipolar world.

Through much of the Cold War, world politics was bipolar. That is, the world was divided into an American led anti-communist group and a Soviet led group. Following the end of the Cold War, the world has been unipolar. The United States as the only remaining super power has been dominant. Some see the maintenance of a unipolar world as essential both for keeping the peace and also for protecting U.S. security. Ira Straus writes

> If we expand NATO in a way that truly engages Russia, we will have a shot at a sustainable unipolarity—a world that is based concentrically on the North/West/America, and that is capable of drawing other countries in as they mature economically and democratically. But if we expand in a way that keeps Russia permanently on the outside, we will slip back into multipolarity—a world in which the dangers of the Cold War have metastasized into a chaotic balance of opposing nuclear powers. (P 41)

In addition, a policy of including Russia within NATO might provide the West with great influence over Russian policy (P Kupchan 26).

How would an alliance with Russia be organized? Straus proposes a detailed list of policies for including Russia in a unipolar world. He suggests cooperation in opposing the Taliban in Afghanistan, working with Russia on a strategic defense program, "joint nuclear programming" as an alternative to mutual deterrence, and a focus on confronting the dangers of nuclear terrorism and China (P 41). In relation to NATO, Straus argues for a three-step process. First, Russia would be invited to attend NATO meetings "as an observer, with a 'voice not a veto,' instead of always holding separate meetings with Russia." Second, the alliance should move toward the "development for the longer term of a procedure for Russia to have a vote in NATO that will be less than a veto, but more than just a voice." The third step would be "the eventual extension of NATO membership to Russia at the same time as the Baltic states or Ukraine" (P 41).

A strong case can be made for the Alliance with Russia policy, rather than continued NATO expansion. Many experts believe that Russia poses little danger to the world today, but that NATO expansion could make it dangerous. If that is the case, then a radical shift away from current policy might be sensible.

On the other hand, the advocates of NATO expansion would find the call for an alliance with Russia to be ridiculous. They would reject the idea of a grand alliance in which Russia joins NATO as inconsistent with the very premise upon which NATO was founded, the need for a Western alliance to keep Europe safe from the threat of Russian domination. In addition, the Russians themselves recently rejected such an approach. Foreign Minister Primakov came out against Russian membership in NATO (P "Eastern cheers" 7). Finally, nearly all of the general arguments for NATO expansion serve as reasons to oppose inclusion of Russia within NATO.

Russian Arms Sales

The second major aspect of U.S. foreign policy as it relates to defense issues concerning Russia is arms sales and the export of dangerous technology. Today, Russia is pushing arms sales as a means of bringing in vitally needed foreign currency. One source projects total arms sales for 1997 of over $4 billion, which is roughly one-third of the arms sales of the world's leading exporter, the United States (P Ford 1+).

The issue is not so much the quantity of arms being sold, but the particular nations to which Russia is selling them. One concern is the large Russian sales to China over the last few years. Russia has sold China 72 fighters comparable to F-15s and may sell 200 more. Russia also has sold China four submarines and several destroyers (*Economic Review* of Hong Kong in "China's Buying" 11).

Of still more concern, Russia has sold China the "Sunburn" missile, which has been labelled "the most vicious antiship missile in the world" (Representative Solomon in CR "Reauthorization" H8380). Arguably, this missile could effect the balance of power in certain regions. According to Representative Rohrabacher, "This advanced cruise missile system endangers the lives of countless American service men and women and could alter the balance of power in key strategic areas such as the Straits of Taiwan and the Persian Gulf" (CR "Foreign Relations Authorization" H3626).

An additional risk relates to Chinese transfer of the missiles to Iran. Since "China has become the primary arms source for the Iranians" (Representative Rohrabacher in CR "Foreign Relations Authorization" H3626) there are substantial risks. He goes on to note that "An SSN-22 [the Sunburn] mounted on a mobile land platform would be extremely difficult to defend against and would threaten any of the ships in the Straits of Hormuz" (Representative Rohrabacher in CR "Foreign Relations Authorization" H3626).

In addition to the sales to China, Russia has been criticized for selling a number of weapons systems to Iran, including three diesel submarines, MIG-29 fighters, SU-24 fighters, and two different kinds of bombers and tanks (P "Bill and Boris" 16). Apparently, Russia also has sold Iran advanced "hand-held antiaircraft" missiles, which it has been reported Iran may make available to terrorist groups (CR Solomon "Let's Apply" E717).

In addition to the arms sales, Russia has been accused of selling "high-strength metals, other materials and sophisticated technology to Iran" (P Towell "House Passes" 2863). The fear is that these materials will be used by Iran "to extend the range of its Scud missiles to the point where they would pose a more serious threat to U.S. forces in the Middle East and U.S. allies such as Israel and Turkey" (P Towell "House Passes" 2863). Some experts believe that the technology would give Iran the ability to fire missiles as far as 1,240 miles, bringing sites as far away as central Europe within range (P Cassata "Support" 194). It recently has been reported by a Clinton Administration official that Iran "seems to be making progress at a very rapid pace" (qtd. in P Cloud 11) in the development of this technology.

The new missiles could have very serious regional effects. *The New Republic* argues that "The balance of power in the Middle East—the same one that we went to war to restore in 1991—is seriously imperiled" (P "Go Ballistic" 9). And Representative Gilman claims that "In the arsenal of a rogue regime like Iran, these weapons pose a significant threat to the security of the United States forces in the area, the safety of all ships passing through the Straits of Hormuz and the stability of the entire Persian Gulf region and beyond" (CR "General Leave" H10124). Understandably, the Israelis believe that the new missiles pose a threat to their security (P Cassata "Support" 193).

An additional problem is that "Russia has also sold Iran a light-water nuclear reactor and 2,000 tons of uranium" (P "Bill and Boris" 16). This sale is of concern since it has been reported that Iran has an active program to develop nuclear weapons (see Representative Berman in CR "Iran Missile Proliferation" H10657).

Finally, it has been reported that 800 high technology gyroscopes were sold by a Russian firm to Iraq in 1995. The sales occurred because Russia did not adequately enforce its export control laws (P Isachenko A3). On the other hand, the gyroscope issue may not be very important since apparently they did not reach their destination. They were confiscated by the Jordanians (P Isachenko A3).

What should be done about Russian sales of dangerous arms or technology to nations like Iran, Iraq, and China? According to the advocates of a tough policy toward Russia, the answer in each case is the threat of trade sanctions or an aid cutoff.

In relation to Iran, proposed legislation would establish tough economic sanctions, including denial of economic assistance. The sanctions also would be aimed at the company or organization carrying out the research or selling the goods to Iran. Two key points of dispute concern the standard for imposing sanctions and whether the President should be allowed to waive application of the sanctions to protect larger U.S. foreign policy interests. Generally, economic sanctions legislation uses a "preponderance of evidence" of violation standard (P Towell "House Passes" 2863). However, some argue that this standard is so high that it makes it virtually impossible to meet the threshold. An alternative would require only that there be "credible information" of a violation. The obvious problem with this standard is that there easily could be credible, but false, information indicating a violation.

The other issue relates to whether the president should be allowed to "waive" sanctions in order to serve larger U.S. interests, as generally has been done in other foreign policy legislation.

In relation to the arms sales to China, some in Congress have called for cutting off Export-Import bank assistance if "a transfer of these missile systems [Sunburn and another cruise missile] takes place" (Representative Solomon in CR "Reauthorization" H8380). Another proposal would cut almost $100 million in foreign assistance funding for 1998 and 1999 if Russia sent the cruise missiles to China (see CR "Foreign Relations Authorization" H3626).

While there is no question that the transfer of Russian arms and technology to rogue states like Iraq and Iran is unfortunate, there are strong arguments that can be made against imposing tough sanctions. First, Russia denies that it has sold any dangerous materials to Iran. Russian Foreign Minister Yevgeny Primakov told *Newsweek* "There are no deliveries to Iran from Russia which could lead to the creation by Iran of nuclear weapons or the development of long-range missiles. . . . I must tell you that the checks have been carried out, and they have shown that the charges fly in the face of reality" (P 43). Primakov concluded with a very powerful statement, "But Iran is situated next to our borders. We have no interest in Iran producing missiles or nuclear weapons" (P 43).

In other cases, Russia does not deny that the sales have been made, but they do deny that they have violated any agreements or provided any nation with destabilizing weapons.

Second, Russia has been tightening its polices concerning arms sales. For example, in January 1998, Russia announced that it was tightening its policy concerning the export of technology that could be used in the development of nuclear weapons (P Cassata "Support" 193). Under the agreement "The Kremlin canceled an Iranian contract with a Russian rocket-engine manufacturer and expelled a Tehran diplomat seeking missile technology" (P Cloud 11).

Third, some argue that the danger posed by the arms systems has been overstated. For example, the Iranians already have North Korean plans for the extended range missile (P Friedman A19). Clearly, the Chinese have access to those plans as well. Nor is it clear why the range extension of the missiles is that important. In both the Persian Gulf and the Straits of Taiwan, the older shorter-range missiles have adequate range to hit the key targets.

Fourth, the president already has the power to punish Russia if they do not change their policy. For example, the 1998 spending bill for foreign affairs included a provision that allowed the president to hold back 50% of foreign assistance if the Russians continued to provide crucial missile technology to Iran (P Cassata "Support" 194).

By all accounts the administration is working hard on the arms sales issue. According to Representative Lee Hamilton: "The administration is working as hard as it can" on the Iran missile technology issue. He adds that "Senior Russian officials have already indicated that Iranian missiles are not in their interest. Our diplomacy is beginning to achieve results . . ." (CR "Iran Missile" H10656).

Fifth, there is also serious question as to whether the problem can be solved. For example, in the case of Iran, it appears that the Iranians now have the expertise to complete their missile program in approximately two years. David S. Cloud argued recently in *The New Republic* that "the damage is largely done" (P 11). In this view, the cow is out of the barn already. A similar point could be made about the other arms sales.

Sixth, opponents of sanctions argue that they would reduce U.S. flexibility in negotiations with Russia and that such negotiations are a better way to stop the transfer of dangerous arms. In congressional debate on the proposed aid cutoff, both Representative Wexler and Representative Gilman argued that the cutoff would be acceptable if it included a provision allowing the president to waive application of the restriction "if he found it to be in the national security interest of our Nation" (Representative Gilman in CR "Foreign Relations Authorization" H3626). That waiver provision was needed, it was argued, to maintain the flexibility of U.S. foreign policy. According to Representative Wexler:

> The amendment [applying sanctions to Russia] gives the President absolutely no flexibility and raises one issue above every other priority in United States-Russian relationships. The amendment distorts United States policy toward Russia, and in fact what it is saying is there would be absolutely no circumstances in which there would be a valid security interest of the United States to provide aid for Russia once the transfer of such an antiship missile was made. I do not believe that is a plausible policy for the United States. (CR "Foreign Relations Authorization" H3627)

Why isn't it a plausible policy? First, such a sanction places all U.S. foreign policy goals behind the specific policy under question. That reduces the ability of the United States to act to achieve other goals. Second, the amendment eliminates the ability of the president to negotiate with the Russians. With a waiver position, negotiation is still possible. Third, the sanction has the effect of limiting possible U.S. reaction to a crisis. For example, if a major problem were discovered in relation to Russian security at a chemical, biological, or nuclear site, the sanction would prevent the United States from acting to solve the problem. Finally, the sanction policy violates the principle that the Congress should not micromanage foreign policy. Of course, Congress has the right to set priorities via the authorization process. But if U.S. foreign policy is to be effective, Congress must give the president the authority to act. Without that authority the president will not be able to solve problems and his/her credibility could be damaged.

Could this problem be solved simply by including the waiver. In one sense the answer is yes. The problem is, however, that with the inclusion of a waiver, the policy looks very much like the present system. As Representative Rohrabacher noted in his response to the comments of Gilman and Wexler, "The bottom line is when we put waivers into these bills, what we do is we are really making them into a sense-of-the-Congress resolution and not changing a darned thing" (CR "Foreign Relations Authorization" H3627).

The upshot of this situation is that a sanctions plus waiver policy essentially defines the present system. This also means that advocacy of such a policy would not necessarily be sufficient to be labelled a "substantial" change in U.S. foreign policy.

Seventh, a fund cutoff in response to any of the arms sales would stop the Nunn-Lugar program that has been so effective in reducing the risk of nuclear war. (This program will be discussed in the next section.) In this regard, Representative Spratt noted that the Sunburn has a range of 60 nautical miles and that India already has deployed a similar system (CR "National Defense Authorization" 23 June 1997 H4199). His point was that while the missile is dangerous, "it does not constitute by any stretch of the imagination a strategic threat to the United States" (CR "National Defense Authorization" 23 June 1997 H4199). In contrast, "Russian ICBM's, however, and Russian SLBM's and the fissile materials that must be secured from nations hostile to the United States are a strategic threat" (CR "National Defense Authorization" 23 June 1997 H4199).

Finally, there is a strong argument that use of sanctions of any kind inevitably would "exacerbate U.S.-Russian relations" (P Cassata "Support" 193).

Technology Transfer

An issue that is closely related to arms sales is technology transfer. Recently, some have called for tighter regulation of U.S. technology exports to Russia, because of Russian purchases of high tech computers (see P Gerth). In 1996, a Russian nuclear laboratory purchased 16 advanced IBM computers (P Barry and Matthews 87). According to the Russians, "We were quoted a price, and we paid it, just like you would buy salami" (P Barry and Matthews 87). Some see such purchases as dangerous because they facilitate Russian arms development and sales to other nations.

On the other hand, there is good evidence that the technology transfer issue is not a very significant problem. For example, in the case of the computer sale experts argue that the computers by themselves will not assist the Russians in designing new weapons (see P Gerth and Gordon). In fact, the computers are not exceptionally fast. IBM has sold more than 1000 of them to colleges, investment firms, and so forth. They are nothing like the most advanced computers available to the military in the United States (P Mathews 6). Given the spread of computer technology throughout the world, it is hard to see why the sale is an issue.

It is also important to recognize that the Russians wanted the computers to help them simulate nuclear weapons testing. They needed the capacity to carry out such simulations because of the ban on nuclear testing that both the United States and Russia have been following. Thus, the computer sale, regardless of whether it occurred legally or illegally, may have been good for U.S. security and the world environment.

Nuclear Weapons Policy

There are three fundamental issues involved in U.S.-Russian foreign policy concerning nuclear weapons. First, some argue that the risk of nuclear war would be reduced if both nations would move away from what is known as a launch-on-warning policy. Second, there are serious questions about the security of Russian nuclear materials. Consequently, some experts argue that the United States should do more to assist the Russians in protecting those materials. Third, there is a risk that U.S. policy actions could derail arms control negotiations with the Russians. Before considering these three policy areas, however, it is important to review the development of arms control negotiations between the United States and Russia.

Status of U.S.-Russian Nuclear Arms Agreements

There are three primary sets of agreements relating to nuclear weapons. First, the United States and Russia have been involved in the Strategic Arms Limitation Talks (START). Second, a number of treaties and other actions were agreed to at the time of the death of the Soviet Union. Third, the United States has enacted policies to assist the Russian government in reducing its nuclear arsenal and making that arsenal more secure. I will describe each in turn.

In relation to START, the United States and Russia agreed in 1991 to a strategic arms treaty (START I) that called for both nations to reduce their nuclear weapons to the range of 8,000 to 9,000 each. This treaty went into effect in December 1994 (P Myers A5). The second of the two strategic arms reductions treaties (commonly labelled START II) was signed on January 3, 1993, and ratified by the United States Senate in 1996. It has not yet been ratified by the Russians. This treaty calls on both nations to reduce their storehouse of nuclear weapons to 3,500 weapons.

In September 1997, the United States signed a groundbreaking agreement with Russia relating to a number of strategic issues. Under the agreement, Russia would be given an additional five years to completely dismantle weapons systems covered in START II. Russia still would need to disable all of these weapons by 2003, but would have an additional four years to destroy them (P Myers A1).

The United States agreed to the delay because of difficulties that Russia was having in complying with the original treaty. The problem was with the nature of the limits established in the START II treaty. Under that treaty, both the United States and Russia were to have no more than 3,500 strategic nuclear weapons by the year 2003 and of that number only 1750 could be on submarines. This created a problem for Russia, which has less than 500 weapons on bombers. Under the treaty, the remaining weapons would be single-warhead land-based ICBM's. However, Russia only has 500 missiles that carry single warheads or could be converted to carry single warheads (P Arbatov 108-109). Thus, the treaty created the odd situation where Russia would be required "to procure and deploy 500 single-warhead ICBM's" to meet the required standards (P Arbatov 109). In contrast, the United States has few problems complying with the standards (P Arbatov 109). Thus, the United States agreement to delay full treaty implementation was not a retreat from arms control, but actually a method of advancing it.

One sign that the agreement was useful is that in April 1998, Yeltsin submitted the amended START II treaty to the Duma and it has been predicted that the agreement will be passed (P "START II" A3).

The September 1997 agreement included other important provisions as well. The United States and Russia agreed to changes in the 1972 Anti-Ballistic Missile (ABM) Treaty. These alterations, placed "new limits on the speed and range of future systems by restricting the targets the missiles may be tested against" and also barred "the United States from testing or deploying any space-based missile defense system" (P Myers A1). These actions were aimed at reassuring "Russia that as the two sides move to cut their nuclear arsenals still more under a future Start 3, the United States would not deploy new missile defenses that could counter Russia's remaining weapons" (P Myers A1).

The speed limitation was established to allow the United States and Russia to develop theater missile defense systems, similar to, but more advanced than, the one used by the United States in the Gulf War to defend U.S. troops, Saudi Arabia, and Israel.

The aim of the ABM agreement was to clear away problems and allow for the negotiation of further significant reductions in nuclear weapons (see P Goshko A16). Some believe that a detailed START III treaty could be negotiated relatively soon. That treaty would build on an arrangement at the March 1997 Helsinki summit in which Clinton and Yeltsin agreed to further reductions to the range of 2,000 to 2,500 nuclear weapons (P Myers A5).

Up to this point, I have focused on actions within the START process. But there have been other consequential nuclear agreements as well. One of the most important was achieved based on presidential action. In 1991, the Bush administration withdrew tactical nuclear weapons (smaller nuclear weapons that are designed to be delivered by planes or missiles within a given region) from bases near the then Soviet Union. Soviet President Gorbachev responded in kind and withdrew Soviet tactical weapons from the Soviet republics back into Russia proper (see P Turner). This action clearly reduced the risk of war.

The United States and Russia also have agreed to stop targeting each other with nuclear weapons. President Clinton often touts this development. It should be noted, however, that either the Russian or the American missiles could be retargeted in a very short period (see P "A Perilous" A14). According to Representative Weldon, the retargeting can be done in as little as "10 seconds" (CR "National Defense" 20 June 1997 H4111).

Russia and the United States also have agreed to an "Open Skies" agreement that has not yet been ratified by the Russians. The agreement is aimed at building security by allowing overflights of territory to provide information to verify arms agreements. The United States already has allowed Russian planes to overfly our territory. In September 1996, the United States and Russia signed an extension of the Nuclear Test Ban treaty (P Barry and Matthews 87).

There are several accords that were made in response to the death of the Soviet Union. In December 1991, Russia reached an agreement with Ukraine, Kazakhstan, and Belarus under which remaining tactical weapons were returned to Russia. This occurred in 1992 (P Garthoff 306).

Over a three year period, from 1991 to 1994, negotiations were held among Russia, Ukraine, Belarus, Kazakhstan, and the United States concerning strategic nuclear weapons that remained in the borders of the old Soviet Union, but outside the borders of Russia. Garthoff explains that "In a 'Lisbon Protocol' to the United States-Soviet/Russian Strategic Arms Reduction Treaty (START I), Ukraine, Belarus, and Kazakhstan agreed to assume nonnuclear weapons status and remove all nuclear weapons to Russia" (P 306). Further negotiations occurred over the three-year period, primarily dealing with the desire of some in Ukraine to remain a nuclear power. After considerable U.S. pressure and promises of assistance, Ukraine agreed to the withdrawal of the weapons (P Garthoff 306). All three of Ukraine, Belarus, and Kazakhstan have signed the Nonproliferation Treaty (NPT) and all strategic weapons had been sent to Russia by the end of 1996 (P Garthoff 306).

The United States has made two main agreements with Russia relating to the security of the Russian nuclear arsenal. As I noted in Chapter Two, the United States agreed to buy 500 tons of highly enriched uranium from Russia to reduce the risk that this material might be stolen by criminals or terrorists.

The uranium deal has proceeded slowly because of "petty commercial considerations" (P Calogero 20). The agency assigned to implement the deal within the U.S. government, the U.S. Enrichment Corporation, tried to negotiate a very low price with the Russians. It took the personal intervention of Vice President Gore and Russian Prime Minister Chernomyrdin to salvage the deal (P Calogero 20).

In addition, under the Nunn-Lugar Act, Congress has appropriated several hundred million dollars to assist the Russians in disposing of nuclear weapons that are to be eliminated under the START process. Some of that money also has gone to increase the security of the sites where Russian nuclear weapons and high-level nuclear wastes are stored. There also have been any number of "confidence building" measures. For example, "in 1995, video cameras and other security monitoring equipment were installed in both U.S. and Russian storage facilities containing highly enriched uranium" (P Scott 45). Another program created a joint effort in the area of Warhead Safety and Security (P Scott 45).

Clearly, the United States and Russia have been very active over the last decade in attempting to reduce the risk of nuclear war. While much has been accomplished, there are three primary areas where experts believe that more can be done.

Proposals Fitting Within the START Process

There are several possible actions that might be taken by the United States to achieve stronger limitations on nuclear weapons. We could ban missile defense systems, expand missile defense systems, or initiate a new arms control process.

Limiting Missile Defense Systems   Some argue that additional actions need to be taken in relation to missile defense systems. Arbatov suggests that the United States and Russia should share information on Theater Missile Defense systems. He says "This is a completely rational suggestion, since neither side has theater missiles within range of the other's territory or forces. Cooperation would make the TMD systems more cost-effective and provide additional insurance that they would not have dedicated strategic capabilities" (P 111). Interestingly, former U.S. Ambassador to Russia Jack Matlock supports a similar view. He suggests that "A revival of proposals for joint research on ballistic missile defense would also be welcome" (P 50).

Why is it important for the United States and Russia to consult concerning missile defense? The Russians believe that the United States has started down a dangerous path. The Clinton administration has agreed to conservative calls for development of what is known as a "thin" missile defense system "that could be deployed as early as 2003" (P Lewis and Postol 23). Such a system easily could be expanded to a thicker missile defense system. In the view of some, the actions taken at Helsinki could have the effect of allowing the United States to implement an ABM system that could be destabilizing.

It could be destabilizing by making a U.S. first strike seem a plausible option. If either Russia or China feared that the United States might be able to launch a first strike that would take out nearly all of their nuclear arsenal and the United States also had an ABM system that could defend against any remaining missiles, that might seem a very dangerous situation. Rodney Jones and Nikolai Sokov note, "Russian military leaders have long contended that a national missile defense in the United States would undermine the deterrent value of Russian strategic forces, rendering Russia vulnerable to a theoretical first strike" (P 27).

To deal with this risk, some believe that the United States should abandon any missile defense research relating to strategic defense. Strategic defense systems can shoot down ICBM's; theater defense systems only deal with shorter range missiles. This action is necessary, in the view of some, because the current agreement concerning testing missile defense systems could actually undercut the ABM treaty. In this view, "the ABM Treaty will survive in name only and will cease to exist as an agreement enforcing any limitations of substance" (P Lewis and Postol 18).

Thus, by enacting a stricter policy on missile defense, the United States would reassure the Russians and make it easier to achieve additional arms agreements. It also might encourage Russia to move away from a launch-on-warning posture. I will discuss that issue in the next section.

There are, however, strong arguments that can be made against a proposal that the United States share information with the Russians concerning theater missile defense and ban the development of strategic defense systems. First, the Helsinki accords include measures aimed at increasing cooperation on missile defense systems. Paul Mann reports that the agreement included "Direct consultation in the event new technologies arise for TMD [theater missile defense] systems." The agreement also called for "TMD cooperation" including "integrated defense efforts for sharing early warning support of TMD activities, technology cooperation and expanded cooperation in the on-going program of joint TMD exercises" (P "Helsinki" 26). Moreover, it is already United States policy to "share TMD information with the Russians to assure them that U.S. systems are intended only for protecting American troops" (P Mann "Helsinki 27").

Second, conservatives argue that the United States desperately needs a strong missile defense program. They point to a variety of dangers including nuclear blackmail from a rogue state with ICBM's, the increasing number of nations that will have access to ICBM's or mid-range missiles over the next several decades, the possibility that a terrorist or someone else might get control of a Russian weapon, and other risks as well. In response to these risks, they argue that the United States should build a missile defense system that could stop a small attack on the United States, either a single or a small number of missiles (see the testimony of former CIA director James Woolsey in D *ABM Treaty* 5-16). An agreement restricting missile defense research would make the United States vulnerable to these risks.

In response to the conservative argument, arms control advocates claim that there is no significant threat against which a missile defense system would be useful in today's world. They also argue that if such a threat develops, that would be the time to develop the missile defense system (see testimony of Jack Mendelsohn of the Arms Control Association in D *ABM Treaty* 64–70). Moreover, terrorists or rogue states are unlikely to rely on ICBM technology to strike the United States. Why would they make the effort to develop such a complex system, when they could hide a nuclear weapon on a freighter and sail it into New York harbor?

Expanding Missile Defense Systems   The second proposal for altering U.S. foreign policy toward Russia in relation to the START process is the opposite of the first. Some conservatives argue that the Helsinki agreement overly restricts U.S. research on missile defense (see P Weinberger "The Helsinki Summit" 37). In fact, Newt Gingrich labeled the agreement as a "deliberate weakening of our national defense" (qtd. in P Mann 26). In their view, the United States should scrap the agreement and move full-speed ahead in the development of a missile defense system. The advantage of such an approach would be that it would protect the United States from the dangers that I mentioned earlier.

While the idea of missile defense is on first glance quite appealing, it probably isn't sensible for the United States to abandon the ABM treaty and make a major commitment to missile defense. First, as I already have explained, such an action could derail the arms control process. Second, it would encourage the Russians to rely on a dangerous hair-trigger alert posture to make sure that the United States did not destroy all of their weapons in a first strike. Third, developing an ABM system would be extremely expensive. Fourth, it is not at all clear that an ABM system could in fact be effective. There are a variety of technical problems that would have to be solved to create such a system. And even if they were solved, a rogue state could circumvent the system in a variety of ways, such as the bomb on the freighter.

Reagan's threat to develop a space-based missile defense system clearly scared the Soviets to death. It encouraged them to participate in serious arms control negotiations. It would be very foolish of the United States to throw away the benefits achieved with that threat for very speculative advantages of a real missile defense system.

Unilateral Arms Reductions   Stansfield Turner, a former admiral and CIA chief, claims that unilateral presidential action could reduce the threat of nuclear war. He argues that the president should unilaterally remove approximately 1,000 weapons from strategic launchers and put them in what he labels "strategic escrow." The Russians would be allowed to observe this process to verify that the weapons were being removed from the missiles, placed in escrow, and not replaced with other warheads. Turner believes that such unilateral action would not harm U.S. security in the slightest and would encourage the Russians to respond in kind (see P Turner). If that happened, then the threat of nuclear war would be diminished.

Turner's suggestion is consistent with a proposal produced by the National Academy of Sciences, which suggests that both Russia and the United States should reduce their arsenals to a few hundred nuclear weapons in order to cut the danger of war (P Weiner A5).

There is some reason to believe that the Russians might go along with a proposal for unilateral action resulting in further reductions in the nuclear arsenals of both nations. Yeltsin publicly has advocated a lower level of nuclear weapons.

On the other hand, a strong argument can be made that the United States should continue to work through the START process. That process has been very successful. Moreover, the difference in risk of war between having a few hundred nuclear weapons and the couple thousand envisioned under the latest agreement does not seem to be very large. In fact, there is an argument that the world is more secure with slightly more weapons because there is much less risk that either side will fear a first strike. If you fear a first strike, that creates incentives for very risky nuclear strategy.

Launch-on-Warning

Some claim that one of the greatest threats to the world is the chance that a nuclear war could occur because of the nuclear launch policies of the United States and Russia. The argument concerns a nuclear policy called "launch-on-warning" (LOW). Under this policy, the United States or Russia would not wait for a nuclear attack to actually hit the ground, but would instead launch while the attacking missiles were still in the air. Russia currently embraces LOW and recently has endorsed what is known as a "first-use" policy (P Nelan 47).

LOW is dangerous because of the risk that missiles could be launched when there was not in fact an in-coming first strike. In January 1995, a frightening incident occurred in which the world was perilously close to nuclear conflict. The Russians detected a rocket launch in the Norwegian sea that seemed to be streaking toward Russia. In response, "a warning of the possible nuclear attack [was sent] to an underground control center south of Moscow" (P Nelan 46). This set off a nuclear alert in which Yeltsin was presented with various options for responding to a nuclear attack. It was over ten minutes before it became clear to the Russians that the missile was not launched at their territory (P Nelan 46). Russian technicians determined that the missile was not part of a nuclear attack "just a few minutes short of the procedural deadline to respond to an impending nuclear attack" (P Blair, Feiveson, and von Hippel "Taking" 75). The rocket actually was a Norwegian scientific experiment and the Russians had been informed, but that information had not been relayed to the proper sources. As a consequence, in the words of Russian Duma member Sergei Yushenkov, "the world was on the brink of nuclear war" (qtd. in P Nelan 47).

One problem with a LOW policy is the danger that a technical error or misunderstanding of radar data could lead to a nuclear response when no real attack had occurred. The dangers associated with LOW have been exacerbated by the failure of a portion of the Russian early-warning system (P Steinbruner B5). Blair, Feiveson, and von Hippel put it succinctly, when they note that such a policy "heightens the possibility that one day someone will mistakenly launch nuclear-tipped missiles" (P "Taking" 76).

Given these risks, why do Russia and the United States retain a launch-on-warning posture? The answer varies between the two nations. The United States has not sworn off a LOW because the possibility that we could launch before enemy missiles hit our nation has the effect of enhancing deterrence. Under current policy, no foreign adversary can know for sure whether the United States would wait for missiles to land before launching. The Russians have an additional motive to maintain a LOW posture. They have far more warheads than the United States that are vulnerable to a first strike (see P Blair, Feiveson, and Hippel "Redoubling"). As a consequence, Russia believes that it needs a launch-on-warning policy to maintain adequate security. As Blair, Feiveson, and von Hippel have noted, "The [Russian] General Staff evidently fears that if its nuclear missiles are not launched immediately, then only tens of them would be able to respond after absorbing a systematic U.S. attack" (P "Taking" 78).

The problem for Russia has been exacerbated by lack of funds. Currently, Russia doesn't have the money to have some of its most survivable forces available. Only two of twenty-six nuclear missile submarines are kept on patrol and missiles on railway cars and mobile trucks are kept at fixed sites (P Blair, Feiveson, and von Hippel "Taking" 78).

It seems clear that moving away from launch-on-warning would be a very good idea. Bruce Nelan notes that "a large part of the risk could be eliminated by . . . 'de-alerting' the forces, taking them off their hair-trigger posture" (P 48). Former Senator Sam Nunn of Georgia and George L. Butler, who commanded U.S. strategic forces from 1991 to 1994, suggest that the United States and Russia should each take actions to de-alert their forces (cited in P Blair, Feiveson, and von Hippel 79). Something similar happened during the Bush administration, when the president "ordered an immediate stand-down of the many U.S. strategic bombers that had remained ready for decades to take off with only a few minutes warning" (P Blair, Feiveson, and von Hippel "Taking" 79). Soviet President Gorbachev reciprocated this action and the risk of conflict was reduced (P Blair, Feiveson, and von Hippel "Taking" 79–80).

Thus, one possibility would be for the United States to change its policy toward Russia by publicly renouncing LOW and providing the Russians with means to verify that action. A more radical option would be to implement technical means that temporarily disabled nuclear missiles. Special pins might be inserted in rocket engines that prevented them from flying. Of course, those pins could be removed, but that would take some time and thus make it impossible to launch the missiles using a LOW posture.

Some experts argue that the best way to deal with this problem is for the United States to take the first step in swearing off launch-on-warning. If that were done, it is argued, the Russians then could respond and the danger eliminated (see P Blair, Feiveson, and Hippel "Redoubling" A23). Why should the United States act first? The answer is that such action is needed to provide a justification for Russian action. Moreover, the United States possesses an adequate supply of truly invulnerable missiles and, therefore, can afford to be the first to act.

What specifically should the United States do? Blair, Feiveson, and von Hippel propose moving the warheads off the MX missile into storage, taking other actions to disable missiles that might be used in a first strike by the United States, reducing the level of alert of U.S. submarines, and allowing the Russians to verify that these actions have been taken (P "Taking" 81). They argue that such actions "would persuade the Russians to follow suit and take most of its missiles off hair-trigger alert" (P "Taking" 80). At the same time, the United States would still maintain several hundred "invulnerable" missiles on submarines to preserve our security (P Blair, Feiveson, and von Hippel 80).

There are two arguments against moving away from launch-on-warning. First, some argue that such an action could have the effect of undercutting a more radical call for the elimination of nuclear weapons altogether (views of former Assistant Secretary of Defense Ashton Carter in P Nelan 48). Second, proposals to technologically disable nuclear weapons might have the effect of destabilizing the nuclear balance. The problem is that such a policy would create an incentive for a preemptive first strike. If nation x knew that nation y could not respond to a nuclear attack for 10 or 12 hours, then nation x also would know that if they could find a way to launch a significant number of weapons, that it would be possible to obliterate the nuclear forces of nation y and prevent any second strike.

While there are arguments against unilateral U.S. action to reduce the risk of LOW and there is no guarantee that the Russians would respond, the evidence suggests that the proposal is a good gamble. Recall that when President Bush implemented similar proposals, Gorbachev responded and the chance of conflict was reduced.

Russian Nuclear Security

The third alternative for changing U.S. policy toward Russia would be for the United States to take action to increase the security of Russian nuclear forces.

There are several problems with Russia's nuclear system that conceivably could lead to war. One difficulty is that "The delicate computer networks at the heart of the nuclear force are not being maintained properly, and the safeguards that prevent accidental or unauthorized launches are fraying" (P 47). It has been estimated that Russia only spends roughly 10% of what is needed to maintain the command and control system (P Nelan 47). Additionally, there have been strikes against the Russian Strategic Rocket Force and even the threat of electricity cut-offs. "Worse yet, the equipment that controls nuclear weapons frequently malfunctions, and critical electronic devices and computers sometimes switch to a combat mode for no apparent reason" (P Blair, Feiveson, and von Hippel "Taking" 76). It even has been reported that the "nuclear suitcase" containing the codes to launch a nuclear strike is "falling into disrepair" (P Blair, Feiveson, and von Hippel 76).

There are also people problems in the command and control system. "Crews receive less training than they did formerly and are consequently less proficient in the safe handling of nuclear weapons" (P Blair, Feiveson, and von Hippel 76). And the people in command of the strategic nuclear system are very poorly paid, housed, and clothed. These problems could get much worse. Igor Rodionov, Russian Defense Minister, has stated that "if the shortage of funds persists . . . Russia may soon approach a threshold beyond which its missiles and nuclear systems become uncontrollable" (qtd. in P Blair, Feiveson, and von Hippel "Taking" 76).

An additional problem is the horrible poverty in which the Russian military controlling nuclear weapons live. They often are not paid for months at a time. In that circumstance, there are several possible scenarios that end in disaster for the world. One is that unpaid nuclear commanders might sell their expertise or their weapons. Another is that they could threaten war in order to be paid. Bill Powell wrote about this risk in *Newsweek* at the time of the Helsinki Summit, "But what, in truth would make everyone feel safer now would be if Yeltsin could find a way to pay the commanders of the nuclear-submarine fleet in Murmansk. They haven't had a paycheck in four months. And it's hard to think of a greater post-cold-war security threat than the issue of 'loose nukes'" (P 32).

Another threat is "a nuclear civil war. If a region in Siberia were to declare its independence, a retired senior officer in Moscow speculates, 'the entire missile force in the area might cut itself off from the chain of command and control and get programmed to be able to launch at will" (P Nelan 48).

An additional threat "is a possible miscalculation of U.S. actions during some kind of crisis" (P Nelan 48). The danger of "miscalculation" has been "greatly increased because the Russian early-warning system is not what it used to be" (P Nelan 48). In fact, "The high command is now partially blind, which increases its apprehensions, produces false alarms and makes good decisions harder" (P Nelan 48).

It is also disturbing that under the Russian system, individual nuclear commanders might be able to program their missiles and launch (P Blair, Feiveson, and von Hippel "Taking" 77). Unlike the United States, these commanders would not necessarily need access to secret codes possessed only by top officials (P Nelan 48). According to John Steinbruner, a senior fellow at the Brookings Institution, "a breakdown within the Russian military command system is far and away the No. 1 danger to the United States in the world" (qtd. in P Cooper "Expanding NATO" 437).

Finally, there is a significant risk that Russian nuclear materials might be stolen by terrorists or the mafia or sold to the highest bidders. In fact, several commentators have argued recently that the theft of nuclear materials from Russia depicted in the film, "The Peacemaker," easily could happen. For example, John Pastore and Peter Zheutlin cited the testimony of Alexander Lebed that Russia does not know the location of 100 suitcase sized nuclear weapons (P 19). Even if the 100 figure is an exaggeration, it would be quite dangerous if only ten weapons were missing. According to Representative Weldon, one of these weapons "could destroy a major portion of one of our cities in this country. It could kill tens if not hundreds of thousands of people" (CR "The Trip" H7824).

In the *Boston Globe,* Graham Allison pointed to the danger that nuclear materials could be stolen and then exported for use in the United States. This risk was backed up by the citation of six documented instances in which nuclear materials have been removed from sites in the former Soviet Union (see P Allison). Clearly, there is a grave danger that criminal gangs or criminal nations (like Libya or Iran) might try to buy access to nuclear materials (see P "A Perilous" A14). Another risk is that Russian nuclear scientists might sell their knowledge or even the weapons themselves. The rise of organized crime in Russia makes the threat of nuclear theft still more frightening (see P "A Chilling" A30). FBI Director Louis Freeh has warned of the dangers posed by theft of nuclear material, even arguing that there is now greater risk of nuclear attack from that source than from the Soviet Union during the Cold War (cited in P Farah "FBI Chief" A18).

Nuclear weapons also could be sold simply to generate desperately needed revenue for the Russian military. Graham Allison of Harvard cites an instance in which the director of a major facility took out loans to pay workers and when it became impossible to repay the loans, committed suicide. Allison noted that the outcome could have been different: "If this man wanted to put 20 weapons in a plane [and fly off], he could have done so without question" (qtd. in P Anselmo 47). In sum, the theft of nuclear material poses, in the words of Francesco Calogero, "the most serious clear and present danger faced by the United States" (P 21).

What could be done to reduce the risks I have described? The United States could take three actions that might cut the danger of nuclear war. The first would be to take the unilateral steps I mentioned earlier to encourage further reductions in nuclear weapons and to get the Russians off LOW. Second, the United States could implement expanded programs to improve nuclear security and safety in Russia. This nation could establish or expand programs to deal with each of the risks I described.

Third, the United States could expedite the program to purchase the 500 tons of high-level wastes that I described earlier (P Calogero 20). One option might be to transfer highly enriched uranium directly to the United States, as opposed to having Russia convert it to low-enriched uranium, prior to shipment. That action would eliminate material "that could be used to make upwards of 10,000 nuclear weapons" (P Calogero 20). It also would "pump many billions of dollars into the Russian nuclear complex" (P Calogero 20). That money, in turn, could be used to upgrade Russian nuclear security and reduce the risk of theft of nuclear weapons. Another option would be to "earmark" 20% of the payment "for the disposal of Russian weapons of mass destruction" (P Calogero 21). That would aid the Russians in disposing of both nuclear and chemical weapons. This approach would be good for both the United States and also Russia, which has indicated that it favors a faster purchase (P Calogero 21).

In sum, there is a compelling case that the United States should do everything possible to reduce the "loose nukes" problem.

Against the "control loose nukes" proposal, there are several important arguments. First, some experts suggest that the dangers have been overstated. For example, a CIA study has reported that the chance of accidental launch was "low" (P Nelan 48). Even in the case of the Norwegian rocket, the system worked.

In addition, so far, at least, according to the CIA and other sources, there has not been a significant theft of Russian nuclear materials (P Anselmo 50). And a National Security Council official estimated that the probability of such a theft was "low," but also admitted that "the consequences are enormously far-reaching" (P Anselmo 50).

Also in relation to terrorism, some argue that terrorists are unlikely to use nuclear weapons both because they can be traced easily and also because their use could result in massive retaliation. On the other hand, "Biological weapons . . . are much more difficult to trace, because international regimes to control them are weak" (views of Zachary Davis of the Congressional Research Service cited in P Anselmo 50).

Second, a strong argument could be made that the United States already has taken adequate action to deal with problems in the Russian nuclear system. Recently, Representative Spratt commented on the accomplishments of the Nunn-Lugar program:

> So far Nunn-Lugar has helped deactivate 4,500 nuclear warheads, put over 200 ICBM silos out of operation, destroyed 20 heavy bombers, eliminated 64 submarine launched ballistic missiles and sealed 58 nuclear testing tunnels. Nunn-Lugar has helped the three former nations of the Soviet Union, Ukraine, Belarus, and Kazakhstan totally denuclearize. This is one of the crowning successes of the post-cold-war world. (CR "National Defense" 23 June 1997 H4199)

These successes have been achieved at a "cost of less than one-third of 1 percent of the Department of Defense's annual budget" (Senator Lugar in CR "National Defense Authorization" 7 July 1997 S6878).

Moreover, the program is not yet complete. Representative Spratt refers to the "work order" for the future:

> Dismantle 130 SS-19 heavy throw-weight ICBM's, dismantle 54 SS-24 mobile ICBM's, fill in 148 SS-18 silos in Kazakhstan, eliminate 492 SLBM silos, destroy 10 more heavy bombers, complete the construction of a facility in Siberia to safely store over 12,000 nuclear warheads, dispose of 100,000 metric tons of liquid propellants, scrap 916 ballistic rocket motors. (CR "National Defense" 23 June 1997 H4199)

Senator Lugar emphasizes in particular the continuing importance of the program for improving security at Russian nuclear sites to minimize the risk of terrorism or theft. He notes:

> The Department of Energy, in co-operation with Russia, the newly independent states, and the Baltic States, has put in place equipment at 18 sites to safeguard plutonium and weapons usable uranium, and agreements are in place to enhance safety and security at over 30 additional sites, including research laboratories and storage sites. (CR "National Defense Authorization" 7 July 1997 S6878; also see the comments of Senator Bingaman in CR "National Defense Authorization" 7 July 1997 S6883).

Clearly, there is important work still to be done.

The Nunn-Lugar program also provides "employment and economic incentives for former Soviet weapons scientists to avoid the temptation that they will sell their know-how to buyers from nations and organizations that support international terrorism" (Senator Kennedy CR "Cloture Motion" S6974). For example, a grant of $22 million was given to Moscow's International Science and Technology Center for nuclear scientists to work on non-nuclear projects (see D *Newly Independent States* 22).

On the other hand, the advocate of change might build a a strong argument that the Nunn-Lugar program is insufficient and should be dramatically expanded. Senator Lugar himself argued in the summer of 1997 that the budget for fiscal 1998 was "a bare-bones request" (CR "National Defense Authorization" 7 July 1997 S6878). He also noted that "Many programs that Congress supported in the past failed to make the list" (CR "National Defense Authorization" 7 July 1997 S6878).

The key question in regard to a proposal to expand Nunn-Lugar support is whether such an action would constitute a "substantial" change in U.S. foreign policy. It could be argued that, given the funding shortfalls, the action would be a major change. On the other hand, it also could be argued that an alteration in funding levels does not constitute any kind of substantial change. All the funding level increase does is let the United States get to certain projects faster than it otherwise would do so. That does not constitute a substantial change.

All of this means that the negative should argue that the present Nunn-Lugar program is sufficient to minimize the problem of "loose nukes" and that any expanded program would not constitute a "substantial change" in U.S. policy.

Finally, the negative should argue that an expanded program risks nationalist backlash from Russia. Russia has accepted the Nunn-Lugar program. The danger in creating a new program is that they might perceive the program as infringing on their sovereignty. If that were to happen then the positive effects of Nunn-Lugar might be lost.

Biological and Chemical Weapons

While Russia's "loose nukes" are the greatest threat to the security of the United States in the world today, Russian biological and chemical weapons are also a security problem.

Biological Weapons

During the Cold War, "the former Soviet Union had the world's largest biological warfare program, more than 100 times larger than Iraq's" (P Zilinskas A39). With the end of that conflict, it appeared that the biological weapons problem would be solved.

Biological weapons are forbidden by the 1972 "Biological and Toxic Weapons Convention" and in 1992 Yeltsin pledged to "dismantle" the Russian program (P Zilinskas A39). He also signed an agreement with the United States and Great Britain and allowed in inspectors in 1992 and 1993 (P Zilinskas A39).

There are reasons to believe, however, that Russia has not followed through on these agreements. For one thing, in 1994 and 1995, the British and American inspection team "was denied access to military installations and eventually was barred from all Russian sites" (P Zilinskas A39).

In addition, some say that Russia retains an active program of research on biological weapons and has dismantled neither laboratories nor the facilities needed for production of the weapons (see P Garthoff 311). And The Center for Security Policy cites a report in *Jane's Air Defense 1997–1998* which "confirms that

Russia has developed a new variant of lethal anthrax toxin that is totally resistant to antibiotics—in flagrant violation of an earlier 'international norm' governing biological weapons activities" (D *Chemical Weapons Convention* 279).

The problem is not primarily that Russia retains an active weapons program, although that is a worry. United States nuclear weapons are probably an effective deterrent against Russian use of biological weapons in the United States. And biological weapons are dangerous, not only to the target, but also for the country using them.

Rather than the risk of use in war, the primary dangers are accidental release, terrorism, and theft. A particular worry is that "scientists may be tempted to offer their expertise to the highest bidders, who could turn out to be outlaw nations or terrorists eager to acquire weapons of mass destruction" (P Zilinskas A39). Another danger is that criminal gangs might make biological weapons "available on the international black market" (P Zilinskas A39). These risks are of special concern given a recent test of U.S. defense capabilities that revealed the United States "is still unprepared to respond to biological terror weapons" (P Miller and Broad A1).

What can be done about the biological weapons problem. There are two basic alternatives. First, the United States might threaten sanctions, either an aid cutoff or trade restrictions, unless the Russians open up their biological weapons sites and demonstrate that they are complying with agreements to destroy their program. Such action is subject to all of the arguments that I have discussed previously in relation to sanctions.

Raymond Zilinskas of the University of Maryland Biotechnology Institute argues for a second approach. He suggests that the United States should take the evidence of violations to the U.N. Security Council, but also provide additional support for Russian scientists and expand general economic assistance to Russia. He hopes that this carrot and stick approach might encourage the Russians to act.

How can present U.S. policy be defended? Unfortunately, the evidence strongly suggests that Russia continues to carry out dangerous biological weapons research. And the risks associated with terrorism and creation of a black market are real. The two primary arguments against a change in policy relate to current actions and doubts about whether an altered approach could be effective.

First, the carrot and stick approach advocated by Zilinskas is arguably essentially the same as the position of the Clinton administration. Thus, a strong argument could be made that such an approach does not represent a substantial change in U.S. policy.

Second, there are reasons to doubt that a changed U.S. policy would accomplish much. Of course, all of the arguments against aid programs apply in this instance. And clearly there would be risk of nationalist backlash in Russia if it were perceived that the West was forcing a given policy on their nation. More than anything, biological weapons research programs are difficult to control. Even Zilinskas admits that "None of these measures singly or together will solve the problem. But we must begin somewhere" (P Zilinskas A39). That is hardly a ringing defense of the effectiveness of his own proposal.

Chemical Weapons

The United States and Russia have agreed to destroy stockpiles of chemical weapons and ban future production. This accord was formalized in a 1990 Bilateral Destruction Agreement. Under this agreement "Moscow promised to provide a full and accurate accounting and afford the U.S. inspection rights" (Center for Security Policy D Chemical Weapons Convention 295) as part of a program in which all Russian chemical weapons would be destroyed by 2005.

Additionally, under the Nunn-Lugar "Cooperative Threat Reduction Program," the United States has provided more than $150 million to assist the Russians in destroying their chemical weapons (Senator Kyl in CR "Cooperative Threat" S7250).

There is also a chemical weapons treaty. The treaty "bans the development, production, sale, purchase, possession or use of chemical weapons" (P Towell "House Passes" 2863). It requires that existing stocks of chemical weapons and production facilities be destroyed within a decade, although a five-year extension is possible (P Hoffman "Lower House" A22). It has been ratified by more than 100 nations. The United States Senate ratified this treaty on April 24, 1997. The Russian parliament ratified the convention in fall 1997 (see P Hoffman "Lower House" A22).

So far, Russia has "failed to meet its promised schedule for destroying old chemical weapons stocks and surplus armaments earlier withdrawn from Europe beyond the Urals" (P Garthoff 311). At a more fundamental level, there is some question as to whether Russia intends to follow the two agreements made with the United States almost a decade ago. Texas Senator Hutchison commented that Russian Prime Minister Chernomyrdin had told Vice President Gore "that both agreements have outlived their usefulness." Her conclusion was that "the Russians do not intend to honor these agreements" (CR "Chemical Weapons Convention" 24 April 1997 S3592). Similarly, the Center for Security Policy reports that the Kremlin has reneged on the joint destruction agreement (D *Chemical Weapons Convention* 279).

And there is some evidence that Russia has continued a secret program to "develop nerve agents so lethal that microscopic amounts can kill" (J. Michael Walker of *The Wall Street Journal* in CR "Chemical Weapons Convention" 24 April 1997: S3589). Russia also appears to have developed a new nerve agent which is not covered under the new chemical weapons treaty (*The Wall Street Journal* in CR "Chemical Weapons Convention" 24 April 1997 S3590). The Center for Security Policy cites a report in *Jane's Air Defense 1997–1998*

> that the Russians have also developed three nerve agents "that could be made without using any of the precursor chemicals, which are banned under the 1993 Chemical Weapons Convention." It added that "two of the new nerve agents are eight times as deadly as the VX nerve agent that Iraq has acknowledged stockpiling." (D *Chemical Weapons Convention* 279)

These new weapons clearly pose serious dangers.

It also should be recognized that many experts doubt whether the United States should rely on the effectiveness of the treaty. In April 1997, four men who had served as Secretary of Defense, Donald Rumsfield, Caspar Weinberger, James Schlesinger, and Richard Cheney, testified before Congress that they did not believe the treaty adequately protected U.S. interests (see D *Chemical Weapons Convention*).

Advocates of a tougher policy on chemical weapons argue that sanctions are needed. They claim, in fact, that assistance programs have been diverted by the Russians to pay for chemical weapons research. In this view, the chemical weapons development process has proceeded using U.S. money "that we sent over for economic development" (testimony of former Secretary of Defense Caspar Weinberger in D *Chemical Weapons Convention* 11). Even the Nunn-Lugar program may have been counterproductive in this case. Senator Kyl argues that "United States assistance to Russia for CW destruction has, in fact, had the perverse effect of underwriting Russia's offensive chemical programs" (CR "Cooperative Threat" S7251).

What are the risks associated with the Russian chemical weapons program? It is important to recognize that Russia has very large stockpiles of dangerous weapons. The stocks are officially estimated at 40,000 tons of chemical weapons, but in actuality may include 75,000 tons of weapons (Senator Helms in CR "Chemical Weapons Convention" 24 April 1997 S3611). Again, the primary risk is not use in an attack against the United States or our allies. Rather, it is unauthorized use, terrorism, or sale on the black market that is the biggest threat. Senator Helms cited an instance in which the Russian former chief negotiator for the Chemical Weapons Convention was removed from his command because "in 1993 [he] sold 1,800 pounds of chemical agents to terrorists in the Middle East. He was caught attempting to sell another 5 tons a year later" (CR "Chemical Weapons Convention" 24 April 1997 S3609).

What can be done about the Russian chemical weapons program? There are two possible solutions. One would be for the United States to negotiate a new agreement and provide greater financial resources to essentially pay for the Russians to destroy their chemical weapons program. It has been reported that the Russians will not follow through on destruction of their stockpiles unless the West agrees to pay for it (Center for Security Policy D *Chemical Weapons Convention* 296). One obvious thing to do would be for the United States to substantially expand the Nunn-Lugar program and provide the estimated $3 billion that would be needed to take care of the problem (Center for Security Policy D *Chemical Weapons Convention* 296). With effective monitoring, such an approach could be useful, just as it has been in the area of nuclear weapons elimination.

On the other hand, if Nunn-Lugar money has been shifted from weapons control to weapons development by the Russians, there are good reasons to be skeptical about an expansion in such a program. And all of the arguments against expanded assistance that I have summarized previously apply in this instance as well.

The other option would be a sanctions policy. Senator Kyl argues that the Russians have not paid their fair share of the cost of the Nunn-Lugar program and that, as a consequence, restrictions should be established, which the Russians must fulfill prior to additional funds being spent. The most important requirement would be that the Russians "show reasonable progress toward implementation of the 1990 Bilateral Destruction Agreement [which applies to chemical weapons]" (CR "Cloture Motion" S6987). The argument here is that applying this restriction would force the Russians to take action to destroy their chemical weapons stockpile and cease the production of new weapons.

On the other hand, it may be that further restrictions would not do much good, because the Russians simply would maintain "a sizable, covert chemical stockpile" (Center for Security Policy D *Chemical Weapons Convention* 296). Here, it is important to understand how "binary" chemical weapons work. Binary weapons produce a deadly substance from the combination of two other substances that are, by themselves, not deadly at all. In the chemical weapons shell, these two substances are combined, producing the poison. However, since the constituent parts of the binary weapon are not deadly, this makes enforcement of either the treaty or any other agreement quite difficult. And of course, all of the other arguments against a sanctions policy apply in this case. It is at least arguable that the best approach is to maintain the policy of the present system, which combines Nunn-Lugar aid with tough negotiations from the State Department.

A strong argument can be made that there is not much else that the United States can do about Russian chemical weapons. This argument has two parts. First, there are structures in place for dealing with chemical weapons, including bilateral actions and the chemical weapons treaty. Second, the problem seems to be the ease of circumvention of such agreements and the difficulty of verifying them. But there is little that can be done about either of these problems. In the words of *The Wall Street Journal* concerning the chemical weapons treaty, but equally applicable here, "Verification is an insurmountable problem" (in CR "Chemical Weapons Convention" 24 April 1997 S3590).

Chechnya

As I noted in Chapter Two, the war in Chechnya resulted in the deaths of tens of thousands of innocent people. The argument could be made that by not protesting vigorously enough, the United States bears partial responsibility for the disaster in Chechnya. Representative Frank Wolf very pointedly stated to a representative of the Clinton administration that "your policy in Chechnya has resulted in the death of a lot of people" (D *Russia's Election* 13).

Even if true, it could be argued that the past failure of the Clinton administration to protest adequately is irrelevant since the war is now over. An agreement was signed ending the conflict in May 1997.

However, some argue that the United States should change its policy to one of protesting Russian actions such as the war in Chechnya more vigorously. The advocates of this position note that the agreement ending the war establishes a moratorium on complete independence for five years (P Goltz 21). At the end of that period, renewed conflict is possible. They also argue that there is a substantial risk of wars similar to Chechnya in the future. The conflict in Chechnya could be a preview of what the Russians will face in the future in areas of their nation possessing a significant Islamic population.

There is no question that the war in Chechnya was both a tragedy and a disaster for Russia. However, there is little ground for altering U.S. policy in relation to a conflict that is now over. First, there is little reason to believe that the conflict will heat up again. Russia was soundly defeated in Chechnya and no one wants a return to conflict. In addition, so far Chechnya is the only place in Russia where there has been any significant rebellion against Russian control.

Second, a strong argument can be made defending U.S. policy in the conflict. The Clinton administration claims that strong protests were made to the Russians. Ambassador James Collins notes

> Our message in all of this [to the Russian government] has been, I think, clear. The cessation of violence and a resolution of this conflict through political peaceful means is in the critical interest of Russia and Russian reform. We've also made clear it's in the U.S. interest.
>
> We have also emphasized to the Russian leadership that continued violence and bloodshed in Chechnya can endanger Russia's developing relations with the West. We have encouraged Russian officials to cooperate with international organizations and humanitarian relief agencies to ameliorate human suffering and assist in ending the conflict. (D *Crisis in Chechnya* 49)

Moreover, it is almost impossible to draft a proposal that mandates a tough U.S. negotiating position but also maintains diplomatic flexibility. Thus, the events in Chechnya do not provide a strong rationale for making a substantial change in U.S. foreign policy toward Russia.

Space Policy

The United States and Russia have been involved in a cooperative program of space development. Several American astronauts have visited Mir, the Russian space station, for extended stays. And Russia is heavily involved in the development of the International Space Station. Some argue, however, that this partnership has not worked out well. In this view, the Russians have not fulfilled their end of the bargain, and the United States should not continue to work with them.

In relation to Mir, some argue that putting U.S. astronauts on the space station has become so dangerous that it should be stopped (see P Spotts 3). As is well known, the Mir has suffered numerous problems with oxygen generators, computers, and so forth. These problems were serious even before a June 1997 event in which a cargo resupply ship crashed into the station, causing severe damage and forcing one entire part of the spacecraft to be abandoned. Given this situation, many experts say that the Russians should close Mir down and the United States should refuse to send any more astronauts to Mir.

On the other hand, since the United States agreement for the use of Mir is up in mid-1998, the issue would appear to be moot (see P Spotts 3). And numerous experts argue that U.S. participation in Mir, even with all of the problems, has been quite valuable. In fact, there is a strong position that the problems have added to the value of the Mir as a scientific platform. The cosmonauts and astronauts on Mir have been forced to cope with a variety of practical problems, including sudden loss of power, puncture of a portion of the craft, and so forth. These situations have provided valuable experience in dealing with crises in space. In addition, the recent history of the Mir has demonstrated the capacity of humans to cope with problems in space, surely a very valuable discovery as we begin the process of building the International Space Station (see P Karash A19).

In relation to the International Space Station, the Russians are responsible for the first module and also for providing freight and personnel carrying rockets (P "Mir's Honorable" 20). The space station project has been delayed because of the inability of Russia to produce its portion of the project on time (see P Sawyer). And there are reasons to believe that these delays may continue. The Russian space program faces a major funding shortfall (P Cooper "Space Program's" 378). That problem is so bad that NASA has agreed to "advance" the Russian program $20 million for two visits to Mir (P Nesmith D2).

Some argue that because Russia has fallen almost a year behind in building the first module for the station, the United States should no longer work with them (see Representative Roemer in CR "Civilian Space Authorization" H1844).

Moving away from cooperation with the Russians in space also might free up money for the U.S. space program. Representative Roemer estimates that the United States has paid the Russians almost $1 billion that could have been spent on "good projects in NASA" (in CR "Civilian Space Authorization" H1844).

While there obviously have been problems in U.S.-Russian cooperation in space, it probably does not make sense to end the relationship. NASA Administrator Daniel S. Goldin estimates that including the Russians in the development of the space station will result in savings of $2 billion and eighteen months of construction time (P 377). In addition, he argues that the United States "would gain enormously from the Russians' expertise and it would give us critical redundancy in the functions of life support, attitude control, extra-vehicular activity and launch support" (P 377).

In addition, pulling out on the Russians at this point would result in increased costs that in turn could destroy the space station project altogether (Representative Sensenbrenner in CR "Civilian Space Authorization" H1844).

In sum, despite all of the problems, maintaining U.S.-Russian cooperation in the development of the International Space Station is probably a sensible policy choice.

Conclusion

In this chapter, I have discussed the primary defense issues involved in relations between the United States and Russia. Of these issues, the most important relate to strategic nuclear weapons, especially the dangers posed by LOW and "loose nukes."

5 Strategic Dimensions in Debating About U.S. Foreign Policy Toward Russia

The focus of this chapter is on the strategic dimensions involved in debating about U.S. foreign policy toward Russia. In the first section, I discuss general affirmative strategy. I then move to negative strategy and conclude with outlines of sample arguments. In relation to the strategic concerns relative to U.S. foreign policy and Russia, it is important to understand that the arguments on this topic are tied to the specifics of the subject area to a greater degree than on many debate resolutions. Therefore, my focus has been on topic-specific positions, as opposed to broader generic arguments that are not tied to the subject area of the resolution.

Affirmative Strategy

There are two primary factors that constrain the affirmative from a strategic point of view: the specific topic wording and the relative weakness of sanctions and aid programs for influencing Russian policy.

The topic wording focuses debate on actions that directly alter U.S. foreign policy in relation to Russia. In the first chapter, I explained in detail why broader interpretations of the policies that are "toward" Russia are difficult to defend. Therefore, it is in the interest of the affirmative to pick a case area that falls clearly within the resolution. There are a number of strong proposals for changing U.S. policy. Why pick a case where you also have to contend with topicality arguments?

The second constraint on affirmative strategy is that neither sanctions nor aid works very well in influencing Russian actions. In addition, current U.S. policy is to rely on a mixture of aid programs and negotiations in which sanctions are an implicit threat at all times. Why is this important? The problem is that in relation to most of the issues involving U.S. relations with Russia, the only possible solutions are for the United States to expand aid or apply sanctions. But it is difficult to argue that such a policy will be effective. And in many cases, use of sanctions or aid actually represents the policy of the present system. It is not at all clear, for instance, that expanding aid would constitute a substantial change in our foreign policy.

The foregoing suggests that the affirmative would be wise to pick a proposal on which direct U.S. action can be used to implement the program or to pick a proposal where the potential harms are so large that weaknesses in solvency are not a fatal problem. In relation to direct action, a strong case can be made that the United States should back away from further NATO expansion and instead work to include Russia in the alliance. In relation to nuclear weapons, there is very strong support for backing away from ABM research and also taking unilateral steps aimed at convincing the Russians to move away from launch-on-warning. These proposals clearly would represent a substantial alteration in U.S. policy and do not require reliance on aid or sanctions.

The other alternative would be to focus on an area where the problem is so large that doubts about solvency become less important. The obvious policy area where a major expansion in U.S. aid might be useful relates to "loose nukes." Given the host of problems facing the Russians in regard to the command and control of nuclear weapons, security at nuclear sites, and so on, it certainly would be prudent for the United States to invest significantly more resources in a program to control these problems. Put differently, the magnitude of the risks associated with "loose nukes" means that it will be very difficult for the negative to outweigh the potential affirmative advantage. And since the "loose nukes" problem is inherently international, expansion of an aid program in the area is not subject to the argument that the United States is paying for a purely Russian domestic problem.

I am particularly skeptical about proposals that rely on the imposition of sanctions. Sanctions do not have a good track record of effectiveness. And applying sanctions to Russia, when there are so many crucial areas where the United States needs cooperation from the Russian government, seems foolish. Yes, there are circumstances where sanctions are justified, but even in those cases it generally makes more sense to let the Secretary of State privately threaten action in order to move forward the negotiation process.

Negative Strategy

The negative faces two significant general problems in debating about U.S. foreign policy toward Russia. On many of the case areas within the resolution, there are very significant problems that are difficult to deny. Launch-on-warning illustrates this point. There is no question that the world came uncomfortably close to a disaster with the launch of the Norwegian science rocket. A similar point can be made about "loose nukes," biological weapons, and other issues. There are problems out there.

Second, unlike most resolutions, the negative has few options for defending a policy other than the present system. The word "change" in the resolution means that any alteration in policy fulfills the resolution. Unless one accepts the legitimacy of topical counterplans, this rules out nearly all negative ground in relation to counterplans.

How should the negative respond to these problems? It is essential that the negative have developed positions in the following areas.

Topicality

The negative needs to be well prepared to argue for a narrow definition of the phrase "foreign policy toward Russia." In the first chapter, I cited the contextual and theoretical reasons for preferring such a definition. In addition, the negative should develop the argument that proposals to expand aid are not a "substantial change" in current policy, but rather reflect merely adding marginal economic resources to the current program.

Solvency

Since on many cases it will be difficult for the negative to win that there is no harm to be solved, the negative clearly needs to focus on developing strong positions that U.S. foreign policy cannot influence Russian actions or solve problems in Russia. The most important solvency arguments relate to the effectiveness of aid and sanctions in dealing with Russia. The negative should develop these arguments in depth. In particular, it would be wise to argue that expanded aid or tightened sanctions would be counterproductive. Taking this tact makes the solvency argument into a net disadvantage.

Additionally, the negative might argue that the United States lacks influence in Russia. Any number of commentators have noted a decline in U.S. influence over Russia (see P Hoagland C9). One possibility is that the United States used up a great portion of our influence in the deal on NATO expansion. Richard Pipes agrees with this judgment. He concludes that "the West can influence the decision only marginally" (P 77).

Another possible solvency argument relates to infrastructure. A number of experts argue that economic development in Russia will be slow until the necessary infrastructure is developed. Infrastructure, in this case, refers to more than merely an adequate stock of energy and transportation. The communist government of the Soviet Union controlled all aspects of the economy. As a consequence, Russia lacks many of the institutions found in market economies. For example, since the banking system was run by the state, Russia lacks a developed system to make commercial loans. Moreover, the Soviet system was incompatible with the work ethic. Hard work did not necessarily pay off in the Soviet Union. This created cultural barriers to economic development.

Another barrier to political and economic development might be labelled the lack of moral infrastructure. Some experts on Russia point to the terrible effects of the Soviet era on Russian society and essentially argue that Russian civil society lacks a commitment to core moral values (see P McMillan and Massie A29). Without these core values, it is argued, both economic and political development will be problematic. The lack of values also exacerbates problems with corruption and overly bureaucratic decision making.

Another related solvency position is the argument that money isn't enough to deal with the problems facing Russia. In this regard, Joseph Anselmo quoted an official in the Energy Department concerning U.S. aid to assist the Russians in securing and disposing of nuclear weapons: "There's no amount of money we could ever make available that could [by itself] solve this problem" (P 47).

Another solvency argument applies to proposals to improve the Russian economy. Some argue that the major problems in the Russian economy mean that the normal economic principles do not apply. A Russian specialist in defense economics, Vitaly V. Shlykov, recently argued that "the technological and structural imbalances between the ex-Soviet military and civilian sectors had severely limited the usefulness of the monetary, budget and credit tools that are considered instrumental in managing Western economies" (in P Mann "Economic Morass" 70). If Shlykov is right, then there is relatively little that Western nations can do to assist economic reform in Russia. The problem is that Western reform efforts of necessity must use the specific tools that Shlykov argues don't work.

Another important solvency argument is that the central government in Russia lacks the authority to control public policy. Sherman Garnett explains:

> The emerging pattern in nuclear technology transfers, arms sales, and military intervention on the periphery is one of initiatives by individual ministers or coalitions of local, ministerial, and industrial representatives, all without benefit of advance coordination. The Kremlin may decide to take advantage of these initiatives, ignore them or provide them with ex post facto strategic justification, but it has lost the ability to set the strategic agenda. (P 65)

He goes on: "Confusion at the center, coupled with the proliferation of decision-makers has made it difficult for both Russians and outside analysts to state precisely what Russian policy is" (P 65).

Stephen Blank notes that this problem exists even in the area of arms sales. He explains that the "Russian government has lost control over its arms sales program" (P 71). Another example concerns the war in Chechnya, where, astoundingly, "the Ministry of Defense was not told about the planned invasion" (P Blank 72). All of these examples suggest that making agreements with Yeltsin or some other Russian leader may mean relatively little, since the Russian leadership cannot control their own government.

Disadvantages

Given the magnitude of potential affirmative advantages, it is essential that the negative have well-developed disadvantages that they are prepared to defend throughout the debate. As I have noted in past years, I think it is strategic for the negative to defend disadvantages in precisely the same way that the affirmative defends their proposal. This means that the strongest disadvantage or two should be presented in the first negative constructive along with case arguments as the basic negative position. The negative then should extend the disadvantage in the negative block. Taking this approach gives the negative the time to develop compelling disadvantage arguments in depth and has the added benefit of making the basic negative position clear from the beginning.

Clearly, the counterproductivity arguments that I discussed in relation to sanctions and expanded aid programs should be at the core of the negative's arsenal of disadvantages. At this point, I want to sketch other possible disadvantages.

Budget Tradeoff   One of the most important disadvantages relates to the budgetary implications of expanded assistance for Russia. The basic argument is that increasing support for Russia will lead to cutbacks in other crucial programs. Those cutbacks could occur in other aid to Russia, or potentially a massive cutback in all foreign assistance. Alternatively, the negative could argue that expanded funding for Russia could undercut the budget agreement and result in a new budget crisis. Given the projected $50-plus-billion surplus, this final argument may not be sensible.

In relation to the chance of a budget tradeoff, Sherle Schwenninger argues that NATO expansion could produce that result. She claims that "Western assistance programs may also be affected, since resources going into military modernization will not be available to countries that still need Western help" (P 29). The conclusion that expanded support for one program could result in cutbacks elsewhere applies more broadly than merely to NATO expansion. Former U.S. Ambassador to Russia Jack Matlock puts it succinctly: "Economic and technical assistance programs will be sharply reduced in budget squeezes" (P 50).

It also should be recognized that there is very little support for expanded foreign aid in the United States and much strong opposition to any such proposal. As a result, NATO expansion "further reduces the chances for real assistance for the Eastern European countries still struggling with painful structural adjustments" (P 29).

There are two key issues relating to the foreign assistance tradeoff argument. First, under current budget law, an expansion in one area of the budget must be offset by a cutback within that same area. Of course, the budget system could be changed. But absent that change, expanded foreign assistance to Russia will be offset by cutbacks in other foreign assistance programs, either to Russia or elsewhere.

Second, there is a strong congressional attitude supporting this tradeoff position. Foreign assistance is among the least popular programs supported by Congress. Aid to Russia is easily attacked. For example, in recent Congressional debate, Representative Traficant attacked a program which provided aid for housing to Russian soldiers. To the Congressman, the program seemed positively absurd, especially since "American families are being uprooted with military base closings" (CR "Providing Housing For Russian Soldiers" H3172). A closer look reveals that the program is quite sensible. If Russian soldiers lack places to live, that obviously increases the risk of an angry backlash. A little U.S. support for Russian housing may be a very good investment. However, the anger of the Congressman's response is indicative of a general (although not as strong) attitude among many in Congress.

Other evidence supports this conclusion. Schwenninger notes: "The mere mention of coordinated economic assistance—a true Marshall Plan—prompts pained looks on the faces of Clinton administration officials wary of any new foreign assistance commitments" (P 29). And Francesco Calogero, chairman of the Pugwash Council, notes that it would be difficult to get financial support for programs that everyone agrees would be valuable. Writing of a plan to speed up the payment of $12 billion to Russia to remove highly enriched uranium to the United States in order to keep that uranium out of the hands of terrorists, he said

> There is no way, goes the argument, that the administration could come up quickly with $12 billion for Russia, for any purpose. Congress would never allow it. (P 21)

He is undoubtedly right.

The negative attitude toward foreign assistance means that any program that substantially increases aid to Russia likely would result in the kind of tradeoff mentioned earlier.

One other point is relevant here. While a substantial expansion of foreign assistance is not politically feasible in the present system, that does not mean that it is illegitimate to advocate such expansion. One of the great values of academic debate is that it focuses on what "should" be done as opposed to what will be done. In the 1950s, civil rights programs seemed utopian and unlikely to be implemented, but that did not mean that they were not right.

On the other hand, the political situation does act as a constraint on action. In the present situation, a major increase in foreign assistance likely would lead to one of the following results. One option is that there would be Congressional backlash and the expanded foreign assistance would be curtailed. Another possibility is the one mentioned earlier: expanded assistance in one area might lead to cutbacks in other areas. Finally, expanded foreign assistance could lead to a massive political response, such as a curtailment of all foreign assistance. In a debate about NATO enlargement, Representative Frank noted that "The American people will more willingly support international engagement, militarily, economically, and other sorts, if they feel they are being treated fairly, if they do not think it is coming at their expense" (CR "European Security Act of 1997" H3716). He went on to say that the United States "is prepared to support foreign assistance to people in need, to deal with disease and poverty and economic development" (CR "European Security Act of 1997" H3716). The implied point was that we were not willing to support foreign assistance if it did not fulfill such crucial goals or if it seemed to unfairly burden us as a nation. Thus, a major expansion of foreign assistance for some specific program, like Russian pollution control, is likely to produce a backlash against all U.S. foreign assistance. Members of Congress will ask why we should subsidize their government when there are Americans in need. All of this means that a substantial expansion in foreign assistance arguably would be counterproductive because it could undercut crucial foreign assistance programs to Russia and other nations.

Increase/Decrease Defense Spending   An alternative spending issue relates to the linkage between public threat perception and defense spending. Recently, Representative Weldon of Pennsylvania observed that defense spending is tied to how the general public perceives the world environment. He noted that

> the funding level for what our military needs are is largely determined by the threat that is perceived by the American people and by Members of Congress. So if the American people perceive that there is no threat, then in fact they want us to cut defense spending. If they in fact think there is an emerging threat, then they respond and say increase defense spending. (CR "National Defense" 20 June 1997 H4110)

This means that the American people's perception of Russia may have a major effect on the amount of defense spending that they will support.

There are two ways that a substantial change in U.S. foreign policy could influence public perception in relation to defense. First, by raising issues relating to U.S. security, the advocates of change might increase the public's perception that the United States was threatened. If that were to happen, the result would be increased defense spending, which might trade off against domestic spending or even impact the budget deal. The trouble with this argument is that Congress is always discussing this threat or that threat, without producing much effect on public attitudes.

The second alternative may be more plausible. The effect of the policy change in relation to Russia would be to raise an issue in terms of public concern and then resolve that issue. Thus, after the policy change, the public would feel less threatened and, consequently, support a lower level of defense spending. It then could be argued that this lower level of defense spending would be insufficient to protect U.S. security. The most obvious type of program that might be cut would be some sort of missile defense system. The argument would be that the primary factor motivating public support for missile defense is fear of Russia. The elimination of that fear might lead to destruction of the program. It then would be argued that theater missile defense programs are crucial for protecting U.S. troops and in the future could evolve into a strategic defense program that the United States could use to defend against nuclear attack from China or from rogue states like Iran, if they were to procure nuclear weapons.

Destabilize Russia   Another potential disadvantage argues that a change in U.S. policy could result in destabilizing Russia. In the present situation, there is a risk that any major policy change could have unforeseen effects which could lead to the destabilization of Russia. Recently, Lila Shevstova and Scott Bruckner of the Carnegie Moscow Center, noted that "it would appear that Russia is barely in balance and that any move to restore equilibrium might risk sending the economy into a nosedive, provoking a devastating social outburst, or causing the Federation to collapse" (P 36). Thus, a strong argument can be made for maintaining present policy as it is.

Backlash   There is a good argument that the United States should not alter its present policy because of the danger that any new policy initiative might seem to Russian elites to be telling them how to run their country. Such an action could produce major backlash. Richard Pipes, one of the foremost experts on Russia, emphasizes the importance of using U.S. influence only on issues that are truly crucial. He writes:

> Western leaders should consider ways of avoiding actions that, without any real bearing on their countries' security, humiliate Russians by making them keenly aware how impotent they have become under democracy. (P 78)

Pipes even includes NATO expansion within this category. This same point applies to assistance programs as well. Pipes notes that "Assistance of any kind, no matter how well-meaning, must take into account Russian people's suspicions of the motives behind it, irrational as they may be" (P 78).

Nunn-Lugar Cutoff   The final disadvantage may be the most important. A strong argument can be made that the single most important United States policy action toward Russia in the post-cold-war era was passage of the Nunn-Lugar act. As I noted earlier, this act already has funded programs to destroy many Russian nuclear weapons. And much remains to be done with money that already has been appropriated.

A good case can be made that any action which threatens Nunn-Lugar cannot be justified. Representative Thornberry notes that the Nunn-Lugar money

> is being used to tighten security on nuclear warheads which could be used against us. It tightens security on nuclear materials which could be sent to other countries, which also could be used against us. It is used to help make sure the expertise on how to build these nuclear weapons is not spread through the world and could be used against us. (CR "National Defense Authorization" 23 June 1997 H4200)

Nunn-Lugar is arguably the most important example of successful bipartisan action on foreign policy in the last two decades.

From this perspective, it is of overwhelming importance to maintain the Nunn-Lugar program in order to improve the security of the Russian nuclear system. Lugar himself argues (quite modestly) that the program is "one of the two most critical programs the U.S. Government conducts for ensuring the strategic national security of this country" (CR "National Defense Authorization" 7 July 1997 S6879). And Senator Bingaman argues that of "the entire U.S. defense budget," the Lugar-Nunn program is one of the places where the nation is "getting the most national security return for the dollars spent" (CR "National Defense Authorization" 7 July 1997 S6882). Therefore, we should take no action that even potentially could harm the Nunn-Lugar effort.

There are two ways that a substantial change in U.S. foreign policy toward Russia could impact Nunn-Lugar. Obviously, expanded assistance to Russia could result in a fund tradeoff in which Nunn-Lugar would be cut. Alternatively, the policy action could offend the Russians and cause them to pull out of the

Nunn-Lugar program, as they apparently have in regard to previous agreements concerning biological weapons.

Conclusion

The topic—Resolved that the United States should substantially change its foreign policy toward Russia—poses somewhat different problems for the affirmative and negative. For the affirmative, the primary problem is to find a problem where U.S. action can make a clear difference. Given the difficulties associated with sanctions and foreign assistance, a focus on policy proposals where the United States can act directly may be sensible. For the negative, the primary problem is that there are any number of aspects of U.S. policy toward Russia where there are enormous problems. This forces the negative to put their primary emphasis on developing appropriate solvency arguments, especially those that claim the affirmative action would be counterproductive, and disadvantages.

Outline of Selected Affirmative and Negative Arguments

Affirmative Case Outlines

ECONOMIC AND POLITICAL REFORM

I. Economic Reform

    A. The Russian Economy Has Suffered a Near Depression

    B. Lack of Developed Market Institutions Prevents Economic Growth

    C. Targeted Economic Assistance Will Improve Russian Economic Performance

II. Political Reform

    A. Instability Threatens the Russian Political System

        1. Instability could lead to a military coup

        2. Instability could lead to a nationalist backlash

    B. Russian Political Institutions Are Weak

    C. Targeted U.S. Aid Could Strengthen Russian Institutions and Protect Democracy

SOCIAL ISSUES

Pollution

I. Russia Faces a Pollution Crisis

    A. Air Pollution Threatens Russian Health

    B. Water Pollution Spreads Disease

II.   Russian Environmental Control Is Inadequate

    A. Russia Lacks the Resources for Environmental Control

    B. Russia Lacks the Technology for Environmental Control

III.   U.S. Assistance Cuts Pollution in Russia by Providing Resources and Technology

Health

I.   Russia Faces a Health Crisis

II.   The Russian Health Care System is at the Breaking Point

III.   Targeted U.S. Assistance Solves the Health Crisis in Russia

DEFENSE POLICY

Launch-on-Warning

I.   Russia Relies on a Launch-On-Warning Policy

II.   Launch-on-Warning Risks Nuclear War

    A. Launch-on-Warning Increases the Risk of Accidental War

    B.   Launch-on-Warning Increases the Risk of Crisis Miscalculation

III.   U.S. Action Solves the Launch-on-Warning Crisis

    A. Unilateral U.S. Action Will Lead to Reciprocal Russian Action

    B. Unilateral U.S. Action Does Not Threaten U.S. Security

Nuclear Weapons

I.   The United States is Committed to Building an ABM System

II.   U.S. Development of an ABM System is Disastrous

    A. U.S. Development of an ABM System Destroys the ABM Treaty

    B. The ABM Treaty Has Played a Critical Role in Strategic Arms Talks

    C. Loss of the ABM Treaty Equals Breakdown in Arms Control Negotiations

    D. Arms Control Agreements Are Essential to World Peace

III.   Banning the ABM System Protects Arms Control

Loose Nukes

I.   Russia Faces a Loose Nukes Problem

    A. Russian Command and Control Systems Are Breaking Down

    B. Russian Nuclear Scientists Threaten World Peace

        1. Scientists are often not paid

        2. Scientists could be hired by rogue states to build nuclear weapons

    C. Russian Nuclear Weapons Are Inadequately Protected

        1. Terrorists could steal a Russian weapon

        2. Organized crime could procure a weapon and sell it to the highest bidder

II.   Inadequate Resources Prevent Russia from Guaranteeing the Security of Nuclear Forces

III.   Expanded Aid Solves Loose Nukes

    A. Aid Programs Can Fix Command and Control Defects

    B. Science Programs Can Hire Russian Scientists

    C. Aid Programs Can Improve Nuclear Security

NATO

I.   Current U.S. Policy Is To Further Expand NATO

II.   Further Expansion of NATO Would Be Catastrophic

    A. Russia Strongly Opposes Further Expansion

    B. Further Expansion Would Cause a Nationalist Reaction in Russia Leading to Rearmament

    C. Russia Would Not Permit Ukraine to Join Nato

III. Alliance with Russia

    A. The United States Should Publicly Reject Further NATO Expansion

    B. The United States Should Initiate a Program of Moving Gradually Toward Accepting Russia as a Member of NATO

Biological and Chemical Weapons

I.   Russian Chemical and Biological Weapons Threaten the World

    A. Russia Has Large Stockpiles of Chemical Weapons

    B. Russia Has Large Stockpiles of Biological Weapons

    C. There Is Substantial Risk that Terrorists Could Steal Chemical or Biological Weapons

II. Russia Will Not Eliminate Chemical or Biological Weapons

    A. Russian Policy Is to Maintain Current Stocks of Chemical Weapons and Develop More

    B. Russia Has Violated Agreements and Continues a Biological Weapons Program

III. Sanctions and Aid Equal the Elimination of Russia's Chemical and Biological Weapons Programs

    A. Tough Sanctions Will Force Russian Concessions

    B. Expanded U.S. Assistance Would Pay for Destruction of Chemical and Biological Weapons Facilities

Negative Arguments

Sanctions Fail

    A. Sanctions Historically Have Failed

    B. Sanctions Will Be Circumvented

    C. Sanctions Will Lead to Backlash

    D. Sanctions Undercut Presidential Diplomacy

Aid Fails

    A. Aid Does Not Reach the People Who Need It

    B. Aid Creates Dependency

    C. Aid Historically Has Failed

    D. Targeted Aid Programs Will Not Work

    E. Aid Programs Produce Backlash

Budget Tradeoff

    A. The Affirmative Dramatically Increases Aid to Russia

    B. A Budget Tradeoff Will Result

        1. Present law requires that increased spending be offset with budget cutbacks

        2. Congressional attitudes will produce major cuts

    C. Nunn-Lugar Will Be Cut

    D. Nunn-Lugar Is a Key to Preventing Nuclear War

Defense Tradeoff

    A. The Affirmative Solves a Russian Military Threat

B. Perceived Threat Reduction Leads to Decreased Defense
    Spending

C. Decreased Defense Spending Will Result in the Abandonment of
    Missile Defense Programs

D. Missile Defense is Essential to U.S. Security

    1. Missile defense protects the United States against accidental
        launch

    2. Missile defense protects the United States against rogue states

Destabilize Russia

A. Russia Faces Grave Problems of Instability

    1. Russia is currently stable

    2. Future instability is possible

B. Policy Change Equals Russian Instability

C. Russian Instability Risks World War

    1. Instability produces loss of control of Russian nuclear
        arsenal

    2. Loose nukes are the greatest threat to world peace

Bibliography

Books and Book Chapters

Aldrin, Andrew J. "Defense Enterprise Adaptation in St. Petersburg." *Commercializing High Technology: East and West.* Ed. Judith B. Sedaitis. Lanham: Rowman & Littlefield Publishers, Inc., 1997. 205–238.

Alic, John A. "Science, Technology, and Economic Competitiveness." *Commercializing High Technology: East and West.* Ed. Judith B. Sedaitis. Lanham: Rowman & Littlefield Publishers, Inc., 1997. 3–18.

Aslund, Anders. "The Gradual Nature of Economic Change in Russia." *Changing The Economic System in Russia.* Eds. Anders Aslund and Richard Layard. New York: St Martin's Press, 1993. 19–38.

―――. "Introduction." *Russian Economic Reform at Risk.* Ed. Anders Aslund. London: Pinter, 1995. 1–8.

―――. "The Politics of Economic Reform: Remaining Tasks." *Russian Economic Reform at Risk.* Ed. Anders Aslund. London: Pinter, 1995. 187–206.

―――. *How Russia Became a Market Economy.* Washington: Brookings Institution, 1995.

Aslund, Anders, ed. *Russian Economic Reform at Risk.* London: Pinter, 1995.

Aslund, Anders, and Richad Layard, eds. *Changing The Economic System in Russia.* New York: St Martin's Press, 1993.

Atkeson, Edward B. "Theatre Forces in the Commonwealth of Independent States." *The Limited Partnership: Building a Russian–US Security Community.* Eds. James E. Goodby and Benoit Morel. Oxford: Oxford University Press, 1993. 113–149.

―――. "US theatre forces in the year 2000." *The Limited Partnership: Building a Russian–US Security Community.* Eds. James E. Goodby and Benoit Morel. Oxford: Oxford University Press, 1993. 150–168.

Balzer, Harley. "Dismantling Russia's Technotopia: Six Ministries in Search of an Industrial Policy." *Commercializing High Technology: East and West.* Ed. Judith B. Sedaitis. Lanham: Rowman & Littlefield Publishers, Inc., 1997. 51–74.

Bezrukov, Mikhail E. "The creation of a Russian foreign policy." *The Limited Partnership: Building a Russian–US Security Community.* Eds. James E. Goodby and Benoit Morel. Oxford: Oxford University Press, 1993. 81–93.

Blanchard, Olivier, et al. *Post-Communist Reform: Pain and Progress.* Cambridge, MA: The MIT Press, 1993.

Blasi, Joseph R., Maya Kroumova, and Douglas Kruse. *Kremlin Capitalism: Privatizing the Russian Economy.* Ithaca: Cornell University Press, 1997.

Boone, Peter. "Russia's Balance of Payments Prospects." *Changing the Economic System in Russia.* Eds. Anders Aslund and Richard Layard. New York: St Martin's Press, 1993. 210–229.

Boycko, Maxim and Andrei Shleifer. "The Voucher Programme for Russia." *Changing The Economic System in Russia.* Eds. Anders Aslund and Richard Layard. New York: St Martin's Press, 1993. 100–117.

—-. "Russian Restructuring and Social Benefits." *Russian Economic Reform at Risk.* Ed. Anders Aslund. London: Pinter, 1995. 99–118.

Boycko, Maxim, Andrei Shleifer, and Robert Vishny. *Privatizing Russia.* Cambridge: MIT Press, 1995.

Chelishchev, Nikolay F. "New Prospects for Mutually Beneficial Cooperation in Geology and Mining." *The New Chapter in United States–Russian Relations.* Eds. Sharyl Cross and Marina A. Oborotova. Westport: Praeger, 1994. 103–112.

Chubais, Anatoly B. and Maria Vishnevskaya. "Main Issues of Privatisation in Russia." *Changing The Economic System in Russia.* Eds. Anders Aslund and Richard Layard. New York: St Martin's Press, 1993. 89–99.

———. "Russian Privatisation in Mid-1994." *Russian Economic Reform at Risk.* Ed. Anders Aslund. London: Pinter, 1995. 89–98.

Coakley, Lori A., and Linda M. Randall. "Defense Conversion in the Former Soviet Union: The Influence of Culture on the Strategic Planning Process." *Commercializing High Technology: East and West.* Ed. Judith B. Sedaitis. Lanham: Rowman & Littlefield Publishers, Inc., 1997. 167–180.

Cohen, Linda R., and Roger G. Noll. "Research and Development after the Cold War." *Commercializing High Technology: East and West.* Ed. Judith B. Sedaitis. Lanham: Rowman & Littlefield Publishers, Inc., 1997. 19–36.

Connor, Walter D. *Tattered Banners: Labor, Conflict, and Corporatism in Postcommunist Russia.* Boulder: Westview Press, 1996.

Cross, Sharyl and Marina A. Oborotova: "The New Chapter: Opportunities and Challenges." *The New Chapter in United States–Russian Relations.* Eds. Sharyl Cross and Marina A. Oborotova. Westport: Praeger, 1994. 1–18.

Cross, Sharyl, and Marina A. Oborotova, eds. *The New Chapter in United States–Russian Relations.* Westport: Praeger, 1994.

Dabrowski, Marek. "The First Half Year of Russian Transformation." *Changing the Economic System in Russia.* Eds. Anders Aslund and Richard Layard. New York: St Martin's Press, 1993. 1–18.

Delpla, Jacques, and Charles Wyplosz. "Russia's Transition: Muddling Through." *Russian Economic Reform at Risk.* Ed. Anders Aslund. London: Pinter, 1995. 19–52.

Dyker, David, and Michael Barrow. "Monopoloy and Competition Policy in Russia." *Challenges for Russian Economic Reform.* Ed. Alan Smith. Washington: The Brookings Institution, 1995. 79–116.

Ellam, Michael, and Richard Layard. "Prices, Incomes and Hardship." *Changing The Economic System in Russia.* Eds. Anders Aslund and Richard Layard. New York: St Martin's Press, 1993. 39–61.

Ellerman, David. "Spin-offs as a Restructuring Strategy for Post-Socialist Enterprises." *Commercializing High Technology: East and West.* Ed. Judith B. Sedaitis. Lanham: Rowman & Littlefield Publishers, Inc., 1997. 271–282.

Fane, Daria. "Moscow's nationalities problem: the collapse of empire and the challenges ahead." *The Limited Partnership: Building a Russian–US Security Community.* Eds. James E. Goodby and Benoit Morel. Oxford: Oxford University Press, 1993. 55–74.

Fedorov, Boris G. "Macroeconomic Policy and Stabilisation in Russia." *Russian Economic Reform at Risk.* Ed. Anders Aslund. London: Pinter, 1995. 9–18.

— — —. "Privatisation with Foreign Participation." *Changing The Economic System in Russia.* Eds. Anders Aslund and Richard Layard. New York: St Martin's Press, 1993. 112–124.

Gaddy, Clifford G. *The Price of the Past: Russia's Struggle with the Legacy of a Militarized Economy.* Washington: Brookings Institution Press, 1996.

Gardner, Hall: *Surviving the Millenium: American Global Strategy, the Collapse of the Soviet Empire, and the Question of Peace.* Westport: Praeger, 1994.

Gleason, Gregory. "Dynamics of National Independence in Central Asia: Implications for Russian–American Cooperation." *The New Chapter in United States–Russian Relations.* Eds. Sharyl Cross and Marina A. Oborotova. Westport: Praeger, 1994. 193–210.

Gomes, Stephen L. "The Role of Third-Party Facilitators in Public-Private R&D Collaborations in the United States." *Commercializing High Technology: East and West.* Ed. Judith B. Sedaitis. Lanham: Rowman & Littlefield Publishers, Inc., 1997. 239–252.

Goodby, James E., and Benoit Morel, eds. *The Limited Partnership: Building a Russian–US Security Community.* Oxford: Oxford University Press, 1993.

Goodby, James E. "Introduction." *The Limited Partnership: Building a Russian–US Security Community.* Eds. James E. Goodby and Benoit Morel. Oxford: Oxford University Press, 1993. 3–8.

Granville, Brigitte. "Farewell, Ruble Zone." *Russian Economic Reform at Risk.* Ed. Anders Aslund. London: Pinter, 1995. 65–88.

Hagedoorn, John, and Bert Sadowski. "General Trends in International Technology Partnering: The Prospects for European Economies in Transition." *Commercializing High Technology: East and West.* Ed. Judith B. Sedaitis. Lanham: Rowman & Littlefield Publishers, Inc., 1997. 253–267.

Hanson, Philip. "Regions, Local Power and Economic Change in Russia." *Challenges for Russian Economic Reform.* Ed. Alan Smith. Washington: The Brookings Institution, 1995. 21–78.

Hansson, Ardo H. "The Trouble with the Ruble: Monetary Reform in the Former Soviet Union." *Changing The Economic System in Russia.* Eds. Anders Aslund and Richard Layard. New York: St Martin's Press, 1993. 163–182.

Hill, Malcolm R. *Environment and Technology in the Former Soviet Union: The Case of Acid Rain and Power Generation.* Cheltenham, UK: Edward Elgar, 1997.

Ikle, Fred Charles. "The case for a Russian–US security community." *The Limited Partnership: Building a Russian–US Security Community.* Eds. James E. Goodby and Benoit Morel. Oxford: Oxford University Press, 1993. 9–22.

Jancar-Webster, Barbara. "New Directions in U.S. Environmental Relations with Russia." *The New Chapter in United States–Russian Relations.* Eds. Sharyl Cross and Marina A. Oborotova. Westport: Praeger, 1994. 113–136.

Johnson, Simon, Heidi Kroll, and Mark Horton. "New Banks in the Former Soviet Union: How Do They Operate." *Changing The Economic System in Russia.* Eds. Anders Aslund and Richard Layard. New York: St Martin's Press, 1993. 183–209.

Kaiser, David. "Issues and images: Washington and Moscow in great power politics." *The Limited Partnership: Building a Russian–US Security Community.* Eds. James E. Goodby and Benoit Morel. Oxford: Oxford University Press, 1993. 94–112.

Kaser, Michael. "Privatization in the CIS." *Challenges for Russian Economic Reform.* Ed. Alan Smith. Washington: The Brookings Institution, 1995. 117–202.

Kolosovsky, Andrei, and Vadim Udalov. "The New Agenda for U.S.–Russian Relations: Economic Partnership." *The New Chapter in United States–Russian Relations.* Eds. Sharyl Cross and Marina A. Oborotova. Westport: Praeger, 1994. 87–102.

Kull, Steven. "Co-operation or competition: the battle of ideas in Russia and the USA." *The Limited Partnership: Building a Russian–US Security Community.* Eds. James E. Goodby and Benoit Morel. Oxford: Oxford University Press, 1993. 209–223.

Kuznetsov, Yevgeny. "Learning to Learn: Emerging Patterns of Enterprise Behavior in the Russian Defense Sector, 1992–1995." *Commercializing High Technology: East and West.* Ed. Judith B. Sedaitis. Lanham: Rowman & Littlefield Publishers, Inc., 1997. 181–204.

Lachow, Irving. "The metastable peace: a catastrophe theory model of US–Russian relations." *The Limited Partnership: Building a Russian–US Security Community.* Eds. James E. Goodby and Benoit Morel. Oxford: Oxford University Press, 1993. 185–206.

Layard, Richard, and Andrea Richter. "Labour Market Adjustment—the Russian Way." *Russian Economic Reform at Risk.* Ed. Anders Aslund. London: Pinter, 1995. 119–148.

Leitzel, Jim. *Russian Economic Reform.* London: Routledge, 1995.

Linden, Carl, and Jan S. Prybyla. *Russia and China: On the Eve of a New Millenium.* New Brunswick: Transaction, 1997.

Miller, Steven E. "Russian–US security co-operation on the high seas." *The Limited Partnership: Building a Russian–US Security Community.* Eds. James E. Goodby and Benoit Morel. Oxford: Oxford University Press, 1993. 249–271.

Morel, Benoit. "High technology after the cold war." *The Limited Partnership: Building a Russian–US Security Community.* Eds. James E. Goodby and Benoit Morel. Oxford: Oxford University Press, 1993. 169–184.

Mozhin, Alexei. "Russia's Negotiations with the IMF." *Changing the Economic System in Russia.* Eds. Anders Aslund and Richard Layard. New York: St Martin's Press, 1993. 65–71.

Neverov, Igor. "Bilateral Arms Reductions and the Search for Stability: A Negotiator's Perspective." *The New Chapter in United States–Russian Relations.* Eds. Sharyl Cross and Marina A. Oborotova. Westport: Praeger, 1994. 19–38.

Newmann, William W. "History accelerates: the diplomacy of co-operation and fragmentation." *The Limited Partnership: Building a Russian–US Security Community.* Eds. James E. Goodby and Benoit Morel. Oxford: Oxford University Press, 1993. 25–54.

———. "Some limits on co-operation and transparency: operational security and the use of force." *The Limited Partnership: Building a Russian–US Security Community.* Eds. James E. Goodby and Benoit Morel. Oxford: Oxford University Press, 1993. 289–305.

Newmann, William W., and Judyth L. Twigg. "Building a Eurasian–Atlantic security community: co-operative management of the military transition." *The Limited Partnership: Building a Russian–US Security Community.* Eds. James E. Goodby and Benoit Morel. Oxford: Oxford University Press, 1993. 224–248.

Palmieri, Deborah Anne. "American–Russian Economic Relations in the Post-Cold War Era." *The New Chapter in United States–Russian Relations.* Eds. Sharyl Cross and Marina A. Oborotova. Westport: Praeger, 1994. 71–86.

Potter, William C. "U.S.–Russian Cooperation for Nonproliferation." *The New Chapter in United States–Russian Relations.* Eds. Sharyl Cross and Marina A. Oborotova. Westport: Praeger, 1994. 39–56.

Remington, Robin Alison. "Balkan Triangle: Washington, Moscow, and Belgrade." *The New Chapter in United States–Russian Relations.* Eds. Sharyl Cross and Marina A. Oborotova. Westport: Praeger, 1994. 153–168.

Rogov, Sergey. "A national security policy for Russia." *The Limited Partnership: Building a Russian–US Security Community.* Eds. James E. Goodby and Benoit Morel. Oxford: Oxford University Press, 1993. 75–80.

Sachs, Jeffrey D. "Why Russia Has Failed to Sabilize." *Russian Economic Reform at Risk.* Ed. Anders Aslund. London: Pinter, 1995. 53–64.

Sachs, Jeffrey D., and David Lipton. "Remaining Steps to a Market–Based Monetary System." *Changing the Economic System in Russia.* Eds. Anders Aslund and Richard Layard. New York: St Martin's Press, 1993. 127–162.

Sapir, Jacques. "Defense Conversion and Restructuring in the Russian High-Technology Sector: Is There an Alternative to Uncontrolled Exports?" *Commercializing High Technology: East and West.* Ed. Judith B. Sedaitis. Lanham: Rowman & Littlefield Publishers, Inc., 1997. 119–144.

Schwartz, Larry W. "Financing the Commcercialization of Russian Defense Technologies: Venture Capital and Related Transactional Structures." *Commercializing High Technology: East and West.* Ed. Judith B. Sedaitis. Lanham: Rowman & Littlefield Publishers, Inc., 1997. 313–328.

Sedaitis, Judith B., ed. *Commercializing High Technology: East and West.* Lanham: Rowman & Littlefield Publishers, Inc., 1997.

Sedaitis, Judith B. "Commercializing State-Owned R&D: A Russia–United States Comparison." *Commercializing High Technology: East and West.* Ed. Judith B. Sedaitis. Lanham: Rowman & Littlefield Publishers, Inc., 1997. 145–163.

Shapiro, Judith. "The Russian Mortality Crisis and Its Causes." *Russian Economic Reform at Risk.* Ed. Anders Aslund. London: Pinter, 1995. 149–178.

Silliman, Emily, and Edward Kayukov. "New Company Formation in Russia: Legal Regulation." *Commercializing High Technology: East and West.* Ed. Judith B. Sedaitis. Lanham: Rowman & Littlefield Publishers, Inc., 1997. 329–353.

Smith, Alan. "Introduction: The Economic Challenge Facing Russia." *Challenges for Russian Economic Reform.* Ed. Alan Smith. Washington: The Brookings Institution, 1995. 1–19.

———. *Russia and the world economy: Problems of integration.* London: Routledge, 1993.

———. "Trade and Payments Between the Former Soviet Republics." *Challenges for Russian Economic Reform.* Ed. Alan Smith. Washington: The Brookings Institution, 1995. 203–263.

Smith, Alan, ed. *Challenges for Russian Economic Reform.* Washington: The Brookings Institution, 1995.

Sorokin, Konstantin E., and Constantine P. Danopoulos. "Challenges of Military-Civilian Conversion: U.S. and Russian Experiences." *The New Chapter in United States–Russian Relations.* Eds. Sharyl Cross and Marina A. Oborotova. Westport: Praeger, 1994. 57–70.

Twigg, Judyth L. "Defence planning: the potential for transparency and co-operation." *The Limited Partnership: Building a Russian–US Security Community.* Eds. James E. Goodby and Benoit Morel. Oxford: Oxford University Press, 1993. 272–288.

Vasiliev, Sergei A. "Economic Reform in Russia: Social, Political, and Institutional Aspects." *Changing the Economic System in Russia.* Eds. Anders Aslund and Richard Layard. New York: St Martin's Press, 1993. 72–86.

— — —. "The Political Economy of Russia's Reform." *Russian Economic Reform at Risk.* Ed. Anders Aslund. London: Pinter, 1995. 179–186.

Wehling, Fred. "Prospects for U.S–Russian Cooperation in the Middle East." *The New Chapter in United States–Russian Relations.* Eds. Sharyl Cross and Marina A. Oborotova. Westport: Praeger, 1994. 169–192.

Zevelev, Igor A. "New Russia and the United States: Prospects for Cooperation in Human Rights." *The New Chapter in United States–Russian Relations.* Eds. Sharyl Cross and Marina A. Oborotova. Westport: Praeger, 1994. 137–152.

Congressional Record

"Bringing Russia Into the Western World." *Congressional Record* 18 March 1997: H1108–1109.

"Chemical Weapons Convention." *Congressional Record* 23 April 1997: S3468–3486.

"Chemical Weapons Convention." *Congressional Record* 24 April 1997: S3570–3658.

"Civilian Space Authorization Act, Fiscal Years 1998 and 1999." *Congressional Record* 24 April 1997: H1819–1849.

"Cloture Motion." *Congressional Record* 8 July 1997: S6974–6989.

"Cooperative Threat Reduction Funds for Chemical Weapons Destruction." *Congressional Record* 11 July 1997: S7250–7253.

"Departments of Veterans Affairs and Housing and Urban Development and Independent Agencies Appropriations Act 1998." *Congressional Record* 16 July 1997: H5309–5371.

"Emergency Foreign Aid to Russia." *Congressional Record* 16 April 1997: H1546.

"European Security Act." *Congressional Record* 10 June 1997: H3640.

"European Security Act of 1997." *Congressional Record* 11 June 1997: H3706–3717.

"Expressing Concern over Russia's Newly Passed Religion Law." *Congressional Record* 8 November 1997: S12205–12206.

"Flank Document Agreement to the CFE Treaty." *Congressional Record* 14 May 1997: S4451–4478.

"Foreign Operations Export Financing and Related Programs Appropriations Act, 1998." *Congressional Record* 16 July 1997: S7515–7536.

"Foreign Relations Authorization Act, Fiscal Years 1998 and 1999." *Congressional Record* 10 June 1997: H3591–3632.

"Freedom of Religion in Russia." *Congressional Record* 25 September 1997: S9914.

"The Gazprom Deal." *Congressional Record* 22 October 1997: S10915–10917.

"General Leave." *Congressional Record* 6 November 1997: H10124–10129.

"Gulf War Veterans Health." *Congressional Record* 11 July 1997: S7253–7284.

Harman, Jane. "Sanctions on Russian Entities." *Congressional Record* 22 July 1997: E1477.

Hutchinson, Asa. "Sense–of-Congress Resolution." *Congressional Record* 24 October 1997: E2082–2083.

"Iran Missile Proliferation Sanctions Act of 1997." *Congressional Record* 12 November 1997: H10646–10660.

Lantos, Tom. "The President Is Correct—Now Is the Time to Approve The Chemical Weapons Convention." *Congressional Record* 10 Feburary 1997: E191–192.

"The Mir Space Station." *Congressional Record* 24 July 1997: S8004–8005.

"National Defense Authorization Act for Fiscal Year 1998." *Congressional Record* 20 June 1997: H4103–4122.

"National Defense Authorization Act for Fiscal Year 1998." *Congressional Record* 23 June 1997: H4167–4212.

"National Defense Authorization Act for Fiscal Year 1998." *Congressional Record* 7 July 1998: S6877–6906.

"National Defense Authorization Act for Fiscal Year 1998." *Congressional Record* 8 July 1997: S6960–S6970.

"National Defense Authorization Act for Fiscal Year 1998." *Congressional Record* 9 July 1998: S7091–7114.

"NATO Alliance Membership for Romania." *Congressional Record* 16 May 1997: S4625–4628.

"NATO Enlargement after Paris." *Congressional Record* 12 June 1997: S5590–5594.

"Proposal to Reduce Quota of Gray Whales." *Congressional Record* 23 October 1997: H9476–9477.

"Protecting Religious Freedom Worldwide." *Congressional Record* 29 September 1997: S10180–10181.

"Providing Housing for Russian Soldiers While Americans Are Uptrooted by Military Base Closings." *Congressional Record* 22 May 1997: H3172.

"Reauthorization of the Export-Import Bank." *Congressional Record* 6 October 1997: H8373–8382.

"Regarding Proliferation of Missile Technology from Russia to Iran." *Congressional Record* 7 November 1997: S12064–S12065.

"Religious Liberty in Russia." *Congressional Record* 16 July 1997: S7620.

"Religious Persecution in Russia." *Congressional Record* 15 July 1997: H 5189.

"Report on the CFE Flank Document—Message from the President—PM 35." *Congressional Record* 15 May 1997: S4586.

"Report on the CFE Flank Document—Message from the President—PM 36." *Congressional Record* 15 May 1997: S4587–4588.

Sanders, Bernard. "If NATO Is Expanded, Our Allies Must Pay More of the Costs." *Congressional Record* 10 June 1997: E1159–1160.

Smith, Christopher H. "Tajikistan's Peace Accord." *Congressional Record* 15 July 1997: E1426.

Solomon, Gerald B.H. "The Baltic States Are Not Former Soviet Republics." *Congressional Record* 11 July 1997: E1412.

— — —. "Let's Apply the Gore-McCain Act to Russia and China." *Congressional Record* 23 April 1997: E717.

— — —. "NATO Expansion Cannot Be Limited." *Congressional Record* 3 June 1997: E1091–1092.

"Support Rohrabacher Amendment to Foreign Relations Authorization Bill." *Congressional Record* 11 June 1997: H3669.

"The Trip to South Africa." *Congressional Record* 24 September 1997: H7821–7828.

Weller, Jerry. "Vice President to Meet with Russian Prime Minister." *Congressional Record* 5 March 1998: E317–318.

Documents

ABM Treaty and U.S. Ballistic Missile Defense. Senate Hearing. 24 and 26 September 1996. Washington: Government Printing Office, 1997.

The Administration's Proposal on NATO Enlargement. Senate Hearing. 23 April 1997. Washington: Government Printing Office, 1997.

Agricultural Export Credit Guarantees. Senate Hearing. 6 May 1993. Washington: Government Printing Office, 1993.

Challenges to U.S. Security in the 1990s. House Hearing. March, April, June, and August 1994. Washington: Government Printing Office, 1994.

The Chechen Conflict and Russian Democratic Development. Hearing before the Commission on Security and Cooperation in Europe. 6 March 1996. Washington: Government Printing Office, 1996.

Chemical Weapons Convention. Senate Hearing. April 1997. Washington: Government Printing Office, 1997.

Collective Security in the Post-Cold War World. House Hearing. February, March, and May 1993. Washington: Government Printing Office, 1993.

Consideration of the Administration's Fiscal Year 1998 Request for Assistance to Central and Eastern Europe and the Former Soviet Union. Senate Hearing. 7 May 1997. Washington: Government Printing Office, 1997.

Crisis in Chechnya. Hearing Before the Commission on Security and Cooperation in Europe. 19 and 27 January 1995. Washington: Government Printing Office, 1995.

Current Agricultural Situation in Russia. House Hearing. 30 and 31 March and 1 April 1993. Washington: Government Printing Office, 1993.

The Debate on NATO Enlargement. Senate Hearing. October and November 1997. Washington: Government Printing Office, 1998.

Economic Freedom and U.S. Development AID Programs. Senate Hearing. 19 September 1996. Washington: Government Printing Office, 1996.

Foreign Operations, Export Financing, and Related Appropriations. Fiscal Year 1994. Senate Hearing. Washington: Government Printing Office, 1994.

Foreign Policy Implications of a Balanced Budget. Senate Hearing. 20 March, 18 April, and 16 May 1996. Washington: Government Printing Office, 1996.

The Future of U.S. Foreign Policy (Part I): Regional Issues. House Hearing. February and March 1993. Washington: Government Printing Office, 1993.

The Future of U.S. Foreign Policy in the Post–Cold War Era. House Hearing. February, March, and April 1992. Washington: Government Printing Office, 1992.

The Legacy of Chernobyl 1986 to 1996 and Beyond. Hearing Before the Commission on Security and Cooperation in Europe. 23 April 1996. Washington: Government Printing Office, 1996.

Newly Independent States of the Former Soviet Union: U.S. Policy and Assistance. House Hearing. 14 November and 15 December 1995. Washington: Government Printing Office, 1996.

Review of United States Foreign Policy. House Hearing. 31 July 1996. Washington: Government Printing Office, 1997.

Russian Economic Development. House Hearing. 28 June 1993. Washington: Government Printing Office, 1994.

Russia's Election: What Does It Mean? Hearing Before the Commission on Security and Cooperation in Europe. 10 July 1996. Washington: Government Printing Office, 1996.

Treaty Between U.S. and the Russian Federation on Further Reduction and Limitation on Strategic Offensive Arms (The Start II Treaty) Treaty Doc. 103–1. Senate Hearing. May and June 1993. Washington: Government Printing Office, 1993.

U.S. Assistance to the Newly Independent States of the Former Soviet Union. House Hearing. 11 March 1997. Washington: Government Printing Office, 1997.

U.S. Foreign Policy on Privatization: Results for Small Business. House Hearing. 12 May 1994. Washington: Government Printing Office, 1995.

U.S. National Goals and Objectives in International Relations in the Year 2000 and Beyond. Senate Hearing. 13 June 1995. Washington: Government Printing Office, 1997.

U.S. Policy Toward the New Independent States. House Hearing. 21 September and 6 October 1993. Washington: Government Printing Office, 1994.

U.S. Stake in a Democratic Russia. House Hearing. 24 March 1993. Washington: Government Printing Office, 1993.

Wolf, Charles, Jr. *Economic Transformation and the Changing International Economic Environment.* Santa Monica: Rand, 1993.

Periodicals

"Administration Backs Russia On Changes in Arms Treaty." *Congressional Quarterly* 3 May 1997: 1031.

Albright, Madeleine K. "Does NATO enlargement serve U.S. interests? Yes." *CQ Researcher* 16 May 1997: 449.

— — —. "Speaking to Russian Opinion Leaders About NATO Enlargement." *U.S. Department of State Dispatch* May 1997: 16–17.

Allison, Graham. "Nuclear dangers; Fear increases of terrorists getting hands on 'loose' warheads as security slips." *Boston Globe* 19 October 1997: C1.

Anselmo, Joseph C. "Dangers Mount Despite Cooperative Efforts." *Aviation Week & Space Technology* 23 June 1997: 47–50.

Apple, R.W., Jr. "Road to Approval Is Rocky, and the Gamble Is Perilous." *New York Times* 15 May 1997: A1+.

Arbatov, Alexei. "Eurasia Letter: A Russian–U.S. Security Agenda." *Foreign Policy* Fall 1996: 102–117.

Barry, John and Owen Mathews. "The Secret Computer Trade: Did Clinton let banned technology get to Moscow?" *Newsweek* 10 November 1997: 87.

Bayer, Alexei. "Out of the Melting Pot, into the Global Market." *New York Times* 30 November 1997: C11.

Bernstein, Jonas. "Reform Follows Function." *The American Spectator* May 1997: 63–64.

"Bill and Boris (Cont'd)." *National Review* 10 November 1997: 16.

Blair, Bruce G., Harold A. Feiveson, and Frank N. von Hippel. "Redoubling Nuclear Weapons Reduction." *Washington Post* 12 November 1997: A23.

———. "Taking Nuclear Weapons Off Hair-Trigger Alert." *Scientific American* November 1997: 74–81.

Blank, Stephen J. "Sino–Russian Ties: Implications for the West." *Aviation Week & Space Technology* 18 August 1997: 71–72.

Bradley, Bill. "Eurasia Letter: A Misguided Russia Policy." *Foreign Policy* Winter 1995/1996: 81–97.

Browne, Malcolm W. "Money Shortage Jeopardizes Fusion Reactor." *New York Times* 20 May 1997: C8.

Calogero, Francesco. "Fast-track the uranium deal." *The Bulletin of the Atomic Scientists* November/December 1997: 20–21.

Carpenter, Ted Galen. "Should the United States aid the former Soviet Union? No." *CQ Researcher* 5 March 1993: 233.

Carroll, James. "ABM Treaty is not a 'relic of the Cold War'—it must be protected." *Boston Globe* 25 November 1997: A13.

Caryl, Christian. "The sideshow known as Russian reform: Greed, power and a mercurial president." *U.S. News & World Report* 8 December 1997: 54.

Cassata, Donna. "Abortion Compromise Eludes Foreign Aid Conferees." *Congressional Quarterly* 1 November 1997: 2698.

———. "Parties Find Common Ground In Iran Sanctions Bills: Measures aimed mainly at Russia would punish transfers of missile technology." *Congressional Quarterly* 1 November 1997: 2697.

———. "Support for Iran Sanctions Bill Still Runs Strong in Senate." *Congressional Quarterly* 24 January 1998: 193–194.

"A Chilling New Threat from Russia." *Chicago Tribune* 10 October 1997: A30.

"China's Buying Binge in Moscow's Armory." *World Press Review* June 1997: 10–11.

Cloud, David S. "Warheadache: How Russia helps Iran's missile program." *The New Republic* 20 April 1998: 11–12.

Cohen, Stephen F. "'Transition' or Tragedy?" *The Nation* 30 December 1996: 4–5,

Coleman, Fred, and Tim Zimmermann. "Chips off the old bloc." *U.S. News & World Report* 26 May 1997: 33.

Collina, Tom Zamora. "Ratify Test Ban Treaty Now." *Christian Science Monitor* 17 September 1997: 20.

Cooper, Mary H. "Communist Party Rises Anew in Eastern Europe." *CQ Researcher* 3 May 1996: 398.

— — —. "Expanding NATO: Does adding new members pose serious risks?" *CQ Researcher* 16 May 1997: 433–450.

— — —. "Russia's Political Future: Will voters turn the clock back in June?" *CQ Researcher* 3 May 1996: 385–407.

— — —. "Space Program's Future: Is NASA putting safety at risk to cut costs?" *CQ Researcher* 24 April 1997: 361–379.

— — —. "U.S. Invests Its Aid In Trade." *CQ Researcher* 3 May 1996: 396.

Cornell, Svante E. "The Unruly Caucasus." *Current History* October 1997: 341–347.

Cortright, David. "NATO's New Frontier." *The Nation* 31 March 1997: 21–22.

Crossette, Barbara. "Russia and U.S. Square Off Over U.N. Sanctions on Iraq." *New York Times* 25 November 1997: A6.

Danner, Mark. "Still Living In a Cold-War World." *Harpers* December 1997: 19–22+.

Dean, Jonathan. "The NATO Mistake: Expansion for all the wrong reasons." *Washington Monthly* July/August 1997: 35–37.

Deane, Daniela. "Soros to give Russia up to $500 M; U.S. financier targets health, military reform." *USA Today* 21 October 1997: A9.

"Debate on Chemical Arms Pact is Not Over Yet." *Congressional Quarterly* 3 May 1997: 1031.

Doherty, Carroll J. "Armenia's Special Relationship with U.S. Is Showing Strain." *Congressional Quarterly* 31 May 1997: 1270–1271.

— — —. "Clinton Wins First Round in House on Money for Programs Abroad." *Congressional Quarterly* 10 May 1997: 1084–1085.

— — —. "The Heat Is On to Freeze Out China." *Congressional Quarterly* 26 April 1997: 967–972.

— — —. "Pact With Russia Eases Way for NATO Expansion." *Congressional Quarterly* 17 May 1997: 1149.

— — —. "Senate Passes Bill to Reverse Long Decline in Foreign Aid." *Congressional Quarterly* 19 July 1997: 1716–1718.

"Drug-Resistant TB Raises Fear of New Scourge." *New York Times* 23 October 1997: A13.

"Eastern cheers, Russian jeers, American silence." *The Bulletin of the Atomic Scientists* January/February 1997: 5–7.

Ebel, Robert E. "The Oil Rush in the Caucasus." *Current History* October 1997: 344–345.

Farah, Douglas. "FBI Chief: Russian Mafias Pose Growing Threat to U.S.: Freeh Cites Possibility of Nuclear Banditry." *Washington Post* 2 October 1997: A18.

— — —. "Russian Mob, Drug Cartels Joining Forces; Money-Laundering, Arms Sales Spreading Across Caribbean." *Washington Post* 29 September 1997: A1+.

Filipov, David. "Russia, China call for a 'multipolar world': Declaration seen as challenge to US role." *Boston Globe* 24 April 1997: A2.

Fish, M. Steven. "The Pitfalls of Russian Superpresidentialism." *Current History* October 1997: 326–330.

Ford, Peter. "Russia Aims to Be Top Arms Merchant. Cheap, reliable, and up-to-speed new weapons might carry it out of a post-cold-war slump." *Christian Science Monitor* 22 August 1997: 1+.

Friedman, Thomas L. "Missile Myopia." *New York Times* 2 October 1997: A19.

Garfinkle, Adam. "Expanding NATO : Implications for America." *Current* March/April 1997: 23–29.

Garnett, Sherman. "Russia's Illusory Ambitions." *Foreign Affairs* March/April 1997: 61–76.

Garthoff, Raymond L. "The United States and the New Russia: The First Five Years." *Current History* October 1997: 305–312.

Gati, Charles. "Growing Pains." *National Review* 16 June 1997: 27–29.

Gerth, Jeff. "Advance for Bill to Restrict Computer Exports." *New York Times* 29 October 1997: A22.

Gerth, Jeff, and Michael R. Gordon. "Despite U.S. Ban, Russia Buys I.B.M. Computers for Atom Lab." *New York Times* 27 October 1997: A1+.

Gessen, Masha. "Scary Fires, Crashes, and Glitches—Isn't That Just Life in Russia? The Mir Dilemma: Would You Go Up There?" *Christian Science Monitor* 26 September 1997: 18.

Geyer, Alan. "NATO expansion: Dividing the House of Europe?" *Christian Century* 4 and 11 June 1997: 566–567.

"Go Ballistic." *The New Republic* 27 October 1997: 9–10.

"Go East." *The New Republic* 17 February 1997: 7.

Golden, Daniel S. "Should the Russian government be involved in building the International Space Station? Yes." *CQ Researcher* 25 April 1997: 377.

Goldman, Marshall I. "Russia's Reform Effort: Is There Growth at the End of the Tunnel?" *Current History* October 1997: 313–318.

Goltz, Thomas. "Chechnya & the Bear's Long Shadow." *The Nation* 10 February 1997: 20–23.

Gordon, Michael R. "Irking U.S., Yeltsin Signs Law Protecting Orthodox Church." *New York Times* 27 September 1997: A1, A5.

———. "Russians Pass Bill Sharply Favoring Orthodox Church." *New York Times* 20 September 1997: A1, A5, A6.

———. "Searching for the Method in Czar Boris's Madness." *New York Times* 5 April 1998: WK4.

Goshko, John M. "U.S., Russia Reaffirm Nuclear Pact; Leaders Sign Accords to Preserve ABM Treaty and Boost START II." *Washington Post* 27 September 1997: A16.

Graham, Bradley. "U.S. Digs In for 'Long-Term' Struggle over Iraq Arms: Officials Appear to Be Countering Russian Push at U.N. to Secure Easing of Sanctions." *Washington Post* 26 November 1997: A22.

Gray, Malcolm. "Back in the saddle." *Macleans* 24 March 1997: 27.

Griffin, Rodman D. "Aid to Russia." *CQ Researcher* 12 March 1993: 219–234.

Gruenwald, Juliana. "House Panel Takes Bipartisan Tack in Approving List of Bills." *Congressional Quarterly* 19 April 1997: 906–907.

Harris, John F. "Clinton Tells U.N. He's Ready to Forward Test Ban to Senate." *Washington Post* 23 September 1997: A6.

"Helsinki Illusions." *National Review* 21 April 1997: 16–17.

Hoagland, Jim. "Resisting America." Washington Post 9 November 1997: C9.

— — —. "Yeltsin Denies Selling Nuclear Arms to Iran; Russian General Also Says Reports of Missing Weapons Are False." *Washington Post* 27 September 1997: A16.

Hoffman, David. "Lower House of Russian Parliament Ratifies Global Chemical Weapons Ban." *Washington Post* 1 November 1997: A22.

Howard, Glen E. "Oil and Missiles in the Caucasus." *Wall Street Journal* 14 May 1997: A22.

Isachenko, Vladimir. "Russia's laxity nearly sent missile controls to Iraq." *Kansas City Star* 14 April 1998: A3.

Johnson, Rebecca. "Little Orphan Fissban." *The Bulletin of the Atomic Scientists* May/June 1997: 4.

Jones, Rodney W., and Nikolai N. Sokov. "After Helsinki, the hard work." *The Bulletin of the Atomic Scientists* July/August 1997: 26–30.

Kamp, Karl-Einz. "Would expanding NATO to include central and East European countries threaten Russia? Yes." *CQ Researcher* 3 May 1996: 401.

Kaplan, Bernard D. "Yeltsin's odd actions lead to speculation by outsiders." *Kansas City Star* 5 April 1998: A16.

Karash, Yuri. "What the Mir Can Still Teach Us." *New York Times* 19 July 1997: A19.

Karatnycky, Adrian. "Emerging Russia." *National Review* 24 February 1997: 40–42.

— — —. "NATO Weal." *National Review* 10 November 1997: 43–44.

Kempster, Norman, and Craig Turner. "Clinton Says U.S. Won't Join Treaty to Ban Land Mines." *Los Angeles Times* 18 September 1997: A1+.

Kennan, George F. "A Fateful Error." *New York Times* 5 February 1997: A23.

Kissinger, Henry. "Beware: A Threat Abroad." *Newsweek* 17 June 1996: 41–43.

Klare, Michael T. "Beyond the Rogues' Gallery." *The Nation* 26 May 1997: 22–26.

Kotkin, Stephen. "Stealing the State: The Soviet collapse and the Russian collapse." *The New Republic* 13 April 1998: 26–33.

Kovalev, Sergei. "Russia After Chechnya." *The New York Review of Books* 17 July 1997: 28–31.

Kozyrev, Andrei. "NATO Is Not Our Enemy." *Newsweek* 10 February 1997: 31.

Kramer, David J. "Dubious Deals with Gazprom." *Washington Post* 25 November 1997: A19.

Kranz, Patricia. "The Business of Russia is Biznes — And That Could Mean Trouble." *Business Week* 17 November 1997: 143.

— — —. "What's Bringing Moscow Together: Fear of Lebed." *Business Week* 10 February 1997: 59.

Kupchan, Charles A. "NATO Maneuvers on Russia." *The Nation* 15 December 1997: 24–26.

Kyl, Jon. "A Bad Chemical Arms Pact: Proponents urge the US to take high moral ground, but we've already done that to no avail." *Christian Science Monitor* 18 March 1997: 19.

Lake, Anthony. "The Challenge of Change in Russia." *U.S. Department of State Dispatch* 8 April 1996: 181–183.

Lande, Laurie. "Ex-Im Bank Is Expected to Pull Gazprom Funds." *Wall Street Journal* 28 October 1997: A10.

Lewis, George, and Theodore Postol. "Portrait of a bad idea." *The Bulletin of the Atomic Scientists* July/August 1997: 18+.

Lieven, Anatol. "The Future of Russia: Will It Be Freedom Or Anarchy?" *Current* March/April 1997: 15–22.

Lind, Michael. "Looking Past NATO: A Plea for a New Global Strategy." *The New Leader* 30 June 1997: 9–11.

Mandelbaum, Michael. "Our Outdated Russia Policy." *Time* 5 February 1996: 39.

———. "Westernizing Russia and China." *Foreign Affairs* May/June 1997: 80–95.

Mann, Paul. "Economic Morass Foils Military Progress." *Aviation Week & Space Technology* 26 May 1997: 70–73.

———. "Helsinki Summit Spurs Strategic Partnership." *Aviation Week & Space Technology* 31 March 1997: 24–27.

———. "Little Progress On START 3." *Aviation Week & Space Technology* 2 December 1996: 72–73.

———. "Reform Deficiencies Afflict Russian R&D." *Aviation Week & Space Technology* 26 May 1997: 73.

———. "Russia and NATO Agree to Cooperate." *Aviation Week & Space Technology* 2 June 1997: 26.

———. "Russians Sound Alarm Over Stalled Reforms." *Aviation Week & Space Technology* 26 May 1997: 64–69.

———. "Stalled Treaty Jeopardizes Major Nuclear Arms Cuts." *Aviation Week & Space Technology* 2 December 1996: 70–73.

———. "Yeltsin Acquiesces to NATO Charter." *Aviation Week & Space Technology* 31 March 1997: 27.

Martel, William C. "Russia's 'Loose Nukes': a Myth That Distorts US Policy." *Christian Science Monitor* 16 June 1997: 18.

Mathews, Brendan. "Competitive computing and 'creative acquisition.'" *The Bulletin of the Atomic Scientists* May/June 1997: 5–7.

Matlock, Jack F., Jr. "Dealing with a Russia in Turmoil." *Foreign Affairs* May/June 1996: 38–51,

McFaul, Michael. "Democracy Unfolds in Russia." *Current History* October 1997: 319–325.

McMillan, Priscilla, and Suzanne Massie. "We need a policy on Russia." *Boston Globe* 9 October 1997: A29.

Miller, Judith. "Soros to Donate Millions More to Help Russia." *New York Times* 20 October 1997: A1+.

Miller, Judith, and William J. Broad. "U.S. Fails Exercise Simulating Strike by a Germ Weapon." *The New York Times* 26 April 1998: A1, A10.

"Mir's Honorable Record." *Christian Science Monitor* 26 August 1997: 20.

"Mishandling Russian Uranium" *New York Times* 11 June 1997: A24.

Morgan, Dan, and David Ottaway. "Drilling for Influence in Russia's Back Yard; U.S. Woos Oil-Rich Former Soviet Republics." *Washington Post* 22 September 1997: A1.

Muravchik, Joshua. "Why Die for Danzig?" *Commentary* October 1997: 40–45.

———. "Should the United States aid the former Soviet Union? Yes." *CQ Researcher* 5 March 1993: 233.

Myers, Steven Lee. "U.S. and Russians Agree to Put Off Deadline on Arms." *New York Times* 27 September 1997: A1, A5.

Myre, Greg. "Parliament again rebuffs Yeltsin." *Kansas City Star* 18 April 1998: A6.

———. "Yeltsin pushes nominee." *Kansas City Star* 24 April 1998: A15.

"NATO's Growing Pains." *The Nation* 9 June 1997: 3–4.

Nelan, Bruce W. "Nuclear Disarray." *Time* 19 May 1997: 46–48.

Nesmith, Jeff. "NASA to give Russia agency funding boost; $20 million would go to keep factories at work on key module in space station." *Atlanta Constitution* 7 February 1997: D2.

"A New 'Great Game'—for Fuel." *World Press Review* June 1997: 32–33.

Norton, Rob. "The Good News About Russia." *Fortune* 14 April 1997: 32.

Obey, David R. "Does NATO enlargement serve U.S. interests? No." *CQ Researcher* 16 May 1997: 449.

Ogden, Christopher. "A Diplomatic Triumph for Bill Clinton." *Time* 26 May 1997: 51.

Passell, Peter. "Wanted: a global warming policy that stands a chance." *New York Times* 2 October 1997: D2.

Pastore, John O., and Peter A. Zheutlin. "'Peacemaker' Movie an Uncomfortably Real Vision of Future." *Christian Science Monitor* 22 September 1997: 19.

"A Perilous Pause on Nuclear Cuts." *New York Times* 13 October 1997: A14.

Perry, William J. "Would expanding NATO to include Central and East European countries threaten Russia? No." *CQ Researcher* 3 May 1996: 401.

Petrov, Vladimir. "Don't Enlarge NATO—Downsize It." *Washington Post* 5 February 1997: A27.

Pickering, Thomas. "Russia's Journey from Totalitarianism Toward Democracy." *U.S. Department of State Dispatch* 21 October 1996: 528–530.

Pipes, Richard. "Is Russia Still an Enemy?" *Foreign Affairs* September/October 1997: 65–78.

Powell, Bill. "A Summit, but Not of Equals." *Newsweek* 31 March 1997: 32.

"Primakov on Peace: 'I Do Not Envy Madeleine.'" *Newsweek* 29 September 1997: 43.

"A Qualified 'Yes' to the Deal with Russia." *World Press Review* June 1997: 18–19.

Quinn-Judge, Paul. "The Perils of Catching Cold." *Time* 22 December 1997: 38.

Reddaway, Peter. "Beware the Russian Reformer; While the U.S. Depends On Chubais, Accusations Fly in Moscow." *Washington Post* 24 August 1997: C1.

Remnick, David. "Can Russia Change?" *Foreign Affairs* January/February 1997: 35–49.

———. "How Russia Is Ruled." *The New York Review of Books* 9 April 1998: 10–15.

Rohrabacher, Dana. "Should the Russian government be involved in building the International Space Station? No." *CQ Researcher* 25 April 1997: 377.

Rose, Richard. "Teddy Bears." *National Review* 1 September 1997: 42–43+.

Rosenfeld, Stephen S. "Wake Up—The Nightmare's Not Over." *Washington Post* 31 January 1997: A21.

"Russia: Transition to Nowhere." *The Wilson Quarterly* Spring 1997: 139–140.

"Russia in Turmoil." *World Press Review* January 1997: 6–12.

"Russia's Smoldering Anger over NATO." *World Press Review* June 1997: 9–10.

Sanger, David E. "On Russian–Iranian Oil Deal, U.S. Sanctions May Backfire." *New York Times* 16 October 1997: A1+.

———. "Two-Edged Sanctions Sword." *New York Times* 30 September 1997: A12.

Sawyer, Kathy. "Partnership in Space Loses Momentum; Delays from Cash–Starved Russians Trouble International Space Station." *Washington Post* 9 March 1997: A1+.

Schwenninger, Sherle R. "The Case Against NATO Enlargement: Clinton's Fateful Gamble." *The Nation* 20 October 1997: 21–22+.

Scott, William B. "Classification Sensitivities Slow Weapon Dismantlement." *Aviation Week & Space Technology* 23 June 1997: 45–46.

"Senate Resolution Raps Russia For Religious Discrimination," *Congressional Quarterly* 15 November 1997: 2865.

Sengupta, Somini. "Again, It's Diplomats vs. New York, with Both Sides Demanding Apologies." *New York Times* 5 November 1997: B12.

Shargorodosky, Sergei. "Opponents firm on Yeltsin nominee." *Kansas City Star* 14 April 1998: A3.

Sharp, Jane M.O. "Toward a Secure Europe." *Current History* March 1997: 130–134.

Shevtsova, Lilia, and Scott A. Bruckner. "Russian Instability: Heading For Crisis." *Current* May 1997: 32–36.

Shlapentokh, Vladimir. "'Normal' Russia." *Current History* October 1997: 331–335.

Singer, Daniel. "Yeltsin's Summit, Russia's Vale." *The Nation* 31 March 1997: 18–21.

Slavin, Barbara. "Value of sanctions questioned: Economic weapon's power is eroding, critics contend." *USA Today* 3 June 1997: A12.

Smith, Jeffrey R. "U.S. Asks for Assurance on Test Ban After Activity Detected at Russian Site." *Washington Post* 29 August 1997: A34.

———. "U.S. Officials Acted Hastily in Nuclear Test Accusation; CIA Hesitates to Call Russian 'Event' a Quake." *Washington Post* 20 October 1997: A1+.

———. "U.S. Studies Deeper Nuclear Warhead Cuts; Possible START III Pact Could Encourage Russia to Ratify 1993 Arms Reduction Treaty." *Washington Post* 23 January 1997: A4.

Specter, Michael. "AIDS Onrush Sends Russia to the Edge of an Epidemic." *New York Times* 18 May 1997: A1+.

Spotts, Peter N. "Mir's Mission: Science Or Merely Survival?" *Christian Science Monitor* 10 September 1997: 3.

"Start II treaty back to Russia's Parliament." *Kansas City Star* 14 April 1998: A3.

"The State of Boris Yeltsin's Health." *New York Times* 5 April 1998: WK14.

Steinbruner, John. "Russia Faces an Unsafe Reliance on Nukes." *Los Angeles Times* 3 March 1997: B5.

"Stop Stalling on Land Mines." *The New York Times* 26 August 1997: A18.

Straus, Ira. "NATO, Go East." *National Review* 11 August 1997: 39–41.

Talbott, Strobe. "America and Russia in a Changing World." *U.S. Department of State Dispatch* 28 October 1996: 536–540.

———. "The End of the Beginning: The Emergence of a New Russia." *U.S. Department of State Dispatch* August/September 1997: 22–26.

———."Managing the Russian Connection." *Time* 25 November 1996: 59–60.

———. "The Struggle for Russia's Future." *Wall Street Journal* 25 September 1997: A22.

———. "U.S.–Russian Relations: The Next Phase." *U.S. Department of State Dispatch* 15 July 1996: 361–363.

Towell, Pat. "Albright Argues NATO Expansion Would Buttress Democracy." *Congressional Quarterly* 11 October 1997: 2495–2496.

———. "Arms Modernization, Redeployments . . . Would Drive Costs of Expansion." *Congressional Quarterly* 15 March 1997: 650–651. [ellipsis in original]

———. "Chemical Arms Ban's Chances Put at 50–50 in Senate." *Congressional Quarterly* 19 April 1997: 917–920.

———. "Five Amendments to Dominate Debate." *Congressional Quarterly* 19 April 1997: 918.

———. "House Passes Iran Sanctions, but Bill Stalls in Senate." *Congressional Quarterly* 15 November 1997: 2863.

———. "House Poised to Pass Sanctions Against Those Who Aid Iran." *Congressional Quarterly* 8 November 1997: 2780.

———. "NATO Expansion Debate Put on Fast Track." *Congressional Quarterly* 4 October 1997: 2415–2416.

———. "NATO Expansion Forges Ahead with Little Hill Scrutiny." *Congressional Quarterly* 15 March 1997: 648, 650–652.

———. "Panel Gauges Russian Response to NATO Expansion." *Congressional Quarterly* 1 November 1997: 2696.

———. "The Price of Admission." *Congressional Quarterly* 4 October 1997: 2416.

———. "Russia Wins Shift in Arms Limits." *Congressional Quarterly* 17 May 1997: 1149.

———."Senate Boosts Some Arms Programs, Sticks to Clinton's Basic Policies: After low-key debate, chamber adopts amendments on NATO expansion, Bosnia peacekeeping." *Congressional Quarterly* 19 July 1997: 1719–1722.

———. "Senate Passes Domestic Version of Ban." *Congressional Quarterly* 19 April 1997: 919.

Trojan, Jakub S. "NATO expansion: The view from Central Europe." *Christian Century* 4 and 11 June 1997: 567–568.

Turner, Stansfield. "A US Initiative to Cage the Nuclear Genie." *Christian Science Monitor* 29 October 1997: 19.

"Two Dissenting Views: Why the Axis Won't Form." *World Press Review* June 1997: 10–11.

"The U.S. and Russia Issue Joint Statement Supporting Conclusion of a Comprehensive Test Ban Treaty." *U.S. Department of State Dispatch* 29 July 1996: 393.

"U.S.–Russian Relations: Principles and Benefits." *U.S. Department of State Dispatch* 12 February 1996: 40–41.

— — —. "Would-Be Members and Their Prospects." *Congressional Quarterly* 15 March 1997: 649.

Uzzell, Lawrence A. "A Show of Bad Faith: Behind Yeltsin's Betrayal of Religious Freedom." *Washington Post* 2 November 1997: C1, C5.

vanden Heuvel, Katrina. "Russia's Oligarchy." *The Nation* 17 February 1997: 5.

vanden Heuvel, Katrina, and Stephen F. Cohen. "The Other Russia." *The Nation* 11 and 18 August 1997: 24–26.

Weinberger, Caspar W. "The Helsinki Summit: Fiction vs. Fact." *Forbes* 5 May 1997: 37.

— — —. "Russia's Oil Grab." *The New York Times* 9 May 1997: A35.

Weiner, Tim. "Panel Urges Deep Cuts in U.S. and Russian Nuclear Arsenals." *New York Times* 18 June 1997: A5

Wickham, DeWayne. "Soros' giving a blessing—and also a concern." *USA Today* 30 October 1997: A15.

Williams, Carol J. "Yeltsin Hints Again at Land-Mine Ban." *Los Angeles Times* 21 October 1997: A8.

Williams, Carol J., and John–Thor Dahlburg. "Intervention Marks Milestone for Russian Leadership." *Los Angeles Times* 21 November 1997: A14.

Williams, Daniel. "Russia's Efforts in the Iraq Crisis Don't Tip Foreign Policy Balance; Primakov Tries to Retain Independence, Avoid Conflict with U.S." *Washington Post* 21 November 1997: A47.

Woodward, Colin. "In Kyoto, a Try at Next Big Eco-Pact. Countries will gather Dec. 1 to try to put teeth into effort to slow climate change." *Christian Science Monitor* 26 November 1997: 1+.

Yavlinsky, Grigory. "Shortsighted." *New York Times Magazine* 8 June 1997: 66.

Zakaria, Fareed. "The Rising Power We Are Ignoring." *Reader's Digest* June 1997: 207–208.

Zilinskas, Raymond A. "The Other Biological Weapons Worry." *The New York Times* 28 November 1997: A39.